The Transformation of Political Community

Ethical Foundations of the Post-Westphalian Era

ANDREW LINKLATER

Polity Press

The right of Andrew Linklater to be identified as author of this work has been asserted in accordance with the Copyright, Designs and Patents Act 1988.

First published in 1998 by Polity Press
in association with Blackwell Publishers Ltd.

Editorial office:
Polity Press
65 Bridge Street
Cambridge CB2 1UR, UK

Marketing and production:
Blackwell Publishers Ltd
108 Cowley Road
Oxford OX4 1JF, UK

ISBN 0-7456-1335-7
ISBN 0-7456-1336-5 (pbk)

A CIP catalogue record for this book is available from the British Library.

Typeset in Sabon on 10/11.5 pt
by SetSystems Ltd, Saffron Walden, Essex
Printed in Great Britain by MPG Books Ltd, Cornwall

This book is printed on acid-free paper.

The Transformation of
Political Community

Contents

Introduction

Otto Hintze (1975, p. 342) described the early Occidental city as a corporate association of free and equal citizens. 'Sworn union', or *conjuratio*, formed the basis of the association; the social bond was grounded in an 'oath for mutual protection and support'. Modern ideas of political community continue to draw upon such Hellenic conceptions of equal citizens bound together in joint rule. They assume the existence of a high level of solidarity which citizens treasure and for which they are prepared to make significant personal sacrifices. Surrendering life in war for the sake of the greater communal good has long been regarded as the supreme example. Hegel, for one, believed that warfare was essential for the ethical health of political communities. Although this stark claim is hardly in tune with modern sensibilities, it captures the important point that communities will not survive unless their members are prepared to define their interests in the light of a more general good. Of course, citizens may be bound together as members of a community of fate who do not share common sentiments but who recognise in the face of adversity that it is best to hang together. An important strand of political thought suggests that individuals in this sorry condition form an association rather than a community (Toennies, 1955). In Hegelian terms, they may belong to a civil society but they do not enjoy citizenship of an ethical state.

The survival of political community owes much to the fact, which Bodin (1967, p. 21) emphasised, that the social bond between citizens and the state does not extend to aliens. Political communities endure because they are exclusive, and most establish their peculiar identities by accentuating the differences between insiders and aliens. In the history of political community, distinctiveness has often been forged in war or in unifying struggles for national independence. But this phenomenon does not stand on its own: communities do not rely simply on contrasts with the outer world in order to purchase their identities. As Foucault argued, various distinctions between the allegedly competent members of the community and the marginal such as the criminal and the insane also play their part in the constitution of community. Sharp contrasts between the dominant strata and subaltern groups who may well possess citizenship rights but feel less than completely at home within the political community exert their distinctive influence. Citizens who are uncomfortable with, or threatened by, the dominant representations of the community may believe that the general lifting of discrimination – which E. H. Carr (1946, pp. 162–9) regarded as essential for the survival of community – has failed to progress far enough. Their alienation or unrest is further testimony to the exclusionary nature of political communities.

This book considers communities as systems of inclusion and exclusion. The problematical aspects of the social bonds which unite and separate, associate and disassociate, are its principal concern. The argument extends an earlier discussion of the respects in which the sworn union between citizens may clash with obligations to the rest of the human race (Linklater, 1990a). The fact that citizens have to reconcile their identity as citizens with their conception of themselves as subjects of universal duties and rights is central to the analysis. The following discussion is unapologetically universalistic while recognising that many conceptions of cosmopolitan ethics are as exclusionary as the particularistic associations which they are turned against. In any case, universalistic loyalties have to be reconciled with strong emotional attachments to specific communities. While recognising that this is so, one of the central purposes of this book is to reaffirm the cosmopolitan critique of the sovereign states-system and to defend the widening of the moral boundaries of political communities.

Communities are constantly being remade, and their moral boundaries expand or contract on two separate fronts. They can develop more or less particularistic orientations towards the members of other societies. Regard for the interests of outsiders can wax in one epoch and wane in another: hence the importance of a cosmopolitan ethic which questions the precise moral significance of national boundaries. But as with aliens, so with subaltern groups: in one period, efforts to create more inclusive societies may predominate but, in another, the objective of creating more closed societies may prevail: hence the importance of ethical perspectives which reflect on moral deficits in the relations between members of the same society. Moral deficits arise, then, in the relations with outsiders when citizens attach more moral significance than is justified to differences between fellow-nationals and aliens – for example, by denying the outsider any rights in war. They are evident within societies which prevent minorities from preserving their cultural differences; and they occur when the dominant groups appropriate the most important social resources and meaningful opportunities. Visions of the triple transformation of political community to secure greater respect for cultural differences, stronger commitments to the reduction of material inequalities and significant advances in universality resist pressures to contract the boundaries of community while encouraging societal tendencies which promise to reduce these basic moral deficits.

Normative commitments of this kind have not exerted a great deal of influence on the study of international relations. Dominant perspectives such as realism and neo-realism have argued that the international environment is hostile to normative visions of radical political change. The prospects improve radically, the argument continues, within the more secure world of the sovereign state. These are unconvincing allegations, and much recent work in international relations has undermined the stark realist contrast between the peaceful security of domestic politics and the violent anarchy of international relations. Postmodern and feminist writings have argued that the radical distinction between the two worlds of domestic and international politics confers legitimacy on imperfect sovereign states (Walker, 1993). Supposedly neutral accounts of the world out there should give way, they have maintained, to the normative analysis of the possibilities for the transformation of political community. Efforts to create approaches to international relations which are actively engaged in criticising unjust forms of exclusion within communities have also questioned the recurring practice of establishing collective identities by demeaning cultures elsewhere. Problematising the ways in which societies privilege the interests of insiders over outsiders is a complementary exercise advocated by the exponents of cosmopolitan perspectives.

Making the moral case for new forms of political community is an important trend in recent international relations theory. Establishing that modern states are much more precarious and far more susceptible to fundamental change than neo-realism suggests is an equally important development. Sociological approaches which deny that expansive normative visions are bound to be destroyed by the dominant, conflictual patterns of international relations are a necessary part of the critical-theoretical project which has acquired major importance in recent years. Sociological investigation reveals that present structures are not natural and permanent but have a history and are likely to be succeeded by different arrangements in the future. Identifying the seeds of future change in existing social orders is a key feature of sociological inquiry.

Important precedents for current forms of sociological analysis exist. Recognising the need for the passage from ethics to sociology, Kant connected the normative defence of perpetual peace with a sociological account of the prospects for its realisation. He believed that the possibility of extending legal rights not only to the rising bourgeoisie but to the members of other societies was inherent in modern liberal society and its dominant ideology of the freedom and equality of individuals. The emergence of a transnational civil society created the conditions in which individuals could unlearn their perceptions of estrangement from other peoples and learn how to associate with them in more humane arrangements. In Kant's thought, and in Marxism, sociological analysis had the task of revealing that crucial moral deficits in modern capitalist societies could be eradicated by releasing existing potentials for enlarging the sphere in which human beings treat one another as equals.

As a result of the twenty years' crisis, realists were keen to point out that radical projects of global reform had failed to appreciate the strength of nationalism and the tenacity of state power. States contracted the boundaries of the moral community in the first part of the twentieth century by closing the door on aliens, pursuing nationalist foreign policies and tightening the forms of exclusion practised against minorities within their territories. Many contemporary critical analyses of the possibilities of new forms of community also lack the faith in the progressive effects of globalisation which was so pronounced in the writings of Kant and Marx. Many argue that globalisation creates new forms of hegemonic power which threaten cultural differences. But contemporary attempts to reconstruct the reformist project argue that earlier normative visions did not go far enough. Kant and Marx maintained that the dominant patterns of economic change made it possible for human beings to create new forms of universal cooperation; more recent approaches which defend the critical project from realist pessimism are more likely to emphasise the need for learning new levels of respect for the culturally different. In this context, these approaches argue that prevailing conceptions of identity and otherness have a history: they are far from natural or permanent, and they can be unlearned in more dialogic communities. They invite sociological analysis to reflect on the constraints upon and the possibilities for the development of more advanced orientations towards difference.

The status of ethical universalism in the light of these emphases upon the importance of respect for difference is one of the central issues in social and political theory, and in the theory of international relations, at present. Given the normative preferences which have already been mentioned in the preceding paragraphs, the present work argues for modes of sociological investigation which analyse the prospects for achieving progress towards higher levels of universality and difference in the modern world. Political communities embodying higher levels of universality would not attach deep moral significance to differences of class, ethnicity, gender, race and alien status. Political associations incorporating higher levels of respect for difference would display sensitivity to the variations of culture, gender and ethnicity which has been all too infrequent in the past. Societies which sought to realise higher levels of universality and difference would need to add measures to reduce material inequalities, thereby promoting the triple transformation of political community.

With these moral purposes in mind, it is necessary to build on the approaches taken by Kant and Marx by arguing that the logics of globalisation and fragmentation have brought many states to the point where new relations between universality and difference can be built into their political structures. Globalisation and fragmentation erode traditional conceptions of community and reduce the moral significance of national boundaries. They create unprecedented opportunities for overcoming the moral deficits of those states which have been insufficiently universalistic or insensitive to the value which others attach to their cultural differences, but they simultaneously introduce new threats and challenges. Globalisation has the pernicious effect of deepening material inequalities, while ethnic fragmentation produces new dangers of extreme particularism. The point, however, is not to abandon the critical project in the wake of realist or neo-realist objections, but to reconstruct it in the wake of contemporary social and political change. Reconstructing the critical project means preserving the strengths of the perspectives of Kant or Marx and cancelling their profound weaknesses. The most important developments as far as the project of reconstruction is concerned stress potentials for widening the boundaries of dialogic communities. Reworking the critical project requires normative and sociological accounts of more inclusive communication communities which introduce unprecedented forms of dialogue between the radically different.

Critical theory is to be judged not only by its contribution to ethics and sociology but by the extent to which it sheds light on existing political possibilities. Deficiencies in its normative and sociological approaches will inevitably be reflected in its praxeological analysis. Praxeology is concerned with reflecting on the moral resources within existing social arrangements which political actors can harness for radical purposes. It is preoccupied not with issues of strategy and tactics but with revealing that new forms of political community are immanent within existing forms of life and anticipated by their moral reserves. Critical theory arises in the context of social tensions and ambiguities and turns their progressive dimensions against unnecessary constraints. Illustrating the method, Kant directed the liberal notions of freedom and equality which had emerged in response to the growth of state power against political domination and inter-state violence. Marx similarly turned bourgeois notions of liberty and equality against the oppressive nature of capitalist social relations. Of course, these challenges to unjust systems of exclusion did not go far enough. Their response to the ambiguities of modernity sought to realise limited social purposes: bourgeois freedoms for one small segment of the population in Kant's case, and proletarian freedoms which took little account of the needs of the victims of racial, ethnic and gender inequalities in the case of Marx. Modern praxeological analysis must aim for larger objectives but, in so doing, it must replicate important features of Kantian and Marxist inquiry, specifically the project of drawing upon the moral reserves provided by modern ideas of freedom and equality in order to criticise systems of unjust exclusion. As part of this move, critical social theory breaks with the classical Marxist tendency of regarding developments within modes of production as more fundamental for the course of human history than movements within the moral-cultural sphere.

Starting from this premise, the following argument attaches particular importance to modern ideas about citizenship. These ideas first emerged in reaction to increases in state power and specifically in response to what has been called the totalising project. The totalising project refers to the efforts made by central governments to mould homogeneous national communities and to accentuate the differences between citizens and aliens in order to meet the challenge of inter-state war (see Corrigan and Sayer, 1985, p. 4). Modern ideas about citizenship which emerged, first, in response to increasing state demands and, second, in opposition to increasing capitalist inequalities are the most important moral resources which have been accumulated in the struggle against wrongful exclusion. They have been vital in promoting three key developmental tendencies in modern societies. These include, first, questioning the grounds on which the dominant groups deprive significant sections of the population of the legal and political rights which the former already enjoy; second, appreciating that the redistribution of power and wealth is essential because universalising legal and political rights alone will not improve the circumstances of the most disadvantaged groups in society; and, third, realising that such measures to ensure that all citizens feel at home in the political community will not go far enough unless they are accompanied by the public recognition of the cultural differences which exist between citizens and which many are keen to preserve. Citizenship is important because it avails societies of the possibility of overcoming their internal moral deficits by promoting the triple transformation of political community. Creating social relations which are more universalistic, less unequal and more sensitive to cultural differences are the three dimensions of the project of transformation.

Engaging the systematically excluded in dialogue about the ways in which social practices and policies harm their interests is a key ethical commitment for any society which embarks on this process of change. Most members of such a society may share many cultural traits and traditions, but the bond which unites them can owe as much to the ethical commitment to open dialogue as to a sense of primordial attachments. Identification with shared cultural norms need not end in the conviction that some dominant conception of national identity must set the community apart and must be shared by all members. The desire to engage others in dialogue to ensure that the dominant assumptions about the nature and purpose of the community do not harm their legitimate interests can be an overriding consideration. Important implications for the realm of external relations follow. To make dialogue central to social life is necessarily to be troubled by the ways in which society discriminates against outsiders unfairly by harming their interests while denying them representation and voice. The obligation to enlarge the moral boundaries of the political community in order to engage excluded aliens in dialogue is required by the commitment to the ideals of citizenship.

The most effective means of honouring this obligation is to create institutional frameworks which widen the boundaries of the dialogic community. Multiple frameworks are necessary, given the diverse characteristics of nation-states, and the members of the rationalist tradition of international relations theory have contributed more than other perspectives to understanding the principles which can underpin them. They have distinguished between a pluralist international society, in which radically different societies engage in a dialogue which has the singular objective of preserving elementary principles of order and coexistence between sovereign states, and a solidarist international society, in which states cooperate to protect agreed moral principles such as basic human rights. Rationalist thought has often emphasised the powerful constraints which prevent the transition from a pluralist to a solidarist society of states, and it has generally been dismissive of grand visions of global reform. But a parallel line of discussion in rationalist inquiry has stressed that radical encroachments upon state sovereignty are possible within small pockets of international society such as Western Europe. In this region, it has been suggested, significant transfers of state power to sub-national and transnational political authorities are feasible. Rationalist analysis therefore suggests that while the majority of states may remain committed to pluralist principles, others may participate within solidarist arrangements and a small minority may embark upon collaborative projects which breach the sovereign principle which has been central to international relations since the Peace of Westphalia in 1648.

Debates continue about the possibility of progress in international relations, and more specifically about whether it is possible for states to agree on more than the basic principles of their coexistence. What has declined in recent years is the level of consensus about the adequacy of sovereign states and the principles of international relations which have prevailed during the Westphalian era. The level of geopolitical rivalry and the incidence of war between sovereign states has been high for most of this period, as realists and neo-realists have argued, but much recent thought questions the assumption that past patterns of international relations are bound to be reproduced indefinitely. Analyses of the pacification of the core industrial regions of the modern world system point to the end of geopolitics, if not globally then in the relations between the majority of the great powers. Where logics of pacification prevail, the elements of national coherence are more difficult to preserve. Minority nations whose claims for autonomy were denied when state-formation and nation-building were at their height acquire new opportunities for realising their objectives. In this context it is no longer utopian, at least as far as the relations between like-minded states which are exposed to high levels of transnational harm are concerned, to imagine new forms of political community and new conceptions of citizenship which bind sub-state, state and transnational authorities and loyalties together in a post-Westphalian international society. One result of globalisation and fragmentation is that new state structures which combine greater universalism with increased sensitivity to difference become possible in Europe and elsewhere in the pacified core.

The transformation of political community would constitute a revolution in the areas affected because societies would no longer confront each other as geopolitical rivals in the condition of anarchy. More dialogic relations would spell the end of the Westphalian era. Participants in this project could cooperate to engineer a wider process of change which secures higher levels of respect for pluralist and solidarist international arrangements. While designing post-Westphalian forms of cooperation, these societies could work for the establishment of these two additional frameworks in which dialogue and consent replace domination and force. In this way it is possible to approximate the normative ideal of a universal communication community and to ensure that global arrangements have the consent of a greater proportion of the human race. The normative, sociological and praxeological analysis of political community which is developed below is orientated to this goal.

The writings of Kant and Marx exemplify this approach. They developed a critical-theoretical approach to political community which is superior to the neo-realist thesis that competition and conflict between states will endure as long as international society remains anarchic. With this in mind, chapter 1 argues that critical approaches have acquired unusual significance in an era in which globalisation and fragmentation create the possibility of forms of community which are simultaneously more universalistic and more sensitive to cultural differences. Whether universalism can remain an ethical ideal is considered in chapters 2 and 3. Critiques of cosmopolitan morality which have appeared in recent years deny the possibility of an Archimedean viewpoint from which some universalisable conception of the good life can be identified. However, a vision of the dialogic community whose members are troubled by all forms of unjust exclusion, whether practised against insiders or aliens, survives these criticisms and often develops in tandem with them. Chapter 4 notes how exclusionary orientations towards outsiders emerged in the ancient world alongside the development of state power. Many factors encouraged the widening of the moral boundaries of political community in the early empires and in the Greek city-state system, although most conceptions of politics and international relations stopped short of recognising duties to engage the radically different in unconstrained dialogue. By contrast, modern states have developed unprecedented powers over society but they have also generated equally unprecedented claims for freedom and equality. Chapter 5 maintains that the idea of citizenship has been the most potent response to increased state power. Various developmental tendencies pointing towards the triple transformation of political community have existed in societies which are committed to the ideals of citizenship. How the ambiguities of modernity will finally be resolved remains unclear, but modern societies have accumulated significant ethical reserves which can be used to eliminate their most troubling moral deficits. Some of the means by which they can move towards the ideal of a universal communication community which confers rights of dialogue and citizenship on the hitherto excluded are considered in chapter 6. Intimations of the post-Westphalian world are apparent in Western Europe especially but it is not impossible that the erosion of the state's monopoly powers and the emergence of improved forms of political community will occur elsewhere. The modern society of states may yet turn out to be the first international society which is not destroyed by conquest and war but transformed peacefully by the normative commitment to extending the moral and political boundaries of community.

The argument which is developed in this book is the third part of a larger inquiry into the nature and possibility of new forms of political community. It builds on two earlier books, *Men and Citizens in the Theory of International Relations* and *Beyond Realism and Marxism* (Linklater 1990a; 1990b), and integrates several themes drawn from recent papers. The argument will be taken further in a book on the English School and the Grotian tradition which will be written with my Keele colleague Hidemi Suganami. That work will consider the relationship between the Grotian analysis of different forms of international society and the notion of a universal communication community. A final work on the historical sociology of international relations will explore some of the claims made in chapters 4–6. It will consider how different forms of world political organisation (including empires, civilisations and societies of states) understood the moral and political boundaries of community. That book will focus upon their conceptions of the morally relevant differences between insiders and outsiders, and analyse the extent to which they participated in, and anticipated the development of, wider communities of discourse. Some of the claims made about modernity and its potentials in chapters 4–6 of the present book will be investigated further in that work.

The central aim of the present study and the larger project to which it belongs is to develop a critical approach to international relations which embraces normative, sociological and praxeological concerns. A commitment to universalistic conceptions of ethics and dialogue is central to the argument which follows. The argument of *Men and Citizens* which defended more universalistic forms of political organisation that would transcend the ethical limitations of sovereign nation-states is restated in the light of the contemporary politics of difference. The restatement suggests that Frankfurt School critical theory, postmodernism and feminism reflect modern sensitivities about the manifold forms of unjust exclusion. Each denies the legitimacy of systems of exclusion which are imposed on excluded groups which lack effective participation and voice. Each invites movement to wider communities of discourse in which the included and excluded participate as equals to determine the dominant principles of inclusion and exclusion. The defence of universalism in *Men and Citizens* is restated in an argument about recognising that all human beings have a prima facie equal right to take part in universal communities of discourse which decide the legitimacy of global arrangements.

Normative arguments of this kind are incomplete without a parallel sociological account of how they can be realised in practice (see Linklater, 1990a, pp. 165–8); and normative and sociological advances are incomplete without some reflection on practical possibilities (Linklater, 1990a, p. 204; 1990b, p. 172). The latter book made the argument for a sociology of international relations which considered the part that war, production, the quest for international order and moral development have played in shaping the moral and political boundaries of community. Chapters 4 and 5 of the present work return to these themes. Chapter 6 then seeks to integrate the normative and sociological dimensions of critical theory with praxeological concerns. The central argument here is that resistance to unjust systems of exclusion has resulted in the modern theory and practice of citizenship. The idea of citizenship provides modern societies with the moral resources with which to create new and more inclusive arrangements, domestically and in international relations. The prospects for designing forms of political community which are more sensitive to the claims of universality and difference are immanent within existing forms of life which have serious commitments to citizenship.

The argument for a critical perspective which embraces normative, sociological and praxeological analysis was first set out in my paper 'The Problem of Community in International Relations' (Linklater, 1990c). A more involved statement was developed in 'The Question of the Next Stage in International Relations Theory: A Critical-Theoretical Point of View' (Linklater, 1992a). I am grateful to the editors of the journals *Alternatives* and *Millennium* for their permission to incorporate elements of these papers in this book. Various parts of the argument have been developed in papers in recent years. I am grateful for permission to draw on material from 'What is a Good International Citizen?' (1992b), which was published in P. Keal (ed.), *Ethics and Foreign Policy* (Allen and Unwin, Sydney); 'Community, Citizenship and Global Politics', *Oxford International Review*, 5 (1993); 'Liberal Democracy, Constitutionalism and the New World Order' (1993), in J. L. Richardson and R. Leaver (eds), *The New World Order* (Westview Press); 'Neo-Realism in Theory and Practice' (1995a), in S. Smith and K. Booth (eds), *International Political Theory Today* (Polity Press); 'Community' (1995b), in A. Danchev (ed.), *Fin de Siecle: The Meaning of the Twentieth Century* (Tauris Academic Studies); 'Citizenship and Sovereignty in the Post-Westphalian State' (1996b), *European Journal of International Relations*; 'The Achievements of Critical Theory' (1996a), in S. Smith, K. Booth and M. Zalewski (eds), *International Theory: Positivism and Beyond* (Cambridge University Press); 'Hegel, the State and International Relations' (1996c), in I. B. Neumann and I. Clark (eds), *Classical Theories of International Relations* (Macmillan); and, finally, 'The Transformation of Political Community: E. H. Carr, Critical Theory and International Relations', *Review of International Studies*, forthcoming.

A first draft of this book was written while I was a member of the Department of Politics at Monash University in Melbourne. Numerous conversations at Monash with Ian Bell, Scott Burchill, Matthew Gibney, Paul James, Michael Janover, Tony Jarvis, John Mandalios and Heather Rae helped shape the present argument, as did many discussions with Hugh Emy, who offered numerous insights drawn from his extraordinary command of the literature on ancient and modern states. Collaborating with Peter Lawler was one of the great pleasures of the Australian phase of my academic career. Countless debates and discussions with him for more than a decade are a continuing reminder that few minds really meet. Work on an earlier stage of this project was eased by Lesley Whitelaw's exuberant generosity and by Pauline Bakker's reliable assistance. Outside Monash, Jim Richardson and Greg Fry at the Australian National University, Canberra, and Paul Keal at the Australian Defence Forces Academy, also in Canberra, provided valuable support and encouragement.

Most of the work for this book was undertaken during the 1995–6 academic year while I was on sabbatical leave from Keele University. I am grateful to the University for a Keele Research Award which allowed me to turn one semester's leave into a year-long sabbatical. My sabbatical might have been delayed had Alex Danchev not extended his period as Head of Department, and had Dan Keohane not offered to succeed him. I thank them both for their collegiality. With his characteristic intellectual generosity, Alex Danchev has encouraged this project since we first met in 1992. Many colleagues in the Department of International Relations at Keele (including Sarah Orme, Pat Thompson and Julie Spragg) have contributed greatly to the completion of this project. I would especially like to thank two former colleagues, Richard Devetak (now at Warwick) and Richard Shapcott (now at Bristol) for discussing this project with me over many years, and for offering their comments on an earlier draft of the manuscript. Debbie Lisle at Keele also provided valuable comments on a previous draft, as did Chris Brown at Southampton, Tim Dunne and Nick Wheeler at Aberystwyth and Peter Lawler at Manchester. Hidemi Suganami has brought his formidable analytical powers to bear on this project for over twenty years, since we first met as graduate students in International Relations at the LSE. He offered detailed comments on the penultimate draft of this manuscript, and on much more besides. I am immensely grateful to David Held at the Open University and Daniele Archibugi at the Lelio Basso Foundation in Rome for involving me in their workshop on cosmopolitan democracy, and I am especially indebted to David Held for the keen interest he has taken in my work on political community.

Not so long ago, as ageing scholars in the field will recall, international relations theory occupied a place of minor importance on the edges of the discipline. Much has changed. The dark ages would have been darker still but for the late John Vincent, who enthusiastically encouraged the development of new approaches which did not fit tidily within the handy classification of realist, rationalist and revolutionist patterns of thought. Iver Neumann has recorded this point in his astute appraisal of John Vincent's contribution to International Relations. All I wish to add is my sadness that there can be no merry debate with him about the uses and abuses of his rationalist position in the pages below.

Many of the themes discussed in this book were first aired in seminars and conferences in very different intellectual settings. I have benefited greatly from comments made in presentations at my own university and also at the Centre for International and Strategic Studies at York University in Toronto, Deakin University in Melbourne, Edinburgh University, Manchester University, Padjajaran and Parahyangan Universities in Bandung, Pompeu Fabra University in Barcelona, the University of Sussex, and the University of Wales in Aberystwyth.

My work on political community would not have made much progress without Jane's support over a twisting journey which has led from Aberdeen to Keele via Oxford, London, Hobart and Melbourne. Ollie made the latter part of that journey with us. It continues with Lynne and Adam to whom this book is dedicated.

1
Anarchy, Community and Critical International Theory

The neo-realist contentions that the anarchical international system will be reproduced indefinitely and that competition and conflict will remain endemic in the relations between sovereign states – and especially in exchanges between the great powers – have been at the centre of recent disputes in international relations theory. Neo-realism transformed the contemporary debate in International Relations by anchoring realist criticisms of the first and second images of war in improved theoretical foundations (Waltz, 1990). Although neo-realism supersedes realism in the area of methodological sophistication, it preserves its imperfections, which include the failure to recognise that the international system can be transformed by reconstituting exclusionary political communities. Some brief observations about a major weakness which is common to realism and neo-realism form the starting-point of this inquiry.

According to first-image analysis, war can be abolished by eradicating the propensity to use violence which is inherent in human nature. According to the second-image approach, war will end with the spread of enlightened national government. For liberals, such as Kant, the diffusion of republican regimes held the key to the progressive development of international society; for the exponents of Marxist class analysis, the universalisation of socialist rule would cancel the realm of power politics. Third-image analysis in realist thought maintains that war is an ineradicable product of international anarchy. Its key argument is that states are forced to compete for military power and national security because of the absence of any higher political authority, and are repeatedly brought into conflict by forces which elude their control.[1] Neo-realism simplified the analysis by distinguishing between two main strands of international theory: reductionism, which assumes that the nature of the international system is determined by the actions of constituent national regimes, and systemic reasoning, which maintains that international anarchy embroils all states, regardless of the nature of their regimes and societal preferences, in an endless struggle for security and power which frequently culminates in war (Waltz, 1979).

As with third-image analysis, systemic explanation maintains that sovereign states lack the requisite freedom of manoeuvre to bring an end to their anarchic condition. The speed with which revolutionary governments such as the Soviet Union embraced Realpolitik is thought to illustrate the explanatory failures of reductionism (Waltz, 1979, p. 128). Neo-realism has argued that national behaviour is greatly constrained though not wholly determined by the struggle for security and power. It has denied the existence of deep logics which promote radical international political change, and rejected the supposition shared by much liberal and Marxist thought that the extension of the boundaries of moral and political communities can secure the long-term pacification of international relations (Waltz, 1979).[2]

If sovereign states are likely to survive indefinitely – and neo-realism recognises they are unlikely to survive forever – then reflections on alternative forms of world political organisation are futile; and if domestic moral aspirations are invariably overridden by systemic constraints then reflections on the character of ethical foreign policy are largely, but not completely, otiose. All realist doctrines seek to demonstrate that a progressivist interpretation of international relations is impossible, but neo-realism is by far the most powerful attempt to banish idealist sentiments and reformist projects from the study of international society. It has been more rigorous than its intellectual predecessors in developing powerful theoretical buttresses for the critique of reformist approaches to world politics. The proposition that the anarchic international system and the potential for inter-state violence will be reproduced indefinitely has been its pivotal observation in this regard.

Although neo-realism brought greater theoretical sophistication to the discipline, its effort to eradicate normative imperatives has spectacularly backfired. To a far greater extent than any other perspective, neo-realism has highlighted the moral impoverishment of the study of international relations. Its attempt to equip realist pessimism with deeper methodological insight has had the paradoxical effect of promoting the recovery of critical and normative approaches. All such approaches – critical-theoretical, postmodern, feminist and liberal – have defined their identity through a series of challenges to neo-realism. Those approaches have challenged its conviction that the sole purpose of international theory is to explain the indefinite reproduction of the international states-system;

they have contested its account of an allegedly immutable anarchic condition and they have repudiated its effort to reduce rational political action in international relations to technical considerations of national power and self-interest. Such approaches clash with neo-realism but they also question the longer tradition of international pessimism which neo-realism draws on and seeks to refine. Critical approaches to world politics have taken the initiative in recovering the ethical imperative which animated the discipline in the inter-war years (see Long and Wilson, 1995).

Unlike neo-realism, critical approaches take the prospects for ethical foreign policy and the possibility of new forms of political community seriously. Gradually they have brought new images of international relations to the centre of the contemporary debate. These competing images are not concerned with the respects in which human nature, the characteristics of particular regimes or international anarchy cause international conflict, but with the problem of exclusionary political communities and their role in generating conflict and war.[3] On the assumption that the connections between moral exclusion and international conflict are not simply fortuitous, critical approaches argue for a political undertaking which the realist analysis of the three images of war and the neo-realist focus on reductionist and systemic theory have ignored. This is the enterprise of reversing what Corrigan and Sayer (1985, p. 4) call the totalising project, in which states seek to construct homogeneous national communities which are sharply distinguished from the world of outsiders and largely unconcerned about their interests. The critical enterprise has two main parts. Reconstructing the modern state and the international states-system to permit the development of higher levels of universality is one dimension of an alternative practice to state-formation and nation-building. Transforming exclusionary political communities so that higher levels of respect for cultural differences can evolve is a second element of the practice of superseding the totalising project.[4] Each dimension will be considered in more detail later.

This chapter makes the case for envisaging new forms of political community and for reworking international relations theory in the light of a normative commitment to realising higher levels of universality and difference. There are four parts to the discussion. Part one develops recent claims that neo-realism lacks an adequate account of modern political community. It argues that the neo-realist focus on the anarchic condition which compels states to behave in very similar ways ignores the problematical nature of political community, underestimates the potential for the transformation of the modern state and obstructs political practices which can defeat the totalising project.

Part two considers the problematical nature of modern political community in more detail, and argues that neo-realism has ignored its tenuous existence and precarious legitimacy. There are two dimensions to the problem of modern political community. First, although modern states have insisted that obligations to fellow-citizens take precedence over obligations to the rest of humanity, the precise moral significance of the boundary between citizens and aliens has been the subject of continuing ethical debate. The case for more universalistic loyalties and communities has long been important in the theory and practice of international relations. Second, although state-formation and nation-building have reduced cultural differences within many states, the struggle for cultural rights has been a key feature of national and international politics. These reactions against the effects of the totalising project have become stronger in recent decades and create new possibilities for the transformation of political community. The realist analysis of the three images of international conflict, and the neo-realist distinction between systemic or reductionist inquiry, fail to recognise that modern political communities offer a deeply unsatisfactory response to claims for ethical universality and demands for greater respect for cultural difference. Neither approach has considered the possibility that the boundaries of moral and political community could be redrawn to achieve higher levels of universality and difference.[5]

Neo-realism may concede that the legitimacy of the modern state has been precarious yet insist that the nature of international anarchy blocks the development of alternatives to the sovereign state. On this interpretation, critical explorations of alternative forms of political community have the unedifying effect of rediscovering the ancient tension between utopia and reality. Part three briefly considers the changing nature of the modern state in the context of globalisation and fragmentation, and notes how the prospects for new forms of political community have improved in recent decades. This is especially the case in Western Europe, which has become the laboratory for a unique experiment in creating post-nationalist or post-sovereign states which are more sensitive than their predecessors to the need for reconciling the claims of universality and difference, but no region of the world is immune to the politics of resistance to totalising projects. Part four argues that critical theories of international relations which explore normative, sociological and praxeological questions about the prospects for novel relations between universality and difference have acquired renewed political relevance with the decline of the totalising project which frustrated the appearance of alternatives to the territorial state.[6] It locates the origins of this mode of critical inquiry in the project of modernity developed by Kant and Marx and proceeds to ask how this project can be developed under altered historical conditions.[7] The principal aim of the subsequent chapters is to develop an answer to this central question.

The Critique of Neo-realism

The critical turn in international relations has been deeply influenced by debates about the adequacy of the neo-realist analysis of the state. The contention that radically different regimes behave in remarkably similar ways is an instructive theme in neo-realism, but it hardly exhausts the possibilities for theoretical inquiry. Neo-realism maintains that more advanced forms of theory may emerge to explain the respects in which the international system influences the units and is influenced by them. While acknowledging this point, Waltz (1979) argues that the analysis of the homogenising effect of the anarchic system upon national behaviour is the best means of developing the theory of international relations. It will remain so while generalisable statements about the impact of the units upon the anarchic system are unobtainable. Neo-realism does not argue that states are powerless to affect the functioning of the international system but it denies that theory can comment with any precision about any recurrent patterns of behaviour which arise from their limited autonomy and discretion. A role for critical theory which explores the normative purposes to which states can turn their discretionary powers is rejected by neo-realism. Theory is reduced to explaining the patterns of behaviour which result from the eternal quest for power and security.[8]

The positivist dimensions of neo-realist theory have been subject to telling criticisms which meld important themes in the history of reformist international thought with recent developments in social and political theory. Prominent among these criticisms is the arresting liberal claim, first advanced by Kant and Green, which holds that there is nothing in international anarchy itself which imposes competition and conflict upon nation-states (Linklater, 1990a, pp. 30–2). Current reformulations of this argument note that many of the properties which neo-realism imputes to the system of states should be attributed to its constituent national parts. Neo-realism regards the learned and alterable behaviour of the major powers as inherent features of an immutable anarchy.[9] But as an influential formulation correctly maintains, anarchy is what states make of it: the propensity for inter-state violence is not inherent in anarchy itself but is a function of how states have responded to international anarchy by constituting themselves as exclusionary and egotistical units (Wendt, 1992; 1994).[10]

The related argument that neo-realism lacks an adequate account of the relationship between agency and structure has also helped dislodge its dismal assumption that competition and conflict are inevitable features of international anarchy (Wendt, 1987; Hollis and Smith, 1990). Accounts of the ways in which the meanings of sovereignty, territoriality, statehood and associated concepts have shifted since the birth of the Westphalian era further reveal that national responses to international anarchy are socially constructed (Ruggie, 1983; Ashley, 1988; Bartelson, 1995; Biersteker and Weber, 1996). Claims that these concepts are not passive reflections of an immutable reality, but belong to the world of linguistic conventions through which reality is constructed, invite philosophical reflections on alternatives to the sovereign states-system. The positivist approach to social inquiry which informs neo-realism lacks a historical account of the development of social and political categories and fails to develop a critical exploration of alternatives to the structures which currently dominate. The moral limitations of neo-realism can therefore be simply stated. Its observations about the constraining effects of an immutable anarchy have the consequence of absolving states of the moral responsibility for devising practices which will bring more just forms of world political organisation into existence.

Normative international theory would be impossible without the presupposition that states and other actors have the capacity to overcome the constraints which neo-realism imputes to anarchy. For this reason the critique of the immutability thesis in neo-realism which denies the possibility of close political cooperation between the overwhelming majority of states is especially significant. Reformist projects have a long history in the development of international thought but they have often lacked the sophistication of their counterparts in domestic political theory. The recurrence of relatively shallow analyses of global reform which realists could dismember with comparative ease is one of the most unfortunate consequences of the earlier isolation of the study of international relations from ethics, political philosophy and social theory.[11] Important themes from these more critical disciplines have been drawn into the main debates about International Relations in recent years with the consequence that more robust statements of the reformist project have been formulated. In British international relations theory, though not in the United States, the intellectual initiative now lies with the project of reform.

Critical social theory has been centrally concerned with perspectives which purport to distinguish the immutable from the mutable, the natural from the contingent, in human affairs. It has been interested in ideologies which convert historically-contingent and socially-produced phenomena into natural and unalterable facts.[12] Its preoccupation with these forms of alchemy is easily explained. Attempts to justify excluding

various groups from the benefits which others enjoy often rest on a
confident appeal to the authority of nature. Apologists for racial or
gender exclusion have frequently argued that it is nature which deter-
mines social hierarchies, and nature which will be offended by wilful
efforts to modify the prevailing order.[13] During the last 200 years, the
critique of various systems of exclusion has often begun by delivering a
challenge to the accounts of social reality which depict social conventions
as natural and which attempt to place them outside the scope of critical
inquiries into the possibilities for the transformation of human practices.
The Marxist critique of ideology was the decisive intellectual break-
through in this regard because it revealed how the dominant understandings of allegedly natural social relations emerged under specific historical
circumstances, invariably to underwrite and conceal powerful sectional
interests. Efforts to subvert immutability claims, to debunk conventional
assumptions about the natural qualities of social structures or human
behaviour and to identify countervailing and progressive tendencies
within existing societies are the principal hallmarks of critical social
theory.

As with critical social and political thought in general, so now with
International Relations. Critical international theory treats the claim
that inter-state violence is inevitable as long as the anarchic international
system exists with considerable suspicion. These doubts are far from
new, but they are now located in a sophisticated critique of empiricist
and positivist aspirations for developing an objective account of the
world which exists 'out there' independently of the cognitive subject
(Rorty, 1989 p. 5). The crucial argument, which is evident in critical
social theory, in postmodernism and in feminist analysis, invites human
agents to reflect on the disturbing possibility that their efforts to provide
an objective understanding of an independent reality can obscure the
role that knowledge plays in facilitating the reproduction of problematical social arrangements which are not immune from transformation.
This argument has been central to the move beyond neo-realism in
recent years (Runyan and Peterson, 1991).

Cox's argument that knowledge is always for someone and for some
purpose remains the most illuminating formulation of this important
theme. Cox (1981) stresses the ideological consequences of the neo-
realist conviction that systemic theory reveals the impossibility of radical
international political change by peaceful means. Neo-realism, Cox
argues, has an interest in promoting the smooth functioning of an inter-
state order which has thus far defeated efforts to secure peaceful change.
For Cox, the dominant states and social forces rather than the anarchic
states-system are the main source of resistance to the restructuring of
international relations. This observation identifies a central weakness in

neo-realism. In short, Waltz's remarks about the ability of states to influence the operation of the international system prompt the question of whether the possibility of long-term radical change should have been so rapidly discounted. Equally important is the question of whether evidence of resistance to the dominant global political and economic structures should have been so systematically ignored. Troubling consequences result from neglecting the possibility of new combinations of state structures and social forces which are committed to the transformation of political communities and global society. Neo-realism, which is a problem-solving theory committed to promoting the smooth functioning of the inter-state system, has the effect of assisting the reproduction of the very structures which many political actors regard as unjust and which they are evidently keen to transform. Important moral consequences follow from the related observation that no social and political order treats all subjects equally or fairly. To privilege the goal of managing the existing order is to privilege the interests of those who benefit most from its survival – the great powers and the dominant groups within the global system. To privilege that goal is to facilitate the reproduction of arrangements which frustrate the political aspirations of systematically excluded groups such as the global poor and refugees (embracing large numbers of women and children), minority nations and the world's indigenous peoples.

To regard the immutability thesis as an exercise in the politically neutral observation of an independent reality is to lend vital ideological support to the status quo by denying that alternative possibilities are latent within existing social structures or by obscuring their existence. Immutability claims bolster structured inequalities of power and wealth which are alterable in principle. Such claims sanctify historically-specific configurations of power which the weak may resent and which the strong are far from powerless to transform. By converting humanly-produced circumstances into a quasi-natural condition, accounts of the immutability of political orders contribute to the formation of subjects who succumb to the belief that the relations between independent political communities must remain as they are. The immutability thesis conspires to construct human subjects who are resigned to the stultifying distinction, and allegedly unbridgeable gulf, between utopia and reality (Ashley, 1984).

Just as Marxist thought and other radical approaches take issue with systems-determinism, so does the critique of the immutability thesis in neo-realism aim to establish the possibility that human subjects can act together to overcome structural constraints. Critical theory is opposed to theoretical positions which stress political necessity and historical inevitability, and which fail to enlighten human subjects about the

existence of alternative political arrangements. It challenges the positivistic tendency, which is pronounced in neo-realism, of assuming that
actions which recognise the power of existing structural constraints (and
therefore contribute to their survival) are alone in satisfying the criteria
of rationality. Critical theory highlights the fact that by encouraging
resignation to fate, neo-realism denies the higher rationality of efforts to
bridge the gulf between actuality and potentiality. Whereas neo-realism
offers an account of the reproduction of the international states-system,
critical perspectives seek to identify the prospects for change in global
politics – latent though they may be at present. Their interest in
uncovering the first signs of structural decay and social transformation
is influenced by Marx's observation that all that is solid eventually melts
into air, and it is improbable that the future will resemble or repeat the
past.

The recent critical turn in International Relations resumes a discussion
whose existence predates the emergence of the subject as a discrete realm
of academic inquiry, and which has gradually reappeared following the
theoretical advances of recent years. This discussion, which was first
developed by Kant and Marx, was concerned with the possibility of
transforming political community and with the abolition of the constraints which neo-realism assigns to international anarchy. These are
crucial dimensions of the unfinished project of modernity or the Enlightenment. The ethical standing of this project, to which Kant and Marx
were so clearly committed, has been the subject of absorbing disputes in
recent social and political theory, some of which will be considered in
the next two chapters (see also D'Entreves and Benhabib, 1996). Suffice
it to note at this point that what has been retrieved in recent years is one
dimension of the Enlightenment project which realism and neo-realism
virtually erased from the study of international relations. What has been
recovered is the issue of how the future of global society can be
determined by freely chosen moral principles which further the autonomy of all human beings rather than by considerations of national
power or by a concern for maintaining order and stability between the
most powerful or potentially disruptive sovereign states. As the classical
realists argued, this question inevitably requires engagement with the
territorial state; but as the next two sections of this chapter contend, this
engagement requires the move beyond neo-realism to the critical analysis
of political community which first emerged in the writings of Kant and
Marx.

The Problem of Community in International Relations

The theoretical challenge to neo-realism has largely succeeded, and the aim of contemporary international relations theory ought to be to develop more complex analyses of the prospects for, and character of, new forms of political community. Neo-realism poses the searching question of where the sources of change ultimately lie. The response should recall that the modern states-system and its constituent parts have been prone to frequent division and disturbance. As Wight (1977, pp. 35ff) observed, European international society was highly susceptible to patterns of transnational revolutionary fragmentation. By neglecting the existence of these turbulent forces, neo-realism has depicted modern political communities as far more finished and complete than most actually are (Devetak, 1995b; Camilleri, Jarvis and Paolini, 1995, pp. 5–8).[14] Clearly, the states with which neo-realism has been primarily concerned, namely the great powers, have been more complete than most, and such completeness has been an important element of their military success.[15] Nevertheless, the nature of modern political community, including that of the great powers, has been the subject of deep uncertainty and debate since the emergence of the Westphalian states-system.[16] As the next section of this chapter argues, there is mounting evidence that these uncertainties have increased in recent years.

To begin with universality: the guiding point here is that sovereign states emerged within the ruins of a more inclusive civilisation which had been united by the normative and religious power of Christendom. The contention that modern political community is inadequate because it fails to satisfy the claims of ethical universality has been an important theme in much subsequent international thought as a result. Emergent territorial states were anxious to free themselves from the moral and religious shackles of the medieval world, and the history of international theory has been peppered with arguments about the ineradicable tension between ethics and power ever since the dawn of the Westphalian era. Even so, few states have tried to eliminate ethical universalism entirely – an impossible goal in any case – and most have concentrated their efforts on containing the threat which it poses to the ties which bind citizens together. What is more, universalistic ethical commitments have often been integral to the constitution of the modern state, and the claim has frequently been heard that the rights of the citizen give the rights of humanity concrete expression within the boundaries of territorial political communities. Most states proclaim their allegiance, disappointing though the results may be, to lofty internationalist ideals which transcend cold calculations of power and self-interest. Efforts by states to convert domestic moral preferences and interests into a universal morality, and attempts to confer legitimacy upon self-regarding actions by professing that they comply with international norms, invariably provoke cynicism and dissent. Sufficient numbers of citizens recognise the force of the distinction between a transcendent moral ideology, which can be used in criticism of the state, and an immanent ideology, which has no greater goal than fostering solidarity behind national goals, to prevent political communities becoming wholly closed in on themselves.[17]

An elementary universalism underpins the society of states and contributes to the survival of international order. Just as universalism has helped to prevent national communities from turning in upon themselves, so has it prevented the principles of international society from being reduced to a crude instrument of the dominant powers. The elements of a transcendent universalism exist in global society, and the tensions between this morality and the deepening international inequalities of power and wealth have contributed to the emergence of powerful developmental logics, the revolt against the Western dominance of international society being the most striking example (Bull, 1983a). The acquisition of sovereignty by the West's former colonies, the delegitimation of doctrines of racial supremacy and the dismantling of apartheid in South Africa, and the small but important headway in incorporating principles of social justice within the society of states are impressive monuments to the achievements of cosmopolitan morality.

Whether the cultural revolt against the West signifies the decline of attachments to a cosmopolitan ethic in international relations is an intriguing and keenly debated question. Many different interpretations of the meaning of the cultural revolt against the West exist. Some approaches argue that the future lies with the expansion of Western liberal-democratic capitalism (Fukuyama, 1992). Others envisage a new era of transcultural dialogue from which a genuine universal consensus about basic moral and political principles may emerge (Vincent, 1986; Watson, 1987). Predictions of the demise of all but the most rudimentary principles of international coexistence distinguish another perspective on the meaning of the cultural revolt against the West (C. Brown, 1988). Finally, some interpretations of the main directions of contemporary history anticipate increasing cultural variety and renewed civilisational conflict (Huntington, 1993). These disputes have yet to run their course, but it is arguable that the increased regard for cultural difference in international relations inaugurates a new stage in the evolution of cosmopolitan morality. A new universality may yet bring an end to the West's use of universalistic moral concepts to celebrate the achievements of Western modernity and to enlarge its control of other peoples.[18] In the more advanced moral codes, universality embraces greater openness to otherness and increased sensitivity to, and respect for, cultural difference.[19]

Modern citizens learn the language of a transcendent moral code which makes the critique of abuses of national power or cultural arrogance and visions of a less hierarchical international society possible. Modern citizens are aware of the tension between obligations to fellow-citizens and duties to humanity, and recognise that in the course of becoming citizens of particular states they acquire indifference to, and may become enemies of, the rest of the human race.[20] Reworking the social bond which unites a people, but simultaneously separates the community from human beings elsewhere, has therefore been a recurrent aspiration in Western moral and political thought. Images of global citizenship have been advanced by several political theorists, most notably by Kant, in order to make states more open to wider ethical considerations and to reduce the moral significance of the distinction between citizens and aliens (Falk, 1994). One effect of the totalising project, namely the production of estrangement between societies, is resisted by cosmopolitan morality. The cosmopolitan critique of exclusionary notions of national citizenship checks this aspect of the morally problematical nature of bounded political communities. Cosmopolitan morality underpins recurrent arguments in the West for developing stronger international organisations which, whether by supplementing or supplanting the activities of national governments, advance the condition in which citizens and aliens can coexist as moral and political equals (Heater, 1996).

The dialectical interplay between universality and difference is as evident in national societies as it is in the development of international relations. In national societies, the extension of the same legal and political rights to all citizens reveals the influence of universalistic conceptions of ethics which hold that individuals should be treated similarly unless there are morally relevant differences between them. The contention that these rights are a minor victory if citizens lack the power to exercise them marks the growth of the moral concern with the unequal distribution of national wealth and social opportunity. Additional claims that the dominant conceptions of citizenship have tended to privilege the hegemonic culture and to ignore the needs of culturally marginal groups reveal the widening of moral horizons to embrace questions of otherness and difference. Feminist theory and practice, which have argued that decisions to grant women equal access to participation in the public sphere do not go far enough, have further enlarged the realm of significant ethical considerations. Measures to reconstitute the public domain to ensure proper recognition of the interests and needs which are specific to women, or which are important in the lives of large numbers of women, point towards the deeper transformation of political community (Mouffe, 1993; Sylvester, 1994; Steans, forthcoming). The thesis that the public realm can be enriched by drawing on the moral skills which many women develop in the course of caring for family members is frequently linked with this claim. (For further consideration, see below pp. 68–9). The politics of difference intersects with the defence of universality to produce new images of political community. The universalistic response to the problem of community challenges the respects in which the totalising project has estranged citizens from aliens, and the plea for greater respect for difference contests the internal social hierarchies which developed with state-formation and nation-building. (These issues are considered further in chapter 6.)

The upshot of these arguments is that the universalistic solution to the totalising project is radically incomplete where no account is taken of the claims which insiders and outsiders make for the public recognition of their differences. In these circumstances, the problem of modern community is not the absence of ethical universality but insufficient respect for cultural diversity. Past images of international progress which tended to focus on the objective of moving beyond sovereign states to a cosmopolitan community of humankind must be modified accordingly. Some strands of feminist and postmodernist thought prefer a more radical conclusion which argues that universalistic ethical world-views are inherently dominating and underpinned the systematic exclusion of minority cultures within national boundaries and the ruthless exploitation of non-Western peoples. From these perspectives, universalism is part of the problem of modern political community rather than its self-evident solution (Walker, 1993, p. 77). Others have argued that support for the heightened appreciation of the value of cultural differences is ultimately parasitical on universalistic conceptions of ethics (Dews, 1987, pp. 217–18; Neufeld, 1995). This argument points towards the conclusion that it is not ethical universality as such but conceptions of universal morality that are hostile to cultural differences which have been a major failing of the modern form of political community.

Further remarks on the contentious issues which surround current debates about ethical universality can be deferred for the moment. It is sufficient to note the existence of a two-pronged attack on sovereign political communities. On one dimension there is the call for measures which take moral universalism seriously: for example, by increasing the role of authorities above the nation-state. On a second dimension, which is evident in the politics of minority nations and indigenous groups, there is the argument for reducing the influence which sovereign states exert over local communities and subordinate cultures. Feminist political theory enlarges these arguments by claiming that new political authorities, whether sub-state, national or supranational, should be sensitive to the specific needs of women and responsive to an ethic in which care and responsibility for the other displace the logic of social control which has been integral to state-formation and inherent in the totalising project.

These different perspectives converge on one crucial point since they suggest that modern political communities have been too universalistic (too neglectful of the range of differences between citizens) and too particularistic (too inclined to purchase their own national autonomy by limiting or sacrificing the autonomy of aliens).[21] Each of these observations is valid, and neither should be privileged over the other. Whether within states, or in the relations between them, the same issue therefore arises: how to promote universality which respects difference, and how to give public expression to cultural differences without encouraging and unleashing extreme particularism. Neo-realism denies the possibility of institutionalising new articulations of universality and difference on the grounds that efforts to reconstitute political community are domestic matters with little or no significance for international relations or because state-initiated projects of global reform will quickly encounter the unyielding constraints of international anarchy. To define the limits of political action in these terms is to submit to the consequences of the totalising project and to abandon the potentials for alternatives to the modern state to the vagaries of fate or chance.

The Changing Context of the Modern State

States, it has been argued, are less complete than neo-realism recognises, and the totalising project has repeatedly encountered powerful forms of resistance. Political communities which institutionalise new configurations of universality and difference have been one of the directions in which the Westphalian states-system could conceivably evolve. But notwithstanding the predisposition towards division and disturbance which Wight regarded as an inherent feature of the modern system of states, state structures have been able to mobilise sufficient power to prevent the reconstitution of political community. Societal potentials have been frustrated by the monopoly powers at the disposal of sovereign states.

As realists and neo-realists observe, the powers which have accumulated in the hands of modern states are intimately connected with the need to prepare for, and engage in, inter-state war. Sovereign states were suitably adapted for the ordeal of war by virtue of being sufficiently large to withstand external attack and suitably compact to permit administration from a central commanding point (Mattingly, 1955, ch. 5). As Tilly (1992a) has argued, modern states outflanked their competitors – city-states and sprawling imperial structures – by striking the appropriate balance between the accumulation of coercive power and the encouragement of capitalist development. More inclusive and less expansive forms of political association failed in the struggle for survival. The successful mode of political organisation – the sovereign state – created a number of monopoly powers over the territories which came under its jurisdiction. Five monopolies were acquired by states: the right to monopolise control of the instruments of violence; the sole right to tax citizens; the prerogative of ordering the political allegiances of citizens and of enlisting their support in war; the sovereign right to adjudicate in disputes between citizens; and the exclusive right of representation in international society which has been linked with the authority to bind the whole community in international law.[22] These state monopoly powers have been defining features of the Westphalian era.

From the outset, state-formation and the accumulation of monopoly power generated distinctive patterns of exclusion. As the expulsion of peoples in early modern Europe demonstrated (Zolberg, 1985), state-formation was an exclusionary process in the age before territorial boundaries hardened and the dichotomy between internal and external politics became clearly established. However, modern states lacked the capacity to project their power into society and to regulate social interaction within rigorously policed frontiers before the late eighteenth century. One of the hallmarks of the modern nation-state, namely the homogenisation of society and the hardening of the national boundary which separates insiders from outsiders, is a comparatively recent achievement (Giddens, 1985; Mann, 1986, 1994). Armed with unique monopoly powers, and equipped with an increased capacity for social control as a result of industrialisation, the modern state began to nationalise political community, and to marginalise assorted minorities and exclude aliens in the process. The acquisition of monopoly powers which made the totalising project possible undermined alternative sites of power and authority which could compete with the state for human loyalty. The monopolisation of these powers had the consequence of reducing the level of ethical universality and local differences which had existed in pre-modern European states (Mann, 1996, p. 224; Tilly, 1992b, p. 709).

Not only did the state initiate the totalising project: it mastered the political vocabulary with which to legitimate it. The main categories of the Westphalian epoch weakened rival conceptions of political life. Competing political discourses survived but they appeared nostalgic or antiquarian by comparison (as in the case of medieval notions of universal empire and anarchist visions of a return to local communities) or naively utopian (as in the case of Kantian images of world confederation or global government). A powerful statist discourse combining sovereignty, territoriality and citizenship, to which the idea of the nation was subsequently added, made various efforts to give expression to different forms of political organisation seem stumbling and incoherent. This ensemble of concepts has had unambiguous effects upon the constitution of modern political life. Compared with medieval European international society with its overlapping jurisdictions and multiple loyalties, only one sovereign could exercise legitimate authority over the territory and the people which came under its jurisdiction. All citizens have been deemed subject to one and only one sovereign power, and citizenship, which was initially restricted to a small proportion of the total population, has been linked with the supposition that all citizens should possess exactly the same legal and political rights. Nationalism was added to this powerful concoction on the assumption that, ideally, all citizens should subscribe to one national identity conveyed by a common language and culture. The acquisition of state monopoly powers shifted local and transnational authorities and loyalties from centre stage in the Westphalian era. The hegemonic political discourse channelled human loyalties away from potentially competing sites of power to centralising and homogenising sovereign states which endeavoured to make national boundaries as morally unproblematical as possible.

Demands for citizenship rights emerged in response to the accumulation of state monopoly powers, but the dominant vocabulary of politics over the last 350 years has limited the range of imaginable alternatives to the sovereign state.[23] The recurrence and apparent inevitability of war further legitimated sovereign states. In the context of war, as Hegel argued, the state was unrivalled in its ability to promote close political cooperation between citizens as opposed to subjects.[24] Nevertheless, novel interpretations of the prospects for moving beyond the nation-state and ending inter-state violence have made sporadic appearances over the past 150 years. The recurrent motif has been that capitalist industrialisation would no longer interact with war to produce homogeneous communities in which the ideas of sovereignty, territoriality, citizenship and nationalism are forged together into one monolithic political discourse. When unyoked from the state, many have supposed, capitalist development and the spread of commerce would stretch humanity's moral horizons beyond the parochial world of the nation-state and pacify the states-system. So did many liberals and Marxists argue in the nineteenth century.

The question of whether long-term processes of change have begun to fulfil their earlier promise of transforming political life arises once again in the contemporary post-Cold War era (Richardson, 1993). Various disjunctures between the sovereign state and globalisation have been highlighted (D. Held, 1995), and clearer impressions of the impact of long-term patterns of social and economic change upon the state's capacity to perpetuate the totalising project have emerged in recent years.[25] Many analyses of these processes point to the declining import-ance of the state's traditional monopoly powers and observe the erosion of its capacity to promote the closure of political community (Wallace, 1994; Strange, 1996). Many anticipate the imminent demise of the Westphalian era (Rosenau, 1990; Cox, 1992; Zacher, 1992).

Of central interest are the arguments which suggest the obsolescence of war between the major industrial states (Mueller, 1989); the analyses of the rise of new trading states which uncouple economic growth from earlier strategies of conquest (Rosecrance, 1986); and the accounts of the expanding inter-liberal zone of peace (Doyle, 1982, 1986). Each of these approaches to international pacification clearly takes issue with the neo-realist contention that states are powerless to alter the prevalent modes of competitive interaction which are allegedly imposed upon them by international anarchy; and each assumes that the state's monopoly of control of the instruments of violence is less influential in shaping the nature and prospects of international society than it was in earlier epochs. Accounts of the logics of globalisation and fragmentation in contemporary world politics combine with these analyses of the declining significance of force in relations between core states to challenge the neo-realist contention that political life seems likely to revolve around the sovereign state for the indefinite future (Camilleri and Falk, 1992, p. 3; Cochran, 1995). Key features of these accounts are worth noting.

Numerous 'evasions of sovereignty' (Falk, 1990) which are the result of the globalisation of relations of production and exchange undercut the state's traditional power to direct the national economy (Strange, 1996). The state's capacity to regulate the political identities and loyalties of its citizens is weakened by the increase of global interconnectedness which raises awareness of the problems and predicaments of the human species as a whole (Wallace, 1994, p. 55; Strange, 1996, pp. 72–3).[26] The role of the state in securing close cooperation between citizens is reduced as the latter turn to various sub-national and transnational actors to promote, amongst other things, measures to secure environ-mental protection (Hurrell, 1994, p. 162), and look to local or ethnic communities to resist threats to their identity. Pressures on the doctrine of sovereign immunity arise in the context of the state's greater role as a quasi-firm involved in contractual relations with transnational economic enterprises. Inroads into the state's claim to absolute sovereignty within its territory, and infringements of its claim to be the sole subject of international law, have occurred alongside advances in the international protection of human rights (Beetham, forthcoming). Demands for greater international accountability have multiplied with the rising instances and greater possibilities of transnational harm.[27] With globalisation, it is absurd to assume that the most significant moral community comprises fellow-citizens or co-nationals (D. Held, 1995, p. 18). In this context, the question of how the major industrial democracies can preserve democratic governance has emerged as a central problem for political theory and practice (D. Held, 1995). Experiments in national democratic governance have lost much of their value in the context of globalisation, and measures to extend democracy beyond the sovereign state are urgently required, as the advocates of cosmopolitan democracy have maintained (Archibugi and Held, 1995; Habermas, 1994). Seemingly irreversible trends towards the internationalisation of decision-making in economic, environmental and security domains underline the crucial point that national boundaries have become deeply problematical in the modern world (Camilleri and Falk, 1992, p. 9). These are some of the more important developments highlighted in recent accounts of the demise of the Westphalian epoch.

Closer transnational political cooperation is not the only effect of globalisation. As previously noted, war was central to the rise of modern states with their distinctive monopoly powers, high levels of national cohesiveness and clearly defined territoriality. War favoured the survival of the centralised state as the main vehicle for effective political cooperation, and diminished the choices available to minority nations. Faced with the dramatic rise of state power in the nineteenth century, national minorities confronted the difficult choice of whether to struggle to preserve local centres of decision-making power or attempt to democratise the central institutions which followed the growth of state power (Mann, 1994, pp. 250–1 and 354). Warfare settled the matter by promoting the rise and dissemination of unitary states which were hostile to the emergence of potential challengers to their authority in the domestic regions. Intriguingly, globalisation alters the equation. The pacification of core areas of the international system has removed one of the main pillars of national cohesion. Ancient fault lines have been exposed within many national communities, and in several states the myth of national unity and coherence has been shattered. Unprecedented degrees of globalisation and unusual levels of ethnic fragmentation cast doubt on the efficacy and legitimacy of the nation-state as the primary vehicle for successful cooperation in many core regions within the modern world system (Cochran, 1995). Violent transformation is the frequent consequence in the constitutionally insecure and less industrialised societies.

Globalisation and fragmentation develop in tandem, as Aron (1968) observed some thirty years ago, and not only because of the uneven development of capitalism which is the preferred explanation of classical Marxism or because of the uneven development of industrialisation (Gellner, 1983). The members of culturally marginal groups have a long history of declining the state's invitation to shed their supposedly archaic inherited identities and of resisting total incorporation within the dominant national community. As often as not, the revolt against the national-assimilationist ideologies and practices favoured by the majority of nation-states possesses its own distinctive logic which arises out of the humiliation of prolonged cultural domination rather than the resentment of economic inequality.[28] With its homogenising tendencies, globalisation fuels the politics of identity and community. As a result, where cultural and political boundaries do not converge (as in the case of indigenous peoples trapped within settler states, or where migrant populations are exposed to patterns of exclusion in the societies which they inhabit), pressures have mounted to modify traditional conceptions of community and citizenship which are hostile to the creation of group-specific rights (Kymlicka, 1989, 1995; Taylor, 1994). Across the world – and largely because globalisation disseminates similar political projects and creates a common stock of political resources and ideas – minority nations, indigenous peoples and migrant organisations fuel 'the politics of recognition' (Taylor, 1994). Unsurprisingly, since globalisation prepares the way for transnational political activity, these new movements seek global support for their project of reconstructing national communities. One aim of these communities is to create universal norms which establish the principle of respect for cultural differences.[29] The increased prominence of the politics of recognition is one key indicator of movement beyond the Westphalian era.

Of course, the interplay between globalisation and fragmentation does not have a singular effect: their interaction provokes different responses in different societies. In Western Europe, particularly, the future of the modern state with its unique fusion of sovereignty, territoriality, citizenship and nationalism is most obviously in question; new forms of community and citizenship seem most likely to emerge within that region (Waller and Linklater, forthcoming).[30] An important observation about the process of European state-formation indicates one possible trajectory of political development. As Wight (1978, p. 25) argued, the formation of the modern European state involved 'a revolution in loyalties' in which 'the inner circle of loyalty' to an immediate feudal superior expanded, and 'an outer circle of loyalty' to Christendom shrank. The ethnic revolt in Europe, coupled with the internationalisation of decision-making and emergent transnational loyalties, provokes the observation that these earlier processes are now being reversed. If so, then more powerful centres of political authority may emerge above and below the level of national governments to supplement the nation-state (Camilleri and Falk, 1992, ch. 9).

Enthusiasm for these developments should not underrate the power of the nation-state and its enduring capacity to rally support for traditional nationalist projects which oppose substantial transfers of power to new authorities. Nor should it underestimate the tenacity of hierarchical conceptions of race, gender and ethnicity which underpin the modes of exclusion to which the members of national and racial minorities, gypsies, migrants and refugees are regularly exposed. Nationalist social and political forces may be decisive at any historical moment, but the fact that they rarely go unchallenged is also an important feature of modern political community. The debates and divisions which occur as national communities wrestle with three traditional questions about the ethics of exclusion which are posed with renewed urgency throughout the whole of Europe with the passing of the bipolar age are deeply significant. The first of these questions is concerned with what Walzer (1995) calls the distribution of membership – the principles by which political communities decide who to admit and who to exclude from their ranks; the second with what can be called the distribution of citizenship – the principles which define the subjects of citizenship rights and the nature of these rights; the third with the distribution of global responsibilities – the principles which govern decisions about the responsibilities of separate states to the rest of humankind. (For further consideration of these issues, see below pp. 79–85.) Many communities are deeply divided over the answers to these questions which the forces of globalisation and fragmentation have compelled them to reopen, and many have lost their former confidence that these are questions which each sovereign state can rightfully answer on its own. Rightly does Derrida (1992, p. 9) argue that in Europe at any rate – although the same observation applies to many other parts of the world – it is unusual to encounter a political community which is entirely at one with itself (see also Devetak, 1995a, p. 45).

No assumption is made here that some invisible hand steers societies towards a condition in which national governments will despatch their powers to new centres of responsibility within and outside their national territories, and strike a better balance between ethical universality and respect for difference in consequence. All that is argued is that the forces of division and disturbance which Wight identified in past epochs are evident in the current phase of European international society, that a heightened awareness of fluidity and unpredictability prevails, and that less has the air of immutability. Precisely what is in store for the classical sovereign state in Europe and elsewhere remains uncertain, but various trends create the expectation of its steady decline as the most effective and legitimate instrument of close political cooperation (Beetham, 1984; Bauman, 1993, p. 139). The logics of globalisation and fragmentation have disrupted the totalising project and steered many societies to the point where one future course of political development detaches the ideal of cultural distinctiveness from the idea of sovereign statehood and allows new combinations of universality and difference to develop (Tilly, 1992b, p. 705). Under these circumstances it is necessary to reflect upon new forms of political community which sever the links between sovereignty, territoriality, citizenship and nationalism. Increasingly, the central questions of international relations concern the ethical foundations of political community in the post-Westphalian era.

Theorising the Reconfiguration of Political Community

Contra neo-realism, it no longer seems wise to assume that sovereign communities and the anarchic international system will be reproduced indefinitely. A more secure assumption is that globalisation and fragmentation will continue to erode the state's monopoly powers, and that national governments will come under growing pressure to shift important responsibilities to new political authorities (Beetham, 1984). The outline of a post-Westphalian international society has already been traced within Western Europe and may come to include several societies which formerly belonged to the Soviet bloc. Different logics operate in other regions, especially where military regimes dominate weak civil societies, but present trends strongly suggest that globalisation and fragmentation will continue to frustrate the totalising project in the majority of nation-states.[31] Neo-realism is one manifestation of the failure of mainstream international relations theory to consider alternative forms of political community which are relevant in this context; but contemporary patterns of change tax the Western political imagination more generally.

The tyranny of the concept of the sovereign nation-state (Bull, 1977, p. 275) has impoverished the Western political imagination, and left it ill-prepared for the current challenge of rethinking the foundations of modern community. Political thought was divided into two largely self-contained branches which reflected the sharp contrast between the domestic and international realms which appeared with the rise of the Westphalian era. Political Science has analysed the nature of organised life within bounded communities, whereas International Relations has considered their prevalent modes of interaction. Various intellectual encrustations formed around these disciplinary boundaries while the sovereign state remained secure as the dominant form of political community. One of the consequences of distinguishing political theory as the theory of the good life from international theory as the theory of survival (Wight, 1966, p. 33) has been the dearth of analysis of the origins, development and actual or conceivable transformation of the bounded territorial state.

The principal countervailing trend, which is best represented by the writings of Kant and Marx, placed bounded political communities at the centre of social and political analysis. Their writings analysed the processes of change influencing the future of such communities and the fate of the unique distinctions between domestic and international politics, inside and outside, the inner circle of harmony and progress and the outer circle of the eternal recurrence of competition and conflict which have typified the Westphalian era. That there are profound weaknesses in their writings is not in question, and efforts to theorise political community in the contemporary world must go beyond the detailed analysis provided by Kant and Marx. Nevertheless, an insightful account of bounded communities which unites normative, sociological and praxeological inquiry emerges in the writings of Kant and Marx. Any approach to the potential transformation of political community which seeks to integrate normative, sociological and praxeological concerns must first settle accounts with their writings.

One of their shared assumptions was that there are no immutable structures which demand that human loyalties must stay confined within the limits of the parochial sovereign nation-state. There are no systemic forces for Kant and Marx (such as the kind which neo-realism conjures into existence) which dictate that the conscious transformation of human society remains a hopelessly utopian goal. There are no structural logics which prevent human beings from recreating political life, or which decree that a progressivist interpretation of international society will forever be frustrated. Kant and Marx stressed the respects in which the extension of the boundaries of association and the enlargement of systems of cooperation had already occurred in world history. Kant's philosophy of history emphasised the long transition from the original, barbaric international state of nature to the civility of the modern society of states and the growing responsiveness to the demands of cosmopolitan morality. The passage of humanity from an early condition of small and relatively isolated social systems to the modern reality of large, economically interdependent societies governing vast territories was the equivalent theme in the Marxian philosophy of history. For Kant, and even more so for Marx, the destruction of small bounded communities and the dramatic acceleration of the universalisation of social and economic relations were extraordinary dimensions of human history (Linklater, 1990a, chs 6–8, 1990b, ch. 2).

An engagement with these long-term patterns of development underpinned their conviction that it was improbable that the modern sovereign state is the final stage in the development of the human capacity for creating frameworks of close political cooperation. Kant and Marx added specific observations about the main developmental logics in the contemporary era to their reflections on the central dynamics of world history. Kant believed that the universalisation of commerce and the dissemination of republican principles of government in eighteenth-century Europe formed the prelude to the emergence of powerful cosmopolitan sentiments. Marx held that the internationalisation of production and exchange presaged the rise of more universal forms of political cooperation which were embodied first of all in the emergence of transnational bonds and affinities between the members of the world's proletariat. The principal features of their respective sociological accounts of the main universalising processes are sufficiently well known that the discussion can turn to their efforts to integrate a sociology of previous extensions of the boundaries of moral and political community with the normative and praxeological analysis of the emerging post-Westphalian era.

Kant's comments on the ethical limitations of bounded communities indicate that he believed that the bonds between citizens and the state had to be renegotiated since the whole human race comprised a single moral universe. He took issue with the 'miserable comforters', Grotius, Vattel and Pufendorf, who announced that all human beings were obligated by the universal moral principles which reason had the innate capacity to apprehend, but sacrificed or compromised ethical universality whenever it clashed with the interests of the egotistical sovereign state. Kant's response to the conflict between the ties of citizenship and the duties of humanity envisaged a Copernican revolution in political theory in which the international political implications of the cosmopolitanism of the Stoic-Christian tradition would be taken seriously (Gallie, 1978). At first glance, it seems curious that Kant argued that state sovereignty should remain one of the constitutive features of political community. But he believed that the deeper issue was to enlarge the moral, as opposed to the political, boundaries of community, so that stronger cosmopolitan sentiments would cancel the tendency of states to act as self-regarding autonomous units (Hurrell, 1990).[32] Individuals would remain citizens of their respective political communities but they would expose the civic bonds within each independent state to the test of cosmopolitan citizenship. As world citizens, they would exercise their sovereignty with due regard for the principle that all individuals should be regarded as if they were co-legislators in a universal moral community. Kant assumed that the development of a universal communication community would be the defining political aspiration of the post-Westphalian epoch.[33]

Kant's philosophy of world history tried to show that what is true in theory, namely that all humanity should act as if it belonged to a universal kingdom of ends, can become true in practice. Universal commerce and the dissemination of republican principles of government demonstrated that a cosmopolitan kingdom of ends was possible but they did not issue a guarantee that one would ever be realised. A philosophy of ultimate ends and a sociology of the prospects for, and constraints upon, the development of a higher form of life were accompanied by a praxeology which explained the means by which human beings could transcend existing conditions. Kantian praxeology offered a vision of future possibilities in the expectation that theory can play a transformative role by delegitimating existing structures and by steering human action to new political objectives; it also considered how human action could best respond to the new historical opportunities in order to secure the gradual transformation of oppressive structures. Kant's vision of a universal society of co-legislators served this task, as did the inventory of maxims crucial to an ethical foreign policy which was advanced in *Perpetual Peace*. That inventory set out the international moral obligations which republican states had to respect if they were to honour their commitment to publicity, autonomy and consent. Immediately binding objectives, such as complying with just war principles, and longer-term aspirations, including the abolition of standing armies, were identified as the means by which republican states could promote the emergence of a universal kingdom of ends (C. Brown, 1992, ch. 2; Williams and Booth, 1996, pp. 86ff). When specifying these measures, Kant assumed that the possibility of new forms of political community was anchored in the ideas of liberty and equality which were intrinsic to modernity.

Marx's analysis of the prospects for universal emancipation dispensed with Kant's appeal to a system of absolute, universal moral truths. A neo-Hegelian perspective which analysed the historical evolution of more profound understandings of the meaning of human freedom and the development of deeper insights into its social and economic preconditions replaced Kant's belief in the existence of a universal human rationality which had the power to comprehend the principles of an immutable morality. The tension between the language of freedom and equality in capitalist society and the alienating effects of the internationalisation of the modern forces and relations of production was central to Marx's sociology. The powerful ethical themes which run through Marx's analysis of capitalism revolve around this elementary contradiction.

Capitalism compounded the tragic quality of human existence by celebrating freedom and equality as political principles while subjecting increasing numbers of the world's population to universal systemic forces which eluded their control. Marx maintained that traditional conceptions of political emancipation failed to recognise that the problems of modern society could not be solved without reconstructing the totality of social and economic life. His ethical commitment to a universal society of free and equal producers, which is reminiscent of the Kantian vision of a cosmopolitan realm of co-legislators, was inextricably linked with a sociology of the impact of capitalism on human society. The praxeological dimension of his inquiry contained a broad outline of future communist society, assuming in common with Kant that social and political theory can have a transformative role. A more robust articulation of the main political objectives of the leading counter-hegemonic movement, the proletariat, whose growing universal solidarity anticipated a new era of human cooperation, was one dimension of Marx's praxeology. His reflections on the importance of capturing state power and comments on the relationship between class politics and national movements sought to demonstrate that revolutionary actors could solve the mystery of how to progress towards universal socialism. Like Kant, Marx believed that modern commitments to autonomy and equality made new forms of human community possible.

It is the form rather than the substantive content of the reformist project in the writings of Kant and Marx which informs the subsequent discussion; nevertheless a brief account of the principal limitations and shortcomings of their respective approaches is necessary before exploring alternative possibilities. The important point to make about Kant's normative inquiry is that his belief in immutable and universal laws of reason clashes with modern sensibilities which emphasise the social construction of knowledge and the diverse, and changing, cultural conceptions of moral truth. The very possibility of moral universals is precisely what is at stake in much contemporary social theory which has been anxious to stress the threats which universalising moralities pose to cultural diversity. Notwithstanding his opposition to the West's treatment of indigenous peoples (Kant, 1970b, pp. 255–6), the question of cultural difference was hardly a central consideration in Kant's writings. Similar difficulties arise in connection with Marxism. The critics have argued that historical materialism consolidated a binary division between progressive Western civilisation and retarded non-Western humanity which was as problematical in theory as it was pernicious in practice. Marx's exuberance for the loss of self-sufficiency on the part of non-Western peoples (which was echoed in Engels' disparaging remarks about the historyless peoples) revealed an explicit commitment to a process of Westernisation in which little or no value was attached to the survival of radical cultural differences.[34] This inclination to privilege universality over difference was challenged by the Austro-Marxists, who argued that the sovereign nation-state should be replaced by new social formations in which higher levels of universality and respect for cultural autonomy could coexist (Bottomore and Goode, 1978). The critique of Austro-Marxism in the Soviet Union delayed the appearance of the wider regard for national and cultural differences which emerged with the rise of Third World Marxism and which postmodernism in more recent times has been especially keen to support.

The Kantian and Marxist sociologies of bounded communities assumed that egotistical national communities were about to be replaced by new structures of transnational cooperation. Unsurprisingly, given their cosmopolitan ethical commitments, they analysed the universalising processes which promised to widen the boundaries of moral and political community. In this regard, they shared the illusion of the epoch. The supposition that commerce and industrialisation would lead to the growing popular acceptance of cosmopolitan ideals, and eventually to the eclipse of the nation-state, informed many of the leading theories of the rise of industrial society in the nineteenth-century (Kumar, 1981). Three main points need to be made about late eighteenth- and early nineteenth-century explanations of the emergence of a universal political community. First, there was a tendency, which was pronounced in Marx's thought, to underestimate the tenacity of nationalism and the state, and to fail to anticipate the crucial role which war would continue to play in shaping the boundaries of community. Second, although the rise of nationalist feeling and the increased tolerance of violence in international affairs towards the end of the nineteenth century compelled the analysts of community to reconsider their position on the nation-state, many perpetuated the error of assuming that economic forces remained the primary determinants of social and political development. This preference for imputing causal primacy to the sphere of production is most evident in the Marxist theories of nationalism and imperialism (Linklater, 1990b, chs 3–4). The most innovative strands of Marxist thought shared the Austro-Marxist conviction about the significance of language and culture throughout human history. Third, the praxeological observations generated by these sociologies focused on the best means of widening the boundaries of moral and political community to ensure justice for outsiders. The question of how to reconstitute political community so that higher levels of respect for cultural differences would flourish internally was less important.

The substantive analysis of normative, sociological and praxeological questions concerning the future of political community in the nineteenth century cast insufficient light on the issues of the modern age; nevertheless, it exemplified a mode of reasoning which escapes the limitations of later realist and neo-realist thought. Kant and Marx have been described as second-image thinkers who believed that the rise of enlightened regimes would inaugurate a new phase of international history in which cooperation and peace would replace conflict and war. A more accurate interpretation of their writings is that they provided insightful commentaries on the long-term processes of change which disrupted the state's capacity to unify citizens in opposition to aliens. Kant and Marx argued that the primary social bonds which hold societies together but which also separate them from the rest of humanity are more tenuous than much social theory has supposed. They sought to identify immanent forces which ran counter to the state's totalising project, and they offered reflections on how the subjects of independent political communities could gradually replace intersocietal estrangement and conflict with universal harmony. For these reasons Kant and Marx remain important for the critique of the immutability thesis in neo-realism and for efforts to create the condition in which a progressivist interpretation of international society becomes a plausible account of world history.

As members of the Frankfurt School argued, it is necessary for philosophy to move beyond Marx just as it was essential to move beyond Kant and Nietzsche (Horkheimer, 1972). The most convincing efforts to construct a critical analysis of community which remains true to the spirit, if not to the letter, of Kant and Marx's analysis revolve around the idea of expanding the realm of social interaction which is governed by open dialogue. This emphasis on dialogue resonates with the liberal principle of publicising intentions and announcing the reasons for action which Kant's political philosophy stoutly defended. Connections between this ideal and the Marxist tradition are less immediately evident although Habermas (1979a) has argued that Marxism can only realise its critical potential if it is committed to the ideals of undistorted communication.[35] The dialogic turn in recent social theory is not confined to liberal and Marxist political thought, however. Support for dialogic communities is equally central to postmodernist thought (Lyotard, 1993), philosophical hermeneutics (Shapcott, 1994), feminist political theory (Frazer and Lacey, 1993; Benhabib, 1993) and to many other contemporary approaches to international relations (Rosenau, 1994; Blaney and Inayatullah, 1994; Jabri, 1996). Several theoretical approaches converge on this central theme and contribute to the project of reconstructing the three-tiered approach to political community which was developed in Kant and Marx's thought. They place the normative ideal of the universal communication community at the centre of the unfinished project of modernity.

Whereas Kant and Marx were at best unclear about the moral significance of cultural differences, more recent efforts to promote dialogic communities are unambiguous about their importance. Habermas argues that reworking the ethical foundations of Marxism involves a sharp break with any substantive vision of the good society which is assumed to have global validity and significance. The emphasis shifts away from universalisable conceptions of the good life to the procedural universals which need to be in place before true dialogue can be said to exist in any social encounter. Theory neither anticipates the outcome of dialogic relations nor assumes that dialogue must culminate in a consensus about the desirable ends of social and political life. Similar arguments exist in postmodern approaches which are suspicious of, and often opposed to, ethical universalism because of the attendant danger that it will consolidate existing forms of cultural domination and generate new modes of exclusion. Those perspectives do not regard dialogue as a vehicle for reconciling value-differences but defend it as the medium through which greater human variety can be discovered and explored. Dialogue holds out the promise that agreements will not be reached by ignoring or suppressing marginal and dissident voices. The logic of the argument is that dialogic communities will be sensitive to the needs of the victims of the totalising project: namely, aliens beyond secured borders and a range of internally subordinate groups. The recent dialogic turn in social theory points towards a normative approach to community which supports greater universality coupled with a deeper commitment to the wealth of human differences.

The key normative issue, which is that political communities should be reconfigured to combine advances in universality with the heightened appreciation of social variety, has profound implications for the sociology of community. The main sociological question is how far different communities are capable of dismantling the unjust systems of exclusion which are directed against internally subordinate groups and aliens. Sociological investigation ought to retain the Kantian and Marxian focus on the universalising processes which encourage the extension of the boundaries of moral and political community, but it needs to supplement the approach by investigating societal potentials for incorporating greater diversity within modern political life. Social systems reveal different potentials for evolving in this direction. One of the purposes of the critical sociology of bounded communities is to understand them.

Settling accounts with Marxism which made the practice of exclusion central to sociological theory is one central issue. Efforts to transcend Marxist sociology have developed along two fronts. There is, in the first place, the incontrovertible claim that Marxism placed class exclusion at the heart of sociological analysis and neglected the modes of exclusion which are grounded in hierarchical representations of ethnicity, gender and race. In large part because of the influence of Foucault, contemporary critical sociology faces the task of developing a comprehensive analysis of the various barriers to otherness which societies impose (Taylor, 1985). In the second place, there is the equally undeniable argument that the Marxist paradigm of production cannot explain what Habermas has called the grammar of forms of life which includes the sphere of cultural practices (see Roderick, 1986, p. 135). A related point is that the Marxist preoccupation with the sphere of production seriously underestimated the historical importance of the state, geopolitics and war.

Giddens (1985) argues that Marxism failed to understand that the development of the modern state has been shaped by the interaction between internal pacification, geopolitics, capitalism and industrialisation: its evolution cannot be understood as the political effect of the logic of capitalist development alone. Much more is known about the nature of state power as a result of the move to multi-logic explanation (Skocpol, 1979; Mann, 1986; Tilly, 1992a). This critique of Marxist theories of the state also has considerable significance for a sociology of bounded political communities. Mann's inquiry into the development of the forms of social power casts a great deal of light on the expansion of the boundaries of political association and community in the early empires and on the development of the state's capacity to promote totalising projects. That approach intersects with Wight's embryonic sociology of societies of states and with Nelson's analysis of civilisational structures and inter-civilisational relations. All three approaches contribute important resources to the sociology of bounded communities and reinforce the Kantian claim that multiple forces, including commerce, state-building, geopolitics, and developments in the moral-cultural sphere, have interacted to shape the nature of modern political community and its level of responsiveness to universalistic norms. (See below, chapters 4 and 5.) These approaches prepare the groundwork for a sociology of community which analyses societal potentials for developing stronger commitments to universality and difference.

Praxeological innovations are required which correspond with the normative commitments and the sociological project which have already been outlined. One of the functions of praxeology, according to Kant and Marx, was to give direction to the transgressions of state sovereignty and the disengagements from national community which suggested that a cosmopolitan association was slowly emerging.[36] The universalistic commitment which shaped their respective conceptions of praxeology left little scope for measures designed to promote respect for cultural differences. Contemporary praxeological analysis can overcome this limitation by supporting patterns of change which point beyond the totalising project to dialogic communities which are at pains to overcome the exclusion of marginal voices. It can identify ways of institutionalising visions of a universal communication community which diminish the moral importance of shared national identities and embrace the conviction that political decisions lack legitimacy if they are taken without considering their likely effects on systematically excluded groups inside and outside the boundaries of existing forms of life.[37]

To analyse boundaries in this way is to recognise the continuing importance of the nation-state but to argue that it should adopt new political responsibilities. This is to side with Kant against Marx, whose emphasis on the transformation of global capitalism left central questions about the future role of the state and the possibilities for developing the institutions of international society unanswered. It is to seek to reconstruct the Kantian project of defending the transition from an anarchic states-system in which high levels of distrust, competition and conflict prevail to a society of states in which international legal and moral principles tame what Kant called the 'barbaric freedom' of sovereign communities; and it is to support further progress towards a cosmopolitan association in which universal principles unite individuals everywhere while respecting the value they attach to their respective cultural differences. To approach the problem of community in this manner is to endorse the argument that the dominant mode of critical theory in the twentieth century, namely Marxism, paid a high price for its preoccupation with the transformation of capitalist relations of production. Its praxeology was ill-equipped for the crisis of the early twentieth century which revealed the tenacity of nationalism, the state and war, and demonstrated the need for different approaches to the eradication of the totalising project. As Derrida (1992) suggests in his comments about the relationship between Marxism and deconstructionism, critical theory has to become more deeply engaged with the sovereign state, nationalism, international law and citizenship. It has to confront anew the question of how to solve the problem of bounded communities.

The inclusion of citizenship in Derrida's list suggests three further comments on praxeology which complete this part of the discussion. First, various strands of contemporary social and political theory have criticised the exclusionary role of modern conceptions of national citizenship. Recent cosmopolitan democratic theory takes issue with traditional notions of citizenship which deny aliens the right to participate in institutions that make decisions affecting their vital interests (D. Held, 1995). Images of cosmopolitan democracy extend the Kantian theme that moral agents should conceive of themselves as co-legislators within a universal kingdom of ends. They argue for transnational political structures in which citizens and aliens are associated as equal participants in a universal communication community. Second, various strands of contemporary political thought stress the respects in which difference-blind conceptions of citizenship exclude subordinate groups. Group-specific rights are defended by these approaches as a means of breaking with the hegemonic proposition that all citizens must have exactly the same rights and duties notwithstanding their different circumstances and exposure to unequal social possibilities and constraints. Praxeological inquiry can reinforce these pressures to move beyond exclusionary sovereign states by imagining modes of citizenship which weave new relations between universality and difference into the structure of contemporary political life. These are the possibilities which globalisation and fragmentation create within those regions of international society where war no longer plays its traditional homogenising role in the lives of communities.[38]

Third, these remarks do not anticipate the demise of the state but envisage its reconstruction. The task of praxeological analysis is to assist the development of new forms of political authority and novel conceptions of citizenship which strike the appropriate balance between universality and difference. A central ambition is to facilitate the transition to a condition in which sovereignty, territoriality, nationality and citizenship are no longer welded together to define the nature and purpose of political association. This is not to advance the unlikely proposition that conventional state structures either will or should disappear, but rather to suggest that states should assume a number of responsibilities which have usually been avoided in the past. Hegel's conception of the rational state remains insightful in this context. The main insight is that the rational state has ethical responsibilities which other political organisations do not exercise to the same degree. Mediating between the different loyalties, identities and interests which exist in society was, for Hegel, a primary function of the state. The need for political institutions which perform this task would not cease to exist just because national societies had become more responsive to cosmopolitan morality or more sympathetic to claims for the public recognition of cultural differences;

nor would it end were states to share authority with institutions in their domestic regions and international organisations. A crucial responsibility of the modern state is to enable multiple political authorities and loyalties to develop, and to endeavour to bring harmony through dialogue to the great diversity of ethical spheres which stretches from the local community to the transnational arena (Lawler, 1994). The rational state eschews the totalising project, encourages the emergence of new forms of political community in which the potential for higher levels of universality and difference is realised and, in so doing, transcends the limitations of the Westphalian era.

Conclusions

The neo-realist account of international anarchy delivered a profound challenge to the project of the Enlightenment which envisaged the possibility of a cosmopolitan society. Recent responses to neo-realism argue that war is not an inevitable consequence of international anarchy. They take issue with the neo-realist contention that the purpose of international relations theory is to explain the reproduction of the states-system and to promote the smooth functioning of international order. To reduce international relations theory to these tasks is to submit to the consequences of the totalising project. Opposing approaches highlight the incompleteness of states and argue that transforming political community is the primary objective of international relations theory. Practical efforts to promote new relations between universality and difference are a fitting response to the pressures which globalisation and fragmentation have imposed on modern political communities. Critical theory can support these efforts by renewing the normative, sociological and praxeological analysis of community initiated by Kant and Marx. But reconstructing this project is no simple task. Recent developments in social theory have been highly critical of the universalistic normative commitments which were central to their writings. The strengths and weakness of their commitment to the project of universal emancipation are the primary concerns of the next two chapters.

2
Universality, Difference and the Emancipatory Project

A central strand of European thought over the last few centuries has regarded cosmopolitanism as one of the principal achievements of modernity and as one of the key markers which distinguishes advanced societies from parochial forms of life. Enlightenment thinkers were convinced that the steady growth of human reason and the gradual elimination of ignorance and superstition would culminate in the moral and political unification of the entire human race. Marxism argued that the West's faith that its modernising project had universal validity was supported by its cosmopolitan credentials. Assumptions such as these were fostered and continually reinforced by Western economic and political ascendancy over the rest of the world. Nineteenth-century liberalism and Marxism, the two principal heirs of the Enlightenment and the dominant modes of progressivist thought in the later stages of the era of European conquest, exemplified the West's unqualified confidence in the superiority of its own way of life.

Cosmopolitanism has not been without its critics. Powerful challenges emerged in the middle of the nineteenth century as nationalist sentiments became more important and as the historicist critique of Enlightenment conceptions of universal reason and morality gathered strength. These two forces were often interwoven to revolutionary effect. Philosophical criticisms of the liberal belief in the ontological primacy of the individual produced a new emphasis on primordial cultural wholes which intersected with, and helped to legitimate, the rising tide of demands for national self-determination. But, as Mazzini's writings indicated, even in this context cosmopolitanism and internationalism enjoyed a prominence within Western culture which is much less evident today. Despite occasional reinventions of Western cosmopolitan triumphalism – Fukuyama's liberal thesis about the end of history is the best-known recent example – many currents of modern and postmodern social and political theory have been highly critical of universalistic ethical world-views and global political projects. Cosmopolitanism has fallen on hard times in the last years of the twentieth century (Nussbaum et al., 1994).

The contemporary critique of cosmopolitan morality appears at a time when perceptions of Western cultural superiority are significantly weaker than they were even fifty years ago, and when the level of social and cultural diversity is rising sharply across the world after several centuries in which the opposite seemed to be the case (C. Brown, 1988, p. 343). The demise of Western political ascendancy, and the ensuing cultural revolt against Western hegemony, have produced a remarkable retreat from cosmopolitan modes of reasoning. The cosmopolitan backdrop to Western imperialism features prominently in recent social and political thought, which has dramatically represented the violent acts committed against colonised peoples in its name (Todorov, 1992). One of the main contentions of recent social theory is that the potential for domination is inherent in all universalising perspectives. Several strands of contemporary social and political thought extend this argument by rejecting all foundationalist thought and by denying that any ethic can be established absolutely. Epochs are not neatly separated from one another, and anti-foundationalism is opposed just as universalising ideologies were in the nineteenth century, but there is no mistaking the shift away from universalising perspectives and global emancipatory projects during the last ten to fifteen years.

Seldom does the intellectual retreat from cosmopolitanism and the wider project of the Enlightenment lead to a celebration of ethnic particularism or patriotic loyalties which disavows all forms of answerability to others (MacIntyre, 1984; Miller, 1994, 1995). A powerful defence of responsibility to otherness has been advanced by postmodern and feminist social and political theorists in recent years and must count as one of their most significant achievements (White, 1991). The critique of the universalistic principles which were embedded in the grand historical narratives of the nineteenth century takes its cue from this starting-point. Efforts to advance towards the Marxian ideal of socialised humanity are often regarded as having unveiled the totalitarian potential which resides within Western conceptions of the self, autonomy, rationality and historical progress. The critique of the potentials for domination which are believed to be secreted within moral and political universalism is part of a larger challenge to the interplay between constructions of Western identity and the negative representations of non-Western societies which accompanied the West's efforts to universalise its conception of politics and society. The larger challenge highlights the negative representations of non-European peoples which the West employed to construct its own identity as the highest civilisation and to legitimate its project of global domination. The critique of ethical universalism is fundamental to redefining the character of modernity and to eradicating hegemonic constructions of the non-Western world which helped lend cohesion to the modern European state.

Despite the scepticism which is displayed towards universalistic perspectives, a certain resonance with the Kantian principle of respect for persons is evident in the postmodern defence of responsibility to otherness. The next two chapters argue that it is not universalism as such which should be at issue in contemporary debates about ethics and difference but one specific form in which it is supposed that individual reason can discover an Archimedean moral standpoint that transcends the distortions and limitations of time and place. The possibility of occupying an Archimedean standpoint which permits objective knowledge of permanent moral truths which bind the whole of humanity is a claim that has long been denied – by Hegel's famous critique of the Kantian categorical imperative, to cite one of the most influential examples. It is a claim which many of the leading strands of contemporary social and political theory are correct to deny. Precisely where this leaves moral argument is the intriguing question.

Alternative forms of cosmopolitanism are available which dispense with these worn foundations. The approach which will be considered below recognises that human subjects cannot perceive the world other than through the distorting lens of language and culture which has already made them what they are as moral subjects: it therefore eschews any claim that it is possible to have ready access to a privileged Archimedean site. A concern with the unjust systems of exclusion which restrict the opportunities of subordinate groups is the key to this form of ethical universalism. This stress on the ethics of exclusion endeavours to overcome the problems which accompany the quest for an Archimedean standpoint. By virtue of its commitment to the principle of respect for persons, this conception of universalism rejects efforts to impose a single identity upon the whole of humanity. To that extent, its concerns intersect with those of postmodernism. Indeed, it will be argued that postmodern critiques of Western forms of cultural superiority and feminist challenges to universalistic ethics implicitly draw from the reservoir of moral universalism while criticising its philosophically untenable and politically dangerous formulations. Although this is not their central intention, postmodern writings on responsibility to otherness and their related approaches to dialogue and difference contribute to the development of a radically improved universalism.[1]

The upshot of this argument is that a thin conception of cosmopolitanism with no fixed and final vision of the future can replace a thick conception of cosmopolitanism which believes in determining the precise content of a single universalisable conception of the good life. Far from weakening the challenge to the main features of modern political life, the thin account of cosmopolitanism provides a critique of domestic and international political arrangements which is more radical than alternative positions which have sought to incorporate all human beings within a single form of life. Critical social theories which support a thin conception of cosmopolitanism support the development of wider communities of discourse which make new articulations of universality and particularity possible.

This argument about universality and difference is developed in three stages. The first part examines the communitarian argument that cosmopolitan approaches are too inclined to disregard the special ties and affiliations which exist between those who share the same way of life. Hegel is regarded as a key representative of the school of thought which defended the sovereign state from the cosmopolitan belief that all human beings should be treated equally, as if they already belonged to a moral and political community which embraced the whole human race. Hegel's writings defended the arrangements of a pluralist international society while arguing that the sovereign state was the principal expression of the human capacity for close political cooperation.[2] The belief that communities have a fundamental right to protect their different ways of life was a central theme in Hegel's writings which is reiterated in more recent statements of the communitarian position. Walzer (1995) argues that the right of a community to determine its own affairs is incomplete unless it is at liberty to decide who can enter its ranks, and who can be turned away. This position is plainly at odds with those cosmopolitan approaches which maintain that individuals should enjoy the right of free movement in a world society.[3] There is nevertheless a good deal of shared ground between the communitarian and cosmopolitan perspectives, and each contributes important themes to the contemporary project of imagining the transformation of political community. (See below, pp. 51–5.)

The second stage of the argument comments on one issue which communitarian thinking inevitably raises, namely how far duties to other members of a bounded community with its right of closure rule out obligations to the remainder of humanity. One of the oldest problems in international political theory, which is establishing the precise moral significance of national boundaries and determining the moral relevance of shared nationality or citizenship, arises at this point (Linklater, 1990a). A solution has often been thought to require a strict ordering of moral priorities. For many communitarians, duties to other members of a society necessarily come before duties to aliens, and only when the community has looked after its own members can the interests of aliens enter the moral equation. For many cosmopolitans, there are no grounds for privileging those who just happen to have the same nationality or citizenship: the contingent fact of living together within the same national frontiers has no obvious moral significance. The moral issues are rather more complex, however, when communitarians argue that each society has duties to the others as members of an international society of states, and obligations to assist individuals and peoples elsewhere; the ethical questions are more subtle when cosmopolitans argue that special ties and loyalties are valuable and not automatically trumped by the levelling proposition that each member of humanity must have exactly the same duties and rights. The argument below is that loyalties to the community and obligations to humankind both have value; neither automatically takes precedence; and both can be challenged on the grounds that they give rise to unjust modes of exclusion. Whether there are secure foundations for assessing different moral claims and political loyalties with regard to these considerations is the principal philosophical question.

The third stage of the argument extends this discussion by concentrating upon several themes which arise in postmodern and feminist reflections on politics and ethics. The anti-foundationalist claim that there are no stable foundations for ethical judgement, and the related conviction that universalistic moralities are as exclusionary as the varieties of ethical particularism which they purport to overcome, are especially significant in this context. Communitarian ethics also come under fire from the exponents of these claims, notwithstanding general support for their belief that there are no philosophical arguments which secure the case for a universal political association. It should be noted that communitarian thought does not argue that support for sovereign states is the only alternative to the cosmopolitan argument for enlarging the moral frontiers to encompass the whole of humankind. Communitarians take issue with the sovereign state where it deprives local communities of the right of self-determination. What kind of community is being defended here is the primary issue for the critics of communitarianism. The defence of community, it has been argued, often ignores the forms of power and exclusion which communities have imposed on subaltern groups, such as women, in the name of cherished conventions and traditions. Critical social theory, postmodernism and feminism have raised these concerns, and they have made the ideal of dialogic communities which transcend unjust exclusion one of their essential aims. The dialogic ideal clashes with the dominant conceptions of modern political community in which sovereignty, territoriality, citizenship and one dominant nationality are wedded together. It envisages post-nationalist communities which are sensitive to the needs of the systematically excluded within and outside traditional borders – hence its appeal as one of the principal ethical foundations of the post-Westphalian era.

Difference, Self-determination and Exclusion

The political significance of cultural differences was briefly stated over three centuries ago in the writings of Samuel von Pufendorf. Human beings, according to Pufendorf, have an inalienable right to create separate societies because they have not all 'grown out of the earth together like fungi' (Pufendorf, 1931, p. 236). Although they are obliged (albeit imperfectly) to comply with universal moral principles when they deal with the rest of humankind, they are not under any moral obligation to belong to a cosmopolitan political system. Human beings need associate only with those with whom they share 'special inclinations'; the boundaries of a political system should converge where possible with an existing 'harmony of dispositions' (Pufendorf, 1931, p. 236). A similar theme underlies Aristotle's remark that while it might be possible to build a wall around the Peloponnese, no polity would exist there (Wolin, 1960, p. 70). In the nationalism of Herder, chemistry cannot unite what nature has deemed should live apart (Berlin, 1976), and in the cosmopolitan language of Kant (1970b, p. 223), differences of language and religion necessarily prevent 'the peoples from intermingling' though not, he was quick to add, from reaching an understanding about the preconditions of international peace.

The crux of the matter is that morality is social rather than individual, particular rather than universal, diverse rather than uniform, fluid rather than constant. Social-contractarian approaches to the state and international law in the seventeenth and eighteenth centuries were too universalistic and too individualistic to develop a bold exposition of this view. But they were clear that one of the purposes of political society was to overcome the imperfections of the law of reason by establishing several legal frameworks of action which corresponded with different societal preferences. Three of the imperfections of the universal law of reason could be removed thereby: the lack of precision about ethical matters which led to rival interpretations of the nature of right action; the failure to specify the subjects of rights and the holders of corresponding duties; and the absence of a higher authority to ensure that duties were properly observed and noncompliance was effectively punished (O'Neill, 1989b, pp. 224–5). The state removed the imperfections and uncertainties of the state of nature by making rights and duties determinate in law and by enforcing obedience. The achievement of political society was to replace imperfect moral duties with carefully specified legal rights and duties, and to convert human beings into citizens in the light of the special bonds and inclinations which explained their preference for division into separate, bounded communities.

A bolder formulation of the social nature of morality and a richer explanation of the diverse forms of political community are evident in the distinction between *Moralität* and *Sittlichkeit* which is central to Hegel's attempt to defend state sovereignty from a cosmopolitan critique, and especially from the Kantian claim that the moral law urges the human race to enter into a universal association which is authorised to uphold eternal peace. *Moralität* is the approach to ethics which assumes that the solitary individual can use autonomous reason to discover the normative foundations of a cosmopolitan society. It abstracts individuals from concrete social settings and credits them with innate powers of apprehending universal moral truths. *Sittlichkeit* refers to the social institutions and norms which precede the individual and lend shape to the subject's moral life. From its perspective, *Moralität* is based on a distorted account of the relationship between the individual and the social world which fails to recognise that society equips the individual with the power of moral reasoning. Exponents of *Moralität* protest that social norms must have the consent of individual subjects if they are to command legitimacy.

Hegel rejected the conception of the moral self which underpinned Kant's political thought without subscribing to the Burkeian claim that tradition and prejudice provide an authoritative answer to the question of how societies should be organised. The importance of *Moralität* was its requirement that unreflective social moralities should place rational deliberation rather than the reliance on custom and convention at the heart of social and political life. *Moralität* articulated the claim that individuals have the right to lead free lives and to expect that social and political institutions will submit to the imperative of rational criticism and open debate. *Moralität* played a central role in promoting the decisive transition from unreflective to reflective social moralities which enlarged the domain in which individuals could exercise their freedom. However freedom required appropriate social and political institutions which the primitive individualism of *Moralität* could not determine.[4] Hegel believed that the modern state was the only political community which could ensure that individuals enjoyed the institutions which realised their potential for leading free lives. Cosmopolitanism embodied the profound truth that human beings had rights *qua* human beings but it was profoundly at error when it placed citizens at odds with the modern territorial state (Hegel, 1952, para. 209). Beyond the concrete morality of the state there was only the 'void of the rights of man', the 'shapelessness of cosmopolitanism' and the hollow vision of Kant's 'world republic' (quoted in Smith, 1989, p. 75).

An essential theme in Hegel's thought was that freedom must be sought out and won within each society: the precise arrangements which will maximise freedom have to be determined in accordance with the unique experience and distinctive traditions of different forms of life. Freedom cannot be imposed from outside or received in the form of a charitable donation if it is to conform with the special inclinations and harmony of dispositions which Pufendorf regarded as essential for the survival of political community. Hegel's critique of cosmopolitanism was largely concerned with what he regarded as its erroneous political implications rather than with its moral commitment to human equality. He was hostile to the position, which he mistakenly imputed to Kant, that the cosmopolitan principle that all human beings are ends-in-themselves must necessarily deny the moral significance of national boundaries and oppose the principle of state sovereignty. No such implication followed for Kant. Hegel's more telling point was that the most elementary understanding of the importance which human beings attach to their membership of specific bounded communities, each with its distinctive way of life, reveals the impossibility of a universal political association. More recent communitarian thought shares Hegel's conviction that the exponents of an abstract universalism fail to understand the complexities of social solidarity and the necessary division of humanity into separate political associations.[5]

Hegel was vigorous in defending the right of collective self-determination which later theorists from Mill to Walzer have been equally keen to support. Walzer is by far the most explicit about the necessary relationship between political community and the right of closure. He argues that communal self-determination is meaningless if outsiders can enter at will, and if the community is obliged to accept outsiders who do not share its special inclinations. To enjoy self-determination a community must be at liberty to define the boundaries which must not be crossed and the collective rights which cannot be violated (Walzer, 1995, ch. 2). Political communities must have the right to decide who can enter their ranks and who can be directed elsewhere. Honouring the Kantian ethical principle that individuals should be treated as ends in themselves requires, first and foremost, respect for the rights of their communities: hence Walzer's communitarian variant on Kant's categorical imperative which defends the maxim of always acting to defend the right of communal autonomy (see Walzer, 1994b).

It is possible to extend the line of argument which finds support in

Hegel and Walzer by drawing out one theme which is implicit within it. This is the notion that self-government is likely to promote good government even though it does not guarantee it (Miller, 1994). High levels of social trust which result from shared identity increase the likelihood that self-government will promote good government. A state is more likely to be successful in promoting public goods if its citizens have the same nationality; and a people will be more likely to have confidence in the state, and have less reason to fear 'brute force', if national bonds tie them together (Miller, 1994). The contention that collective self-determination facilitates good government strengthens the argument that communities must have the right of closure. Promoting the survival of a common culture requires the unconditional right to decide who can and cannot acquire membership of the society (Walzer, 1995, ch. 2).

The thesis that community necessitates closure runs up against cosmopolitan approaches to the ethics of the refugee problem in which the individual right of free movement overrides the right of any community to preserve its autonomy and distinctiveness.[6] In the main, however, cosmopolitan approaches accept that cultures have the right to preserve their integrity (Carens, 1987; Dummett, 1992). Few would argue that the right of free movement should remain paramount when the evidence is that a society cannot absorb additional refugees without causing serious disruption to its way of life or stretching its material resources to the breaking-point. It is far from obvious that cosmopolitans must take issue with the argument that a liberal society is not obliged to admit aliens who are known to hold racist or totalitarian beliefs which clash with its political ideals (Walzer, 1995, p. 50). One aim of cosmopolitan approaches is to defend the rights of refugees in a world of sovereign states in which no automatic right of refuge is conferred on stateless peoples. Many political theorists who have communitarian sympathies take exactly the same moral standpoint. Walzer argues that communities have a moral duty to help desperate strangers and adds that conferring the right of residence on stateless persons and permitting full citizenship is often the only effective means of honouring that obligation.[7] While defending these cosmopolitan sentiments, Walzer emphasises that communities must retain the right to make their own decisions about their moral obligations to outsiders and about the best means of discharging them. This right of communal self-determination rules out the possibility of alienating the power of decision about such matters to a superior law-making body.

Cosmopolitans are at odds with communitarianism if they argue that political communities should transfer their decision-making powers to a higher international body. But the distance between the two perspectives is less great if cosmopolitanism simply argues that existing political communities ought to increase the impact which duties to the rest of humanity have on decision-making processes. Then their overlapping moral concerns suggest it is unwise to draw a sharp distinction between communitarianism and cosmopolitanism.[8] Nevertheless, the critique of cosmopolitanism has been important in imagining communities which are closed in on themselves. An example is Rousseau's jibe about the cosmopolitans who boast of loving all the world in order to enjoy the privilege of loving no one (Rousseau, 1962, vol. 1, p. 453). Rousseau's preference for a civil religion over universal Christendom expressed the fear that cosmopolitanism would puncture the special ties which hold the community together (Rousseau, 1968, bk 4, viii; Fidler, 1996, pp. 129–30). The contention that cosmopolitanism threatens the survival of workable forms of political life by making communities vulnerable to dissolution through rational criticism stems from a similar source.[9] The logic of this argument is to envisage forms of political community in which the desire for social unity suppresses rational debate about the reasons for closure against the rest of the world and about the point at which rights of exclusion should yield to duties to ensure justice for human beings elsewhere.

Contemporary political theorists who are sympathetic to the communitarian ideal argue that the state has the right to forge appropriate loyalties to the political community but they also stress the importance of wider international moral obligations (Miller, 1994, 1995). In Hegel's terms this is already to imagine forms of political community which have been forced beyond the limits of customary morality or unreflective *Sittlichkeit* by the demands for rational criticism or *Moralität*. The communitarian thesis that those who have special ties have the right to form a political community together and to exercise the right of closure against the rest of humanity does not lose its significance as a result. But the contention that community implies closure has to be balanced with the ethical claims of universality. Quite how bounded political communities should achieve this balance is a complex question, but an unavoidable one if communitarianism and cosmopolitanism identify important moral problems which all bounded political communities must endeavour to solve. The main issues here are still seriously undertheorised but they have more than a passing resemblance to the themes which were at the centre of earlier debates about the relationship between obligations to fellow-citizens and obligations to the remainder of humanity.

The State, Citizenship and Humanity

Questions about the relationship between moral universals and cultural difference have a central place in contemporary debates in international relations theory but they have also been important in associated discussions about the relationship between duties to fellow-citizens and obligations to the rest of humanity. Whether or not shared nationality or common citizenship is a morally significant characteristic which justifies placing the interests of insiders before the interests of outsiders has been the fundamental question of international political theory since the dawn of the Westphalian states-system. Various answers have been advanced. Some have argued that shared nationality or common citizenship is a morally significant difference and that the state has a duty to privilege the interests of co-nationals. Cosmopolitanism is usually assumed to hold that primary loyalties should be directed to the whole of humanity because differences between insiders and outsiders are morally irrelevant. Most theoretical approaches in the second part of the twentieth century occupy some intermediate point between the extremes (as in the case of cosmopolitan and communitarian positions on the ethics of refugees). Some conception of justice in war in which the rights of non-citizens take precedence over military convenience is generally accepted (Norman, 1995). Indeed one of the contributions of international political theory (and practice to some extent) in recent years is its argument for enlarging the circle of human beings who are thought to possess basic rights, irrespective of the society to which they belong. But more recent formulations of universalistic standpoints usually refrain from arguing that all human beings should be absorbed within a cosmopolitan society which removes all trace of cultural difference. Most stress the enriching quality of the diversity of human loyalties (Beitz, 1994).

The import of cosmopolitan reasoning is that loyalties to the sovereign state or to any other political association cannot be absolute; the upshot of the recognition that the diversity of cultures and loyalties has considerable value is that duties to humanity as a whole do not override all other obligations. When faced with diverse loyalties it is always tempting to arrange them into a moral hierarchy. In that spirit, one possible response to the loyalties mentioned above is that the interests of co-nationals should normally take precedence over the interests of the members of other communities but that minor advantages to the state should not be achieved by imposing terrible and disproportionate costs on outsiders. Arguably a moral calculus of this sort is one thread running through the writings of Kant's miserable comforters – Grotius, Pufendorf and Vattel (Linklater, 1990a, chs 4–5). But such a calculus which supposes that obligations to the state should normally have precedence over obligations to the society of states or to humankind is precisely what a second response to the diversity of human loyalties emphatically rejects. What is important from this vantage-point is not the order of priority in a hierarchy of duties but the tests to which loyalties of any kind ought to be subjected.[10] The crucial measure is whether these loyalties are guilty of unjust exclusion. Two ways of approaching this question have been explored in the recent literature.

In his defence of cosmopolitanism, Beitz has argued that its essence is captured by the belief that all human beings possess equal moral standing rather than by a particular preference for a specific form of universal political organisation (such as world government). The cosmopolitan belief in the moral equality of persons holds that sound reasons have to be offered for treating individuals differently (Beitz, 1994, p. 23). On this premise, there are no prima facie reasons for privileging the interests of another person just because she or he is a fellow-citizen – conversely, there are no obviously compelling reasons for disregarding the interests of outsiders simply because they happen to have been born in or belong to another society. The key claim is not that a concern for the welfare of the whole of humanity should displace all other attachments but that political communities have a fundamental moral duty to assess the impact of their actions upon outsiders and to avoid causing them unnecessary harm. Cosmopolitanism argues that political communities should widen their ethical horizons until the point is reached where no individual or group interest is systematically excluded from moral consideration. Expanding the circle of those who enjoy this right is the central moral theme in the Stoic-Christian tradition. The purpose of cosmopolitanism is to protect the alien from the tyranny of one of the fundamental modes of unjust exclusion.[11]

Beitz argues for extending the moral boundaries of the community in recognition of the equality of outsiders. In a different approach to the modes of moral exclusion, Connolly (1994) defends a critical orientation to the ways in which communities have constructed their identity through the production of hierarchies of difference. The role that the construction of the savage has played in the development of American identity is one manifestation of this phenomenon (Connolly, 1995). As with Beitz, Connolly is opposed to any effort to arrange various loyalties in a grand moral hierarchy; instead he argues that all loyalties should be conditional on passing one crucial test which is whether their effect is to construct others as different and unequal (Connolly, 1994, p. 25). A similar approach is evident in the writings of White (1991) and Todorov

(1992). For each of them the value of diverse loyalties is not in question: the important issue is whether political loyalties contribute to the tyranny of exclusion by demeaning other cultures.

The relationship between these two approaches is complex. One of the more obvious differences is that Connolly does not rest his argument on a foundationalist cosmopolitan ethic, although certain universalistic moral commitments underpin his claims, as his reference to 'layered cosmopolitanism' indicates (Connolly, 1994). The two positions have different starting-points but overlap and complement each other in important respects. Beitz's cosmopolitan defence of widening the moral boundaries of communities requires the eradication of the constructions of difference which developed in the era of Western global domination, just as Connolly's approach presupposes a commitment to human equality. However, complex questions remain despite this convergence of views. Quite how the balance is to be struck between loyalties to fellow-citizens and responsibilities to outsiders is one such question which arises whether or not societies depict each other in demeaning ways. As Walzer argues, the central issue is determining the extent to which the right of communal self-determination can be overridden by the principles of a cosmopolitan morality. There are two ways of approaching this question within communitarian thought which warrant discussion at this point. The first defends the notion of a pluralist international society of states; the second envisages a solidarist inter-national society of peoples.[12]

Hegel defends the first approach. As noted earlier, Hegel celebrated the achievements of cosmopolitan *Moralität* but rejected any attempt to place abstract universalism at odds with the sovereign state which was the only effective vehicle of close political cooperation. Hegel was scathingly critical of visions of a cosmopolitical society while stressing the reality of limited political cooperation in the relations between sovereign states. International political cooperation was exemplified by the existence of a rudimentary international law of war which upheld the right of private individuals to be spared unnecessary suffering. International law could not eliminate the tragic conflict between different moralities from the system of states. Deep divisions between incommensurable ethical world-views would often lead to war, which was the only instrument for settling fundamental political disputes. The institution of international law therefore demonstrated the existence of the human capacity for developing a universal system of collaboration; but of equal importance, its inability to solve tragic conflicts in international relations revealed that the capacity for close political cooperation barely extended beyond the frontiers of the sovereign state. Co-existence between states marked the outer limits of effective collaboration.

Hegel believed that the appropriate balance between various loyalties was struck by these three principles: first, political communities have the right to preserve their separateness; second, they are primarily concerned with the welfare of citizens but they are not at liberty to promote their interests without regard for the effects of their actions on outsiders; and, third, while they ought to respect the argument of cosmopolitan *Moralität* that human beings *qua* human beings possess elementary moral rights, they are not answerable for their actions to humanity or to any religious or political institution which may claim to represent its interests. Cosmopolitan morality has the limited, but not insignificant, effect in this approach of placing certain checks upon the untrammelled egotism of the sovereign state. Exclusionary states are restrained by their membership of a more inclusive society of states which embodies a basic commitment to internationalising the politics of dialogue and consent.

This Hegelian claim that respect for the equal rights of other communities is as far as cosmopolitanism can extend in the world of states is close in some respects to the rationalist approach to international relations.[13] According to the rationalist perspective, international society establishes a legal and moral framework which allows national communities to promote their diverse ends with the minimum of external interference (Walzer, 1979; Nardin, 1983). Rationalists lack Hegel's enthusiasm for the virtues of war, and many step outside the Hegelian framework entirely by contemplating humanitarian intervention in exceptional circumstances where, for instance, a people is at the mercy of a genocidal regime (Walzer, 1979; Vincent and Wilson, 1993). But for the most part they deny that cosmopolitan morality can do more than contribute to the maintenance of order between states. The crucial point is neatly summarised by Wight's observation that the rationalist perspective is the *via media* between the Hobbesian image of international anarchy and the Kantian ideal of a cosmopolitan community of humankind (Wight, 1991). For rationalists, as for Hegel, various international institutions such as international law help to balance the claims of universality and diversity within a pluralist society of states.

The problem with leaving the argument there is that many states pose a threat to cultural diversity within their own territorial boundaries. The ideal of communal self-determination is often frustrated by the principle of national sovereignty and by the constitutive principles of international society which regard sovereign states as the exclusive subjects of international law. The balance between universality and difference in the society of states is incomplete because of the large number of states in which cultural and political boundaries are not closely aligned. A more effective balance is promised by the notion of a solidarist international society of peoples in which the rights of national minorities and indigenous peoples are recognised in international law. In certain circumstances, the right of communal self-determination may require a more radical step to which the society of states has traditionally been hostile, namely redrawing traditional frontiers so that minority nations achieve an independent political status.

Communitarian thought defends the right of secession where continued membership of a state is likely to perpetuate extreme forms of discrimination against minority nations and deep material inequalities, or where the very survival of a minority culture is at stake. An important question here is whether a group can exercise the right to secede without regard for the welfare of those who will be left behind. Walzer (1994b) argues that the right of communal self-determination does not exclude wider moral considerations, and there are duties to compensate those who are left behind for the loss of important economic and strategic assets. Obligations do not stop there since acts of secession rarely end by bringing political and cultural boundaries into total alignment. Questions inevitably arise about the status of minorities which have not consented to belong to newly formed states. Consociational arrangements and federal, or confederal, modes of political accommodation which ensure respect for cultural differences may be better remedies than secession (Walzer, 1994b, ch. 4). Such efforts to reconstruct nation-states are necessary to promote the transition from a pluralist society of states to a solidarist society of peoples. Endorsing this point, some communitarians envisage a greater role than exists at present for the international protection of minority rights (Walzer, 1994b).[14]

Communitarianism need not subscribe to a Hegelian doctrine of state sovereignty (Miller, 1994) or propose that all citizens have exactly the same legal and political rights. There are very good reasons from a communitarian point of view for replacing unitary sovereign states with new forms of political community which are more hospitable to cultural difference, and there are equally strong arguments for granting the members of minority groups the right of appeal beyond sovereign states to global legal institutions which give expression to the normative ideal of an international society of peoples. Far from being antithetical, communitarianism and cosmopolitanism provide complementary insights into the possibility of new forms of community and citizenship in the post-Westphalian era. They reveal that more complex associations of universality and difference can be developed by breaking the nexus between sovereignty, territoriality, nationality and citizenship and by promoting wider communities of discourse.

Cosmopolitan theorists and their communitarian and postmodern critics broadly agree that questions about the relationship between obligations to the state and to the rest of humanity will arise as long as human beings believe that national boundaries are neither morally decisive nor morally insignificant. No lasting solution to this, the deepest moral question in international relations, is likely to emerge in theory or in practice – not because neo-realists are obviously right that international anarchy prevents human beings from leading a moral life but because moral tensions inevitably attend the existence of multiple loyalties and identities. The positions surveyed above invite the conclusion that no hierarchy of loyalties and obligations is feasible but that a reflective morality with the following two sensitivities to unjust exclusion is possible: the first is the recognition that the construction of identity needs to avoid the negative representation of alien cultures; the second is the acknowledgement that the right of communal self-determination has to be exercised in ways which accept the cosmopolitan moral principle that the welfare of insiders does not have any automatic privilege over the interests of outsiders and that good reasons have to be offered for treating equals unequally. The principles of a pluralist society of states and the ideal of a solidarist international society of peoples are two approaches to reconciling loyalties to the state or nation with responsibilities to the rest of humanity. Each acts as a counterweight to the exclusionary practices of sovereign states.

Philosophers such as Hegel who believe that the existence of an international society of states marks the outer limits of close political cooperation vigorously defend the idea of sovereignty and non-intervention. Those who support the development of an international society of peoples recognise that the desire to exercise the right of communal self-determination is far stronger than cosmopolitan loyalties to the whole of humankind. But they also observe that a society of states in which the principle of sovereignty is fundamental is exclusionary because it frustrates the political aspirations of subordinate cultures. The communitarian argument that cosmopolitan loyalties will never extend very far does not rule out but requires global political projects to erode the constraints imposed by state sovereignty.

Walzer's injunction always to act in ways which will uphold communal autonomy is a communitarian categorical imperative which points towards a global project with limited universalistic ambitions. Communitarian arguments which support humanitarian aid to individuals and groups caught up in natural disasters or human rights violations similarly envisage an international society of peoples with limited but significant universalistic orientations. The communitarian stress on the importance of special ties and local solidarities does not envisage close international cooperation which emulates the achievements of many nation-states, but its normative aspirations may include international action to encourage consociational rule, active support for secessionist groups and humanitarian intervention to protect the victims of genocide. Communitarian positions therefore suggest that the Kantian project of promoting the transition from a system of states to an international society of states with cosmopolitan aspirations should be revised to ensure respect for minority groups with limited rights of representation within existing sovereign communities; these positions indicate that the Kantian and Marxian projects of extending the boundaries of moral and political community should be reconstructed along the lines foreshadowed by the Austro-Marxists. Such themes reflect the fact that the pluralist society of states acts as a check on exclusionary states but generates its own exclusionary practices.[15]

These efforts to rethink the normative problem of community have clear sociological and praxeological implications. The sociological analysis of community which is developed in the writings of Kant and Marx has to be modified to include discussion of societal potentials for striking an appropriate balance between the universal and the particular; and praxeological discussion has to encompass measures for protecting minority rights including, as already noted, support for secessionist groups and humanitarian intervention in exceptional circumstances. But such efforts to restore global political projects clash with other strands of thought which are as hostile to totalising accounts of the world as they are to universalising aspirations and imperatives. These patterns of thought observe that universalising world-views are as exclusionary as the sovereign states and the international society which they are summoned to reform. Foucault's critique of universal social theory, his enthusiasm for the specific rather than the general intellectual and his related preference for local resistance as opposed to grand projects of social and political reconstruction opened up lines of argument which have been extended in numerous ways by postmodern and feminist writings (Rabinow, 1986). Each of these approaches suggests that cosmopolitan morality may seem to offer the promise of moving beyond exclusionary states and an equally exclusionary society of states yet generate problematical forms of social closure in turn.

Universalism, Domination and Otherness

Obligations to fellow-citizens have been more strongly felt than obligations to human beings elsewhere but their privileged status has had to be justified nonetheless. Moral favouritism has been problematical because of the prominence of universalistic ethical thought in the West (Miller, 1988, p. 647). The need for deeper attachments to cosmopolitan morality may seem more urgent than ever in the age of globalisation notwithstanding the accusation that cosmopolitans care too little for loyalties to bounded communities. The impact of cosmopolitan ideas on Western social and political theory has declined, however, in inverse proportion to the globalisation of social and economic relations. With few exceptions, the main strands of current thought owe little to thinkers such as Kant and Marx, and many abandon their universalistic and emancipatory project entirely. The postmodern critique of state sovereignty is part of a broader and more radical assault on all claims to occupy an Archimedean site and to speak with a sovereign voice. This challenge is directed at the sovereign state and at its cosmopolitan adversaries.

The themes comprising this challenge are complex and diverse, and defy easy summary. C. Brown (1992) maintains that Lyotard's statement that postmodernism displays 'incredulity towards metanarratives' (Lyotard, 1984, p. xxiv) is a useful way of approaching a burgeoning literature. Incredulity towards the Marxist metanarrative arose because it claimed to have grasped the meaning and direction of the whole of human history, the nature and preconditions of universal freedom and the most effective path to the emancipation of the entire species. Postmodernism criticises all such totalising pretensions. Its argument is that grand narratives which purport to explain the purpose of history are simply arbitrary interpretations which have been imposed upon the world. Modernist claims to have established the truth about the world do not mirror reality but seek to bring it under control by forcing order upon it. Emancipatory metanarratives such as Marxism constructed artificial realities which were then deployed for the purpose of freeing others. Contrary to its intentions, its account of human history had the effect of establishing new instruments of social surveillance and political control. Some approaches to the intensification of state power which resulted from efforts to realise Marxism in practice have claimed that it was a tragic but ultimately unintended outcome of the emancipatory project which owed more to the desperate circumstances of the Soviet Union than to the Marxist vision of universal freedom. Postmodernism has argued that potentials for domination are not accidents of history but are inherent in modernist regimes of truth.

Kant and Marx were modernists who believed that critical social inquiry could produce a true account of the world which would explain the meaning of human history, identify the most important logics of development from an emancipatory point of view and sketch the outlines of the first truly free society to embrace the entire species. Postmodernism argues that the loss of coherent accounts of society and history is one of the defining features of the postmodern condition. All modernist claims to possess unrivalled insight into the possibilities for the transformation of society – global as well as national – elicit dismay and suspicion.[16] From the perspective of postmodernism, radical and insurmountable fragmentation is the distinguishing and exalting feature of postmodernity. No single commanding overview of reality is possible; multiple and incommensurable interpretations prevail. No single political consensus about the ultimate purpose of social organisation exists or is likely to appear; multiple political projects flourish with the passing of the modernist quest for coherence and consensus.

Several interlocking themes typify the current phase of incredulity towards grand narratives of universal emancipation. These themes include the problem of 'the elusive foundations' (Bauman, 1993, ch. 3) which troubles all efforts to define an Archimedean standpoint, and the problem of 'elusive universality' (1993, ch. 4) which many Western ethical traditions have aimed to solve but which defies solution according to postmodernism. They also include Foucault's claim that ethical universalism does not represent a major advance in moral consciousness but signifies the emergence of new social systems that possess more subtle technologies of control which rely upon the construction and marginalisation of difference; and finally they embrace feminist claims that the long-standing search for an impartial moral point of view that permits the establishment of universal principles devalues the ethic of care which has been central to traditional female responsibilities for child-rearing. It is important to consider each of these themes in turn.

The belief that the transcendental subject can uncover a system of objective and universal moral principles which are ultimately grounded in human nature or reason has been undermined by the modern sociology of knowledge. From the latter vantage-point, all knowledge is socially constructed, and the criteria which are used to distinguish truth from falsehood change radically over time. A similar point is central to the communitarian critique of the liberal conception of the unencumbered self which assumes that the individual can appeal to some form of cosmopolitan moral reason that exists outside history and tradition in order to criticise social practices.[17] The objection to this position is that individuals cannot escape the moral language embedded in the social conventions which have previously constituted them as moral subjects.[18] Absolute foundations for the assessment of the merits of different cultures or historical epochs will necessarily elude them (Rorty, 1989, p. 46).

Communitarians argue that individuals derive their moral criteria from the particular societies to which they belong. Postmodernists are suspicious of such claims about the nature of the community and its supposedly authoritative norms which underpin the critique of the unencumbered self (Bauman, 1993). They raise the crucial question of who claims to represent the community as a whole, and how far dissenting voices are suppressed or conveniently ignored. But various efforts exist to bring elements of postmodernism and communitarianism together. Some of Rorty's writings are broadly sympathetic with, but not reducible to, communitarianism (C. Brown, 1992; Higgins, 1996, p. 33). But they deny, in the spirit of postmodernism, that community norms embody deep truths about reason, human nature or the meaning of history. Rorty's defence of community is ironic because it argues that moral agents must acknowledge the contingency of their moral beliefs and relinquish any pretence to have uncovered ultimate truths about the nature of reality (Rorty, 1989, ch. 4). The impossibility of living with foundations is a crucial theme in postmodern thought. Moral problems do not dissolve into thin air as a result but they must be approached differently without characteristically modernist appeals to 'absolutes, universals and foundations in theory' (Bauman, 1993, p. 4). Contingent moral standpoints are all that survive the death of the transcendental ego.

If foundations are elusive then moral universals are immediately in jeopardy. The contention that individuals cannot escape the moral categories which they acquire from the societies into which they are born poses a profound challenge to universal validity claims. Meinecke (1970, p. 200) argued that Enlightenment thinkers deceived themselves into believing that they had discovered universal moral truths but they were unaware of the extent to which universalising claims 'always bring with them a clump of native soil from the national sphere, a sphere that no individual can completely leave behind'. The loss of secure foundations means that societies can no longer claim to embody universal truths which others are obliged to follow: there is no 'modern Requirement' and there are 'no sure-fire arguments any more' (C. Brown, 1988, p. 346). The cosmopolitan vision of a humanity united by absolute moral principles is said to dissolve in the process. Addressing this theme, Rorty (1989, p. 59) maintains that it is 'impossible to think that there is something which stands to my community as my community stands to me'; it is simply meaningless to appeal beyond one's community to some larger entity known as humanity which is assumed to possess an 'intrinsic nature' or value.

Historicist thinkers such as Meinecke rejected the Enlightenment dream of a cosmopolitan society but defended a conception of international society in which communities would recognise each other's efforts to express cultural potentials in infinitely varied and frequently incommensurable ways (Linklater, 1990a, ch. 7). Recent efforts to apply Rorty's insights to the study of international relations have argued that they can strengthen pluralist conceptions of the society of states (C. Brown, 1988). In a more detailed elaboration of this approach, Brown (1995, p. 106) argues that a pluralist international society which respects the rule of law but eschews all global projects is the only practicable alternative to the vision of a political community in which solidarity extends to the whole of humanity united in the pursuit of common moral goals. As noted earlier, these communitarian sentiments are implicated in a global project which seeks to narrow the gap between an international society of states and an international society of peoples. Brown (1995) adds that this international political framework should observe a general duty to aid and assist the suffering. The claim that the society of states should embrace an elementary cosmopolitanism has strong affinities with Rorty's thesis that progress towards a more humane morality is centred on the conviction that the differences between groups are ultimately less important than the shared experience of 'pain and humiliation' (Rorty, 1989, p. 192).

As noted previously, this support for progress in the direction of 'greater human solidarity' is ironic since it does not rely on any notion of an essential moral self which is common to all humanity (Rorty, 1989). Rorty rejects appeals to humanity as such, and he is opposed to all efforts to anchor universal moral imperatives in some conception of shared human reason (1989, p. 196). Rorty's constituency is the community of twentieth-century liberals who ought to continue the process of ensuring that traditionally marginalised groups benefit from 'our attempts not to be cruel'; liberals have a duty 'to *create* a more expansive sense of solidarity' rather than to urge others to identify with a pre-existent, if latent, community which encompasses the whole human race (1989, p. 196; italics in original).

Rorty (1989, p. 67) maintains that he is separated from his foundationalist opponents by 'merely philosophical' differences. This seems to suggest that foundationalists will want stronger grounds than his references to liberal irony and the contingency of belief can provide but agree nonetheless with the humanistic ethic which exists in his writings. Postmodern authors argue that the philosophical quest for secure foundations for the moral concern for others cannot surmount the contingency of belief, and they add the deeper claim that foundationalism poses a threat to its own humanistic sentiments. Some differences between foundationalists and anti-foundationalists may be simply philosophical but postmodernists are keen to stress the social and political dangers which are inherent in the ancient search for universal proofs and absolute moral certainties. These are dangers which postmodernists endeavour to avoid.

The belief that complying with universalisable principles is the essence of the moral life is one of the principal targets of the postmodern critique. Bauman (1993, p. 12) argues that the 'arduous campaign to smother the differences' between persons is evident in all universalising ethics which argue that moral subjects should follow principles which bind like persons in like circumstances. Opposing this view, Bauman (1993, pp. 53–4 and 74) argues that humanity 'is neither captured in common denominators' which 'obliterate individuality' nor embodied in the 'character of a rule', but is most fully expressed when moral subjects take responsibility for the radically different other without any demand for, or expectation of, reciprocity. The moral life resides not in the belief that universal rules have been properly observed but in the urge to set new and conceivably unrealisable standards of responsibility for others (1993, pp. 80–1). For Bauman, the supporters of the morality of universal principle desire a level of ontological certainty which is unattainable and which tends towards self-righteousness and complacency. The moral self which seeks to enlarge the horizons of ethical responsibility lacks the security of fixed universal moral rules: its preferred alternative is to conceive of the moral life 'as . . . *always haunted by the suspicion that it is not moral enough*' (1993, p. 80; italics in original).

The objection to universalisable ethics is that they may obliterate individuality; the related objection to foundationalism is that it may lead to political domination (Bauman, 1993, pp. 12 and 53; Campbell, 1994, p. 458). Certain parallels with the Foucauldian claim that all systems of knowledge, including those with the best of emancipatory intentions, generate modes of power and exclusion are evident here. Foucault rejected the idea that a universal ethic based on autonomous reason would free human beings from the tyranny of social convention: the vocabulary of universal moral freedom simply engendered new patterns of social control in which individuals internalised the dominant norms and conventions and assumed responsibility for monitoring and normalising their behaviour. With the emergence of the language of universal freedom, the mechanisms of social control became located deep within the moral self (Foucault, 1979, p. 30). Sharp oppositions between the notions of reason, responsibility, autonomy, individuality, universality and progress and the categories of insanity, criminality, heteronomy, savagery and historical backwardness helped constitute the self-regulating moral subject. The self-monitoring individual in the allegedly more enlightened societies of modern Europe was constructed through a system of oppositions and differences which the existence of prisons and clinics and manifold images of the primitive past and the savage other concretised. The self-congratulatory tone of modern rational thought depended upon the various systems of exclusion established against supposedly less rational subjects. No great moral advance occurred with the rise of modern conceptions of the self and society: new systems of domination replaced earlier forms (see Dews, 1987, p. 208).

Far from defending the vision of universal emancipation associated with Enlightenment thinking, Foucault stressed the dark side of modernity expressed in threats to difference and diversity. His critique of the Western idea of progress was designed to reveal that everything may not be bad, but everything is potentially dangerous (Rabinow, 1986, p. 343). On this interpretation, all claims to truth and enlightenment, and all emancipatory projects, contain the potential for dominating, marginalising and excluding others. All visions of a universal human community or a global moral consensus have potentially catastrophic consequences for Foucault because they contain the seeds of new structures of domination and systems of exclusion (Hoy, 1986, p. 119).[19]

Foucault's writings emphasised the risk that universalising perspectives will privilege one conception of human identity, one vision of the moral self, which can then be imposed on others or used to construct them as backward, inferior or incomplete. In each case supposedly backward humanity can find itself incorporated within dominating social practices. Similar concerns have been central to feminist literature since the publication of Gilligan's influential critique of the account of moral development which was first advanced in Kohlberg's writings on moral development and subsequently integrated within Habermas's project of reconstructing historical materialism.

Gilligan's argument is that Kohlberg's account of moral development failed to recognise that women frequently speak in a different voice from men. In Kohlberg's analysis, the higher forms of moral consciousness are concerned with elaborating abstract principles of justice which regulate interaction between strangers within the public domain. In this sphere, citizens are invited to take an impartial point of view which is free from the distorting influence of private interests, special ties and particular allegiances. Rational moral conduct in the public sphere ignores the particular features of individuals in the belief that the principles which govern this realm should be concerned exclusively with like individuals in similar circumstances. Kohlberg argued that the morality of justice which is concerned with the 'generalized other' is superior to the ethic of care and responsibility which is orientated to the welfare of the 'concrete other' (Benhabib and Cornell, 1987, ch. 4). The ethic of care which has featured most prominently in the lives of women is centred on the development of individual family members rather than on the consistent compliance with generalisable principles (Gilligan, 1993). A highly developed hermeneutic grasp of personal character and social context – the very considerations which an abstract morality of justice deliberately ignores – is one of the main constitutive features of the ethic of care and responsibility.[20]

For Kant, Kohlberg and Habermas the morality of justice is superior because it is universalistic: because it requires the individual to transcend particularism and parochialism, to take the wider moral point of view. That the danger of ignoring the interests of outsiders is inherent in the ethic of care and responsibility is clearly stressed by many thinkers such as O'Neill (1989a) and Tronto (1993). That the ethic of care is unable to deal with relations between strangers separated by considerable distances is also recognised (Tronto, 1993, p. 158). For these reasons many feminists (Gilligan, 1993; Tronto, 1993; O'Neill, 1989a) have argued that the morality of justice and the ethic of care and responsibility are complementary moralities: they should both figure prominently in a just society.

The corollary of this argument is that there are no compelling reasons for granting the morality of justice superiority over the ethic of care and responsibility. To establish this point, Gilligan (1993) argues that the moral skills which are displayed most frequently by women within the family are different from, but not inferior to, the skills which have traditionally been most highly valued in the public domain. Her point is that these skills have not been graded in an objective way but allocated their value on the basis of what is required in the public domain, which has traditionally been monopolised by men. In the decision to assign moral universalism its supreme place an exclusionary practice resides. The public realm has been constructed in a way which devalues the moral skills which are often most highly developed in the lives of women: and the low value placed on the ethic of care and responsibility contributes to the practice of confining women to the private sphere (Benhabib and Cornell, 1987, ch. 4; Young, 1987). It is therefore necessary to subvert traditional dichotomies between the public and the private, the rational and the sentimental, the universal and the particular in order to end the exclusion of women (Young, 1987, p. 59). Were this to occur, the result would be a public domain which is less exclusionary but also significantly more adept at conflict-resolution. Gilligan argues that the hermeneutic understanding of the specific needs and aspirations of specific others which is central to the ethic of care encourages cooperative as opposed to adversarial approaches to conflict. To depict the skills associated with the ethic of care and responsibility as inferior to the ethic of abstract principles of justice is to overlook the existence of powerful moral reserves which can considerably enrich the public sphere.

The postmodern and feminist arguments surveyed above argue that no form of ethical universalism is immune from generating practices of exclusion and subordination. They have suggested that there is no warranty that visions of a universal commonwealth will transcend the negative representations of otherness which have been integral to the construction of individual and social identity. Certain parallels with realism stand out. It is well known that Carr (1946, ch. 4) argued that the nineteenth-century liberal belief in the universal benefits of free trade reflected the standpoint of comfortable powers such as Britain. Industrialising states rightly argued that free trade would place their infant industries at the mercy of more powerful groups in the world economy. Postmodern and feminist critiques of moral universalism operate at a higher level of abstraction but are equally quick to point to the operation of power and exclusion in universal moral discourse. But there the similarities end. Realism is generally regarded as being suspicious of moral universals, noting that they invariably reflect particular configurations of power despite claims to transcend them, and it is critical of the 'utopian' belief that these universals can make serious inroads into state behaviour. As previously noted, some strands of feminist literature are not antagonistic to moral universalism but rather to the supposition that it embodies the highest moral capacities. While they are critical of the traditional defence of moral universalism these approaches allow that new forms of universalism, might yet be constructed. (See below pp. 93–5.) Similar themes have begun to emerge in the postmodern literature (see below, pp. 97–8).

The status of moral universals is one of the more central questions – arguably the central question – in contemporary social and political theory. Frankfurt School critical theory and postmodernism are usually thought to have opposing and irreconcilable positions on the need for, and status of, moral universals. Habermas is frequently associated with the claim that postmodernist and related perspectives lack the moral resources for criticising the structures of power which they oppose. Habermas (1987, pp. 287–90) argued that Foucault provided an account of the intricacies of power which not only neglected developments in the moral sphere but portrayed them as evidence of the creation of more subtle forms of control in modern societies. According to this argument, critical though he was of the modern instruments of power and surveillance, Foucault abandoned the moral ground which makes political resistance possible (Fraser, 1989). Habermas has also contrasted his project of establishing the universalistic moral foundations of effective critique with the conservative implications of postmodern rejections of universal reason. Rather similar themes occur in some branches of feminist literature which are opposed to postmodernism on the grounds that the emancipation of women requires concrete analyses of actual forms of subordination which are oriented towards ascertaining the

truth (True, 1996). The postmodern celebration of competing interpretations of reality, which are all more or less interesting if not more or
less true, is regarded as obstructing the feminist cause (V. Held, 1993,
p. 13; True, 1996, p. 242).

Some postmodern responses dismiss this accusation of conservatism,
relativism and nihilism. They specifically resist the argument that there
is a straightforward choice between rational moral argument based on
secure foundations and the realm of purely subjective preferences,
arbitrariness and irrationalism offered by postmodernism. Foundationalists argue that it is essential to stand on their ground or relinquish the
prospect of ethics; their postmodern critics argue that it is the possibility
of standing on foundationalist ground which is precisely what is in
dispute and that ethics must be constructed differently as a result. If
there are no foundations for moral argument, then the plain choice
between the realm of absolute moral argument and the realm of purely
subjective preferences must be falsely posed (Rorty, 1989, p. 44; Higgins,
1996). Ethics will therefore have to negotiate a different and unfamiliar
terrain.

The postmodern strategy of denying absolute ground to others has
been interpreted as an invitation to licence and as a dangerous flirtation
with the proposition that 'anything goes' (Ashley and Walker, 1990,
pp. 389–90). One postmodern riposte is that an ethic of freedom is
promoted by this strategy of denial. Where such an ethics is practised,
the argument is, no voice can 'stand heroically upon some exclusionary
ground' (1990, p. 395). There are in consequence no grounds for
claiming to enjoy privileged access to necessary truths which can be
imposed on others 'in the name of a citizenry, people, nation, class,
gender, race, golden age or historical cause of any sort. Where this ethic
is rigorously practised no totalitarian order could ever be' (1990, p. 395).
Distinctions between good and bad arguments are upheld but what is
denied is the existence of compelling moral arguments which must
command the consent of the whole human race. No single way of life
can claim to possess the ethical criteria with which to assess the
rationality of other cultures (1990, p. 391).

The postmodern defence of the ethic of freedom may be an ironic and
even self-refuting stance: if the aim is to question established meanings,
to unsettle accepted conventions, to disturb all efforts to speak with a
sovereign voice, then it is difficult to know why an ethic of freedom
should be preferred to an ethic of domination. Perhaps it is sufficient to
argue that the ethic of freedom prevails by default since alternative ethics
of domination which rest on appeals to national, racial, civilisational,
class or gender supremacy have had their foundationalist supports
stripped away; perhaps the ethic of freedom rests on 'invidious compari-

sons' with other perspectives rather than on appeals to absolute truths (Rorty, 1991, p. 211). An ethic of freedom which survives tenuously in the wasteland of derelict utopias and emancipatory lost causes without the assurance of fixed and lasting meanings may be the final repository for the damaged hopes of the Enlightenment and the sole surviving refuge for a modernity which has shed its utopian delusions. Be that as it may, while postmodern thinking eschews grand political projects and universal visions its intent is humanistic and far from conservative. This is evident from its preference for plural over uniform interpretation, for responsibility to otherness over hostility to cultural differences, for dialogue over diktat or decree, and for openness over closure or exclusion.

There are good grounds for arguing that 'a hidden form of universality' underlies the anti-foundationalist plea for 'an active principle of tolerance' and equally good reasons for suggesting that support for diversity is best clothed in unambiguously universalistic garments (R. Bernstein, 1988, p. 590). Arguably, then, the issue is not universality per se but its exclusionary forms. The point is reinforced by the fact that various anti-foundationalist writers display allegiance to a universalism of sorts. Commenting on the plight of the Vietnamese boat people, Foucault is reported as having affirmed the existence of 'an international citizenry' with its own rights and duties, and with a Kantian inclination to 'raise itself up against every abuse of power, no matter who the author or the victims' might be. The state is identified as the most probable source of the abuse of power in this domain. This being so, 'the will of individuals must inscribe itself in a reality over which governments have wanted to reserve a monopoly for themselves – a monopoly which we must uproot little by little every day' (Keenan, 1987, pp. 20–4).[21] Similarly, in his critique of Fukuyama's quaint thesis that history ends with the triumph of liberal democracy, Derrida (1994a, p. 85) argues for a 'new international' on the grounds that 'violence, inequality, exclusion, famine, and thus economic oppression [have never] affected as many human beings in the history of the Earth and of humanity'. Deconstruction supports the 'spirit of Marxism' (1994a, p. 92) and argues for a new conception of the withering away of the state in which the state will no longer possess 'a space which it dominates' and which it has 'never dominated without division' (Derrida, 1994b, p. 58). A recent analysis of Levinas argues that an important element of universality is present in his notion of 'the very particularity' of obligations to others (Campbell, 1994, p. 461). Levinas's thought contains a deeper humanism which is 'attuned to alterity' but is vulnerable nevertheless to the charge that its position on the moral significance of boundaries arbitrarily constrains responsibility for the 'other' (Campbell, 1994, pp. 462–7). Levinas's communitarian answer to the question of 'who is closest to me?' (1994, p. 466) hinders the 'deterritorialisation' or globalisation of moral and political responsibilities.

These formulations inevitably raise some of the oldest normative questions in the study of international relations concerning the relationship between the universal and the particular. They reintroduce questions about the moral significance of cultural differences and national boundaries, about the nature of moral universals and about the moral responsibilities which communities owe their neighbours. As answers to these questions, these formulations are critical of state sovereignty. They deny that the condition of anarchy is immutable and they anticipate new forms of political community which are simultaneously more universalistic and more open to diversity. They prompt the question of whether any account of moral and political obligation can be regarded as complete if it is silent on the matter of what each individual owes the rest of humanity or if it evades the issue of how obligations and responsibilities which transcend the frontiers of states are to be woven into the contemporary society of states.

Important points of congruence exist between postmodernism and Frankfurt School critical theory although they have at times been presented as competing perspectives (Devetak, 1995a, p. 41). Habermas and Foucault were involved in a parallel project of combating systems of exclusion within Western culture (George, 1994, pp. 168–9). Each thinker has enlarged the critical project inaugurated by Kant and Marx which problematised exclusion in its specific legal, political and economic forms. Modern radical perspectives including Frankfurt School critical theory, postmodernism and feminism rework the Enlightenment project in the light of a heightened sensitivity to modes of exclusion embedded in gender, race, language, culture and the structures of cognition. Thinkers as diverse as Derrida, Foucault and Habermas offer variations on the theme of the Enlightenment project (Campbell, 1994, p. 474). Each gives expression to what Foucault described as 'a philosophical ethos that could be described as a permanent critique of our historical era' (Rabinow, 1986, p. 42). Each examines modernity as 'a complex matrix of tensions and critical potentials' (George, 1994, p. 162) with an emancipatory interest in eradicating the surplus social constraints which prevent human subjects from making more of their history under conditions of their own choosing, and in eliminating what is no longer necessary for the constitution of the self.

None of these thinkers supports the grand historical metanarrative evident in Hegelian thought and in classical Marxism, in which the whole of human history is regarded as a process of gradual ascent to the summit of Western conceptions of individuality, autonomy, rationality and universality. However, each subscribes to some notion of progress, which in the language of Habermas (1979a, p. 140) eschews doctrines of historical unilinearity and necessity, temporal continuity and irreversibility. There is apparent agreement within the reconstructed project of modernity that accounts of progress have to be 'stripped' of notions of 'foreclosure against an open future' (Habermas, 1980, p. 250) and there is a general consensus that the ' fully transparent . . . homogenised and unified society' is no ideal at all (Habermas, 1992a, p. 171). Each defends the goal of 'a pluralism of life-forms and interest(s)' (ibid.). Habermas (1994, pp. 119–20) argues for a civilisation which draws upon the 'traces of a reason which unites without effacing separation, that binds without unnaming difference, that points out the common and shared among strangers, without depriving the other of otherness'. Habermas, of course, makes foundationalist claims about essential connections between language and universality which his critics reject. Even so, the different voices are in harmony in believing that one of the primary tasks of social and political theory is to enlarge human understanding about the possibility of new forms of life which shed their resistance to higher levels of universality and difference.

The position which emerges from this encounter with postmodernism and feminism echoes the conclusion reached earlier following the analysis of communitarian thought. There is in the first place no disagreement about the importance of cultural differences, special ties and affinities, and particular obligations to concrete others. Some rights of social closure are immediately suggested by these claims but their precise nature is uncertain because there are also obligations to the rest of humanity. Three ways of negotiating the tension between universality and particularity can be identified in this context: the first takes the form of a pluralist international society of states in which cooperation is limited to defining and preserving the principles of coexistence; the second envisages the transition from a pluralist society of states to a more solidarist society of states and peoples which incorporates basic cosmopolitan principles such as the duty of humanitarian assistance. A third position is suggested by Derrida's remarks on a future European identity which can avoid both the dispersal of identities 'into a multiplicity of self-enclosed idioms or petty little nationalisms, each one jealous and untranslatable' and monopolisation in the form of a 'centralizing authority that, by means of trans-European cultural mechanisms . . . would control and standardize' society (Derrida, 1992, p. 41).[22] This is the notion of a post-Westphalian international society which involves a more radical assault on the modern state and its destructive fusion of sovereignty, territoriality, citizenship and nationality.[23] The main conclusion of this chapter is that this vision of a political community in which the totalising project is brought to an end can command the support of very different critical standpoints.[24]

Conclusions

Different strands of anti-foundationalist thought agree that 'the Enlightenment should not have yearned for a world polity whose citizens share common aspirations and a common culture' (Rorty, 1991, p. 210). Anti-foundationalists have defended difference, noting that the advance of universalism would simply project the dominant identity at the national or civilisational level onto the species as a whole. Support for difference is therefore significantly stronger than support for universality in much recent social theory. But, as befits approaches which are concerned to highlight pernicious forms of exclusion, the defence of difference is heavily qualified. Inherent in the critique of difference is an appeal to universality. Arguably, an account of moral progress is already implicit in the anti-foundationalist support for the recognition of cultural difference. This is especially evident in Rorty's recommended substitution of 'narratives of increasing cosmopolitanism' for 'narratives of emancipation' (Rorty, 1991, p. 213).[25]

Progress in 'the direction of greater human solidarity' involves coming to see 'traditional differences (of tribe, religion, race, customs, and the like) as unimportant when compared with similarities with respect to pain and humiliation' (Rorty, 1989, p. 192). Progress involves the widening of moral horizons to include marginalised groups which we still instinctively regard as 'they' rather than 'us' (1989, p. 196). Anti-foundationalism supports widening the boundaries of moral and political community in keeping with its opposition to pernicious forms of closure. It is tempting to conclude this discussion by stressing parallels with the Kantian project of extending community beyond the state by creating a society of states and by incorporating ethical commitments to the community of humankind, or by emphasising parallels with T. H. Green's argument that moral progress involves the extension of the area of the common good (see Linklater, 1990a). But to conclude in this way would be to ignore some fundamental philosophical differences between these approaches.

The most important philosophical differences between Kant or Green and Rorty concern the way in which these claims are defended. Kant and Green believed that their account of historical progress corresponded with some essential truths about the nature of humanity. But for Rorty (1989, p. 196) the truths of which he speaks are the truths of a particular constituency: the community of twentieth-century liberals. Rorty denies that it is essential to choose between a foundationalist universalism which embraces ultimate truths about the nature of reality and a relativism which in rejecting the notion of truth concludes that 'anything goes'. This quasi-Hegelian aversion to having to choose between fixed moral absolutes and incommensurable social realities abandons the grand metanarrative in which the lower cultures fall by the wayside as reason unfolds in history. What is substituted is a thinner notion of progress that refers to the expanding circle of human sympathy which ought to be the aim of those who identify with the liberal community.

No claims on any other culture are embedded in this perspective. All that is stressed are the obligations and the debates surrounding them which arise for twentieth-century liberals 'who have been brought up to distrust ethnocentrism' (Rorty, 1989, p. 198). On this reasoning, the good liberal will adopt a critical stance towards the boundaries of community on the grounds that there is more to the moral life than the special ties and obligations between fellow-citizens united by the accident of birth. This much transcends the merely philosophical differences between foundationalists and their critics. Anti-foundationalists deny that transcultural validity can be claimed for the liberal stance. They reject the foundationalist claim that it is possible to anchor these arguments about widening the boundaries of moral and political community in a constituency which is as extensive as the human race itself. For their part, foundationalists from Kant to Habermas regard the evolution of a critical orientation towards exclusion and difference as exemplifying progress towards a rational morality with universal significance. The next chapter examines the foundationalist claim that it is possible to provide a rational defence of the project of enlightenment which builds the goal of a cosmopolitan community of humankind on this last conviction.

3

The Dialogic Ethic and the Transformation of Political Community

Anti-foundationalism argues that there is no transcultural standpoint, no view from nowhere,[1] which allows the knowing subject to establish moral principles which are transculturally valid. With the death of the transcendental subject there is no alternative but 'to start from where *we* are' for the purpose of moral reasoning (Rorty, 1989, p. 198). For Rorty, the members of a society can think through the logic of their own cultural beliefs, carefully sifting out weak arguments from strong, but they cannot defend the universalising aspiration that their moral preferences must command the consent of the whole of humanity. Rorty argues that the only compelling moral arguments are those which the members of a society impose upon themselves in the light of their cultural assumptions about the nature and purpose of the self and society. They can defend these moral arguments with vigour by calling upon the most insightful reflections upon moral character and ethical reasoning within their culture. But they cannot escape the fact that their underlying assumptions about self and society are ultimately groundless. Moral convictions may rest on the best arguments available within the culture but they have to be attended by a sense of irony and contingency, given the absence of any secure foundations for the way of life in which they are located (Rorty, 1989, p. xv).

Starting from where *they* are, the citizens of modern sovereign states are increasingly obliged by the prevailing ethic to reflect on how they exclude others within the community and beyond. Significant sections of the populations of modern states do take a critical orientation towards acts of closure directed against marginal groups and are similarly reflective about their rights against and duties to the rest of humankind. Many wish to progress beyond moral parochialism without assuming that there are moral universals which can be grasped from a transcendental point of view and without laying claim to some undisputed right to universalise one conception of the good life.

While the members of such a community may choose to live together because of the special inclinations and the harmony of dispositions which set them apart, they often believe that they are answerable to the claims of universality and difference. The moral status of their principles of association is therefore inherently, even uniquely, problematical. While citizens may wish to perpetuate their association, they cannot justify their desire to do so by appealing to shared practices and common sentiments bequeathed from the past. They can no longer live together in a condition of immediacy, to use Hegel's phrase, because the comfort of social morality or *Sittlichkeit* has already been disturbed by abstract ethical reasoning or *Moralität* (O'Neill, 1988, p. 722). As a consequence, social morality has become highly reflective about practices of exclusion.

How should the members of this society deal with questions about the morality of systems of exclusion? What criteria should they use to distinguish between justifiable and unjustifiable forms of exclusion? What possibility is there that they might be able to claim transcultural validity for their substantive conclusions or for the procedures by which they are reached? Recent philosophical analyses of the debates about the distribution of membership, citizenship and global responsibilities offer important guides to the answers. The first part of this chapter explores some inquiries into membership, citizenship and global responsibilities which confront questions about the ethics of exclusion. It introduces the foundationalist claim that the logic of the cultural beliefs which are influential in many modern states points to these two conclusions: one, there are certain duties which the members of these states owe others by virtue of humanity alone; and two, there are good reasons for believing that the members of other cultures might also assent to this claim.

This is to take issue with Rorty's argument (1989, p. 191) that analyses of duties to others which rest on some notion of the rights which others have simply as fellow human beings are 'weak' and 'unconvincing'. The argument below is that sometimes the strongest defence a culture can give for recognising the rights of outsiders involves nothing other than an appeal to common humanity. Whether other cultures would understand the meaning of these claims (and concur with them if they do) is a crucial question raised by the existence of cosmopolitan claims within any culture. If these claims are incomprehensible to the members of other cultures, or if they are rejected out of hand, then the notion of common humanity is at best confined to one system of cultural beliefs and plainly ethnocentric. But if the reasoning which underpins them resonates with the thinking of other cultures, then certain moral appeals to shared humanity may be deemed to have transcultural validity.

No culture can assume that its moral claims automatically have this transcultural status. Only through dialogue with other cultures can progress be made in separating merely local truths from those with wider acclaim. Part two of this chapter sketches the nature of the dialogic community which is committed to proceeding in this way. Part three explores this further by considering Habermas's account of discourse ethics. It endeavours to show that the normative commitment to universalising the communication community which is central to his work is compatible with the aims of other strands of contemporary social and political theory. It is also important to ask whether one of the supposed consequences of regarding the universalisation of the communication community as a normative ideal can command widespread support. The assumed consequence is that all appeals to discourse and dialogue are incomplete without the critique of the economic and political structures and cultural practices which obstruct the development of a universal communication community. If this is so, then the analysis of the relationship between dialogue and ethics is ultimately engaged in some version of the Marxian critique of the realms of alienation, exploitation and estrangement which obstruct the development of universal freedom.

Limits on Exclusion: Membership, Citizenship and Global Responsibilities

There are no grounds for disputing Walzer's contention that a liberal society is free from the moral obligation to extend membership to outsiders who espouse racist or totalitarian beliefs, or for denying that such a society has the right to preserve its distinctive moral practices by exercising the right of social closure (Walzer, 1995, p. 50). Walzer provides one of the strongest arguments for the right to exclude outsiders and one of the most insightful analyses of the moral considerations which can encroach upon the right to deny membership to outsiders. For Walzer, the right of exclusion does not mean that everything a state does in regard to the distribution of membership is automatically beyond reproach. The United States, for example, restricted access to its soil on the grounds that it was defending a homogeneous white Protestant community but it was clearly involved in a pretence which was as 'immoral' as it was 'inaccurate' (1995, p. 40). The reasons which a society gives for excluding others can be contested by outsiders as well as insiders although Walzer adds that outsiders cannot claim an unqualified right to membership simply because flaws have been discovered in the defence of exclusion. Reasons for refusing membership are matters which outsiders are at liberty to contest but, ultimately, it is up to fellow-citizens to decide the kind of community they want to be. Members are free to choose their future associates; their decisions are 'authoritative and final' (1995, p. 41).

Walzer argues that in the course of reaching their decisions members should heed the moral principle of 'Good Samaritanism' which extends across national boundaries. Members may believe they have a duty to admit a special category of refugees, namely their 'kith and kin' who have been expelled from another society (1995, pp. 41–2). Whether they have a right to deny access to those who do not share their culture, and whether they can insist on their right to maintain their cultural homogeneity and distinctiveness, are more complicated matters. Walzer maintains that an ideological affinity with the persecuted members of other societies can be a strong reason for conferring membership upon them. Cultural affinity between the host society and those seeking refuge is not the only condition of entry: political affinities can suffice.

It is possible to extend this further by arguing that a liberal society ought to be open to the outside world because a commitment to diversity and to a plurality of cultures is inherent in its very character, but that it is not obliged to admit those who are hostile to its political beliefs or bound to absorb large numbers of outsiders without regard for the economic and social consequences. Interestingly, Walzer maintains that Good Samaritanism can outweigh concerns about ensuring that insiders and outsiders must be culturally or politically compatible. Good Samaritanism requires that a society should extend protection to those individuals who have entered its ranks and who seek political asylum knowing that they are likely to be killed if they return to their own society (1995, p. 50). In this case there is a duty to help desperate strangers which represents a significant step beyond the acknowledgement of special duties to kith and kin and special obligations to the persecuted who have similar political convictions. These are obligations which rest on common humanity alone.

On this argument, a society has moral responsibilities to 'necessitous strangers' who are kith and kin, to those who are persecuted for defending political principles which the society also values and to those who simply cannot make a life for themselves anywhere else. But in each case the society retains its right of communal self-determination and its parallel right of social closure. Interestingly, Walzer does not leave the argument there. This right of closure can be qualified, Walzer (1995, p. 46) argues, in exceptional circumstances where 'necessitous' men and women who have been driven by war or famine from their countries of origin clamour for entry into a thinly populated society such as Australia which controls 'great empty spaces' and has a tenuous right to the land which was seized from the first inhabitants. Walzer (1995, p. 46) 'doubts that we would want to charge the invaders with aggression'. Here the right of communal self-determination clashes with, but does not have its usual priority over, the rights of desperate strangers. The choice facing such a society is whether to cede land in order to preserve cultural homogeneity within the remaining territory or to surrender cultural homogeneity for the sake of preserving traditional boundaries. In Walzer's view, there is no other reasonable moral choice (1995, p. 47).

Walzer (1995, p. 48) rejects the principle of global economic redistribution which 'would tend over time to annul the historical particularity of the national clubs and families' but adds that what is true of the abundance of land must also hold for the abundance of wealth. In unusual circumstances the right of communal self-determination must be subject to 'moral encroachment'. A duty to redistribute wealth to the poor should be acknowledged although there has to be some limit on global duties if the right of communal self-determination is to retain any meaning. There is no simple means of determining when the limits of a people's collective liability have finally been reached (1995, p. 51). Walzer emphasises that the right to decide what these limits are cannot be alienated to another community or to an international agency which assumes superior rights. Each society must retain its right of self-determination and seek to ensure justice for others of its own accord but with the inevitable danger, it might be added, that it will deny others just treatment on spurious or questionable grounds.

Walzer is right that there are no simple answers to questions about the ethics of inclusion and exclusion which arise in societies which wish to preserve their cultural integrity but recognise moral duties to the rest of humanity. The tension between collective self-determination and universal duties which Walzer underlines is not easily overcome by specifying the exact moral liabilities of each society. Walzer argues that alienating the power to decide to other agencies is clearly incompatible with the collective right of self-determination. Each society must therefore resolve moral tensions about the distribution of membership in its own way.

Two different obligations which arise in conjunction with the refugee problem challenge this conclusion. There is a duty to grant refugees protection from the tyranny of exclusion which exists in a society of states in which state sovereignty is a central constitutive principle; and there is a duty to assist other societies which may be unable to control the influx of refugees into their territory, with the result that they cannot exercise an equal right of collective self-determination. The cosmopolitan duty to assist refugees and the injunction to act to uphold communal autonomy suggest that all states should acknowledge the duty to enter into close cooperation with one another to ensure that each has an equitable share of the burden of settling refugees. Arguably, the desire to ensure justice for refugees and justice for states points towards a basic international obligation to establish a fair division of global burdens and responsibilities through dialogue with others. Efforts to establish international equity would involve a *de facto* if not a *de jure* encroachment upon the right of the sovereign state to decide questions regarding the distribution of membership on its own accord.

All of this assumes culturally homogeneous societies which are keen to ensure their survival and anxious to balance the right of closure with wider humanitarian concerns. But although the level of reflectiveness about practices of exclusion varies considerably between societies, high levels of cultural homogeneity are remarkably rare. Most societies must not only consider tensions between citizenship and duties to the rest of humanity but also reflect upon the ways in which the dominant conceptions of citizenship exclude culturally marginal groups within national boundaries. A commitment to the right of communal self-determination requires measures to ensure that subordinate cultural groupings within nation-states possess appropriate levels of autonomy. International action to ensure that the rights of minorities receive proper protection is also important since minority problems can have disastrous consequences for neighbouring states and may endanger regional stability.

Support for the right of communal self-determination may clash with the dominant conceptions of national citizenship. As Kymlicka (1989) has argued, the proposition that the members of a society should have exactly the same citizenship rights is one of the central tenets of modern liberalism. Liberal societies claimed to have progressed beyond the feudal order by overturning the principle that different social groups should enjoy different legal entitlements. Many modern societies which classify themselves as liberal have further supposed that all citizens should have a common cultural identity, and many have promoted national-assimilationist policies to ensure that ethnic and other minorities closely identify with the political community. Increasingly, these efforts to achieve the convergence between political and cultural boundaries come up against resistance from ethnic minorities and indigenous peoples. The recurring theme is that the dominant conceptions of citizenship and community are exclusionary, and that the principle of equality to which the community is committed may not guarantee respect for the culturally different.

Kymlicka (1995) argues that where cultural and political boundaries do not converge the challenge is to amend traditional conceptions of community and citizenship by introducing group-specific rights. Consociational arrangements which permit self-government for indigenous peoples are one example of the move beyond traditional constructions of community and citizenship (Kymlicka, 1989, p. 137). Without self-government indigenous peoples cannot protect their special interests within societies which used violence to eradicate or subordinate them and which have long been ignorant of their traditions, needs and aspirations. Some of the rights which are essential for indigenous self-government clash with the traditional rights of liberal society. If, for example, indigenous peoples are to protect their culture and promote their interests they must have the right to regulate access to their land, to prevent outsiders from acquiring property in their territory and to exclude outsiders from participating in their elections. These qualifications of the liberal rights of free movement, property ownership and participation which should be possessed by all citizens are necessary, Kymlicka (1989, p. 183) argues, if vulnerable indigenous cultures are to survive.

Although many societies confer special status on minority groups (on the Amish, for example, within the United States) there are often fears that group-differentiated citizenship will undermine social cohesion and harmony. However, the purpose behind group-specific rights is not to introduce cultural insularity and moral parochialism into society but rather to reduce the forms of cultural provincialism which already exist. Claims for group-differentiated citizenship are compelling when the members of the dominant culture enjoy a right of communal self-determination which they deny to other groups within their midst. Recognising these claims is an important means of promoting the goal which past extensions of citizenship have been designed to realise: namely, the condition in which the systematically excluded feel more at home in the political community (Kymlicka, 1995, pp. 180–1). Dominant groups must pay for that condition by breaking with the assumption which is intimately linked with war and the totalising project that all citizens must share the same national or cultural identity. New social bonds are required which unite citizens around the common aim of eradicating unjustifiable exclusion and promoting deep diversity (Taylor, 1994). Crucial to the new social bond is the desire to engage the members of culturally different groups as equals in wider communities of discourse.

A society which is keen to preserve its cultural distinctiveness but wishes to assist the vulnerable faces hard questions about the distribution of membership; and a society which recognises that the dominant culture has purchased its identity by demeaning minorities faces equally complex questions about the distribution of citizenship. In each case defending the rights of the vulnerable requires efforts to reconcile the right of collective self-determination with duties to engage interested parties in open dialogue. Interested parties can include the members of other societies who are harmed by the consequences of national decisions about the distribution of membership and citizenship. Increasing levels of transnational harm further underline the point that communities should not exercise the power of self-determination without considering their duties to other human beings. At the very least, causing trans-national harm requires a commitment to regard insiders and outsiders as moral equals, and it may involve placing the interests of the vulnerable members of other communities before the interests of co-nationals on the grounds of common humanity. Transnational harm provides one of the strongest reasons for widening the boundaries of moral and political communities to engage outsiders in dialogue about matters which affect their vital interests.

In this connection, Shue's analysis of the export of hazards highlights important respects in which national boundaries do not have any moral significance. Shue (1981, p. 111) discusses corporate decisions in the United States to shift unsafe technologies to other countries rather than install improved technologies within the United States. Two questions arise under these questions: first, is it appropriate to apply lower standards to foreigners than to co-nationals; and second, if not, who has responsibility for ensuring that adequate standards are met (1981, p. 108)? Shue (1981, pp. 116 and 124) argues that the liberal no-harm principle creates a universal moral responsibility not to expose others to damaging or dangerous conditions and certainly 'not to do so without their fully informed consent'. This responsibility is not confined to those who have the same nationality or citizenship but should govern relations with all other human beings. On this argument, the primary duty for protecting the vulnerable rests with the source of transnational harm and not with the national governments of the victims. National bound-aries lack moral significance in these circumstances because they do not mark the point at which the duty to engage in the politics of dialogue and consent can rightly give way to duplicitousness and misinformation. Instead there is a duty to enlarge the boundaries of the moral and political community so that all interested parties – insiders and outsiders alike – enjoy equal rights as co-legislators within an imagined universal kingdom of ends. Many questions about the distribution of membership, citizenship and global responsibilities create this duty to release the Kantian ideal of a dialogic community from the arbitrary constraints of the bounded sovereign state. The argument will be that different conceptions of international society – pluralist, solidarist and post-Westphalian – can contribute in important respects to the realisation of this dialogic ideal. (See below, pp. 206–11.) But first of all it is important to discuss the nature of the commitment to domination-free communication.

The Dialogic Community

Writers such as Rorty argue that an ethic which is critical of exclusion may be significant in the life of the liberal community but it cannot be assumed to have any binding authority on the rest of the human race. Each community can work out the logic of its own cultural beliefs and some may impose cosmopolitan checks upon the ethnocentric tendencies which reside within their own practices and are the source of profound moral unease. But none can issue moral requirements which others are obliged to obey.

This mode of thinking rules out snap judgements about the morality or immorality of other societies and places necessary constraints on intervention to prohibit supposedly immoral practices elsewhere. If societies were largely self-contained and incapable of doing harm to one another, then the boundaries of moral communities could converge with the boundaries of actual political communities, but the reality is quite different and societies are inevitably drawn into complex dialogues about the principles of international coexistence. Some of these dialogues have led to the conclusion that there are obligations to others (to refugees and the victims of transnational harm, for example) which rely on nothing other than respect for common humanity. Most communities rest on special ties and harmonies of social disposition but they are always vulnerable to the claim that they unjustly exclude those who do not share the dominant identity. The goal of dialogic relations with the members of systematically excluded groups therefore emerges as a normative ideal. As in international relations, where it is necessary to enlarge the boundaries of the community to engage non-nationals as equals in open dialogue, membership of wider communication communities does not presume that others must have the same cultural orientations or share similar political aspirations. All that has to be assumed is that cultural differences are no barrier to equal rights of participation within a dialogic community. The duty to associate with others as co-legislators within wider communities of discourse rests on the fact that there are no compelling differences between human beings which can legitimate their prima facie exclusion from dialogic interaction.

Rorty argues that moral progress requires the extension of the boundaries of community as differences between insiders and outsiders come to lose their moral significance. The concept of progress refers not to the evolution of the species as a whole but to developments within the liberal realm of contingent beliefs. No moral judgements about the ways in which other societies treat their culturally different members follow, and no grounds for condemning the decisions which other societies may make on the basis of attaching moral importance to internal cultural differences are assumed. However, complications arise regarding the moral significance which other societies may attach to their differences from alien outsiders. One important historical illustration will suffice. The historical record suggests that many societies which extend basic humanitarian assistance to the shipwrecked – societies, that is, which do not regard the differences of the alien as morally relevant in this respect – believe that those who refuse assistance are barbaric.[2] By the former's standards the latter are wrong to refuse rescue to the culturally different; at least as far as the ethics of rescue are concerned, they are wrong to attach moral significance to cultural differences. Although the former societies may be anxious to avoid ethnocentrism, the logic of their cultural beliefs must mean that they reject the world-views of societies which deny that there is a moral obligation to rescue the outsider.

How then should such societies behave towards other communities which are exclusionary in this way? They may believe that they have been the site for the development of a universal morality of rescue to which other societies should subscribe. They may believe that by denying that cultural differences have any import for the morality of rescue they have made progress in uncovering moral principles which are transculturally valid and which all other societies will eventually embrace. They may believe these propositions are true but they cannot claim absolute certainty for them. All they can do to take their own fears about ethnocentrism seriously is submit the logic of their own beliefs to the test of open dialogue with others. In this case dialogue will require a considered analysis of the extent to which specific cultural differences are morally significant from the vantage-point of the ethics of rescue. If genuine dialogue is to exist, no particular outcome can be anticipated or presupposed. Societies which believe that others are wrong to refuse rescue to the culturally different, and which believe that moral progress revolves around the recognition that specific cultural differences lack ethical force, will seek to win others to their cause. But by entering dialogue they accept that the logic of their beliefs may fail to persuade their interlocutors. Dialogue provides the opportunity to discover whether their denial of the moral significance of cultural differences has transcultural validity.[3] Dialogue may result in an intersocietal consensus that there is a duty to rescue all human beings but it may reveal irreconcilable disputes about the moral significance of differences. It is important not to rule out the possibility that dialogue may produce a change in the societies which denied the moral relevance of cultural differences in the first place. While they may hope that dialogue will confer transcultural status on their position, they have to accept that they may be won over by the argument of the other. This possibility is inherent in any approach to dialogue which is anxious to transcend ethnocentrism.

It is also possible that an intersocietal consensus could be reached in which all agree that the vulnerable should be rescued. As far as this possibility is concerned, it is undoubtedly significant that very different cultures throughout human history have agreed that there are duties to protect the vulnerable by placing limits on violence in war.[4] It is also significant that different societies in the modern world are agreed that apartheid and slavery are universal evils.[5] In circumstances where cultures are otherwise radically different, the commitment to assist the vulnerable rests on nothing other than a sense of common humanity, on sentiments which Rorty regards as weak and unconvincing. If humanitarian principles are to apply in relations between the 'wildly different', to use Rorty's words, then it is difficult to identify any grounds for them other than common humanity. Rorty argues that the sense of cultural affinity with the other provides a deeper moral motive than vague sentiments of shared humanity. But others such as Geras (1995, p. 42) argue that the latter has frequently been the key motive behind efforts to rescue the vulnerable – specifically Jews during the Second World War – and that intellectuals should retreat from weakening the sense of common humanity. This judgement seems right especially at the boundary where the 'wildly different' meet and where there is a primary and universal obligation to engage the other in dialogue on equal terms. The willingness to engage wildly different human beings *qua* human beings, in a dialogue which assesses the rationality of the practices of exclusion, is the hallmark of the communication community.[6]

Dialogue and Discourse

In his answer to the question of what universalism means today, Habermas (1992a, p. 240) argues that it means

> that one relativises one's own way of life with regard to the legitimate claims of other forms of life, that one grants the strangers and the

others, with all their idiosyncrasies and incomprehensibilities, the same rights as oneself, that one does not insist on universalising one's own identity, that one does not simply exclude that which deviates from it, that the areas of tolerance must become infinitely broader than they are today – moral universalism means all these things.

The essence of these claims is captured in recent accounts of dialogue and discourse which are the point at which different strands of critical social theory, postmodernism, feminism and philosophical hermeneutics intersect. These accounts contribute to the project of creating a dialogic cosmopolitanism; they make it possible for ethical universalism to 'be reawakened and further developed in the form of a multi-culturalism' (Habermas, 1990b, p. 211).

Prior to considering the nature of discourse ethics in greater detail, it is important to distinguish dialogic cosmopolitanism from two other forms of ethical universalism. The two principal approaches to ethical universalism in the history of Western political thought have been the ahistorical position adopted by natural law theorists and the progressivist interpretations of human development which were central to the nineteenth-century philosophies of history. First articulated by the Stoic-Christian theories of natural law, the former position argues that all human beings have the same rational faculties which enable them to grasp immutable and universal moral truths. Moral customs and practices vary from place to place, and change over time, but more basic moral truths do not alter. These moral truths are immutable because they are inherent in human nature, but knowledge of them fluctuates across history and varies between societies.

The difficulties with this conception of universalism have already been noted. Vico (1970, p. 51) seems to have been among the first to argue that the belief that certain moral truths are natural and universal is the product of history. Conceptions of universality are therefore tainted by the circumstances of their origins. Similarly, Rousseau (1968, p. 161) argued that all claims to grasp immutable moral truths inevitably confer a wholly spurious universality upon the preferences of a particular time and place. This is the source of the claim that Western conceptions of ethical universality are mired in ethnocentrism.

One path from the blight of ethnocentrism and false universality leads to relativism in which the search for universal moral certainties is abandoned and all cultural claims are deemed to have equal value. The second account of ethical universalism endeavours to finesse the relativist position by arguing that certain universal moral truths have accumulated in the course of human history. Whereas the natural law perspective argues that only human knowledge of permanent truths varies, the progressivist interpretation argues that reason itself has a history and conceptions of freedom are revised and enlarged over time. Universalisable truths emerge out of the struggle between opposing perspectives and from the tensions within social structures. This is a central theme in Hegel's philosophy of history. Interestingly, for Hegel as for Rorty, the progress of human history consists of the gradual realisation that many of the cultural and other differences which have underpinned the practice of granting freedom to some and withholding it from others are morally irrelevant. In this account of history, the spurious grounds for excluding whole categories of human beings from social and political freedom are delegitimated and stripped away until the point is reached where all human beings are understood to have the same prima facie right to, and capacity for, self-determination. Defending this claim, Hegel (1956, p. 19) argued that human history reveals the advance beyond the Oriental world in which only one, the emperor, was free to the Graeco-Roman world in which some enjoyed freedom (adult male citizens but not women, aliens and slaves), and progress to the modern European state in which all human beings enjoy an equal right to self-determination (see also S. M. Bernstein, 1995, ch. 6).

Like natural law theory, the Hegelian belief that the meaning of human history is revealed by some teleology or divine purpose which finds its highest expression in the arrangements of the modern European state cannot avoid the telling criticism of ethnocentrism. Ethnocentrism is all the more plain when the narrative about the universalisation of the right to self-determination was intimately linked with the assumption that modern European states have the unqualified right to conquer other peoples. However, the philosophies of history developed by Hegel and Marx advanced the crucial observation that part of the progress of society involves the destruction of supposedly natural barriers to equal rights to enjoy self-determination. Their critique of allegedly natural foundations for human slavery illustrates the nature of the critical-theoretical project; their failure to problematise the belief that Europeans had the right to exercise dominion over the rest of the world revealed the limitations of that project as it was conceived in the nineteenth century.

It is possible to hoist philosophical history by its own petard by revealing that it provided spurious grounds for denying freedom to non-European peoples and by arguing that its own logic required support for enlarging the circle of co-legislators to embrace the whole of humanity. During the twentieth century the West has come to recognise the principle that non-Western peoples have the same rights of self-determination although these often remain little more than formal in practice.[7] The openness to dialogue with all other human beings as equals is nevertheless one of the most advanced moral themes in modern ethical and political discourse in the West and elsewhere. The fact that there is transcultural but not universal support for this moral theme may be regarded as evidence of the global spread of the Western liberal-democratic ethos which many in the non-Western world emphatically reject (although there have been many efforts to identify the indigenous counterparts of Western notions of consultation and dialogue).[8] Suffice it to add that the force of the better argument requires support for expanding the boundaries of communities of discourse.[9] In this way it is possible to extend the central claim of philosophical history, which is that progress involves the transcendence of the barriers to equal enjoyment of the right of self-determination, while abandoning its faith in the existence of a continuous, irreversible path of historical development. Confidence in the notion of progress is retained but progress clearly does not terminate with the rise of the modern European state and its pernicious assumptions about its superiority over the non-Western world. Progress involves the decentring of world-views in the manner described by Habermas in the citation above; it involves a conception of dialogue in which universality is wedded to multiculturalism; it requires that the moral stance against wrongful exclusion which makes greater universality and respect for difference possible is divorced from notions of inevitable unilinear progress and historical finality (see also Jabri, 1996).

Various strands of contemporary social and political theory have explored the ethics of dialogue. Here the discussion begins with Habermas's conception of discourse ethics which is central to his project of reconstructing historical materialism. Discourse ethics contains the influence of the German tradition of philosophical history without being hostage to the deterministic teleology which is often attributed to Hegel and Marx. Discourse ethics reconceptualises the emancipatory project and retrieves the universalistic position within a complex account of the historical development of species-wide moral competences. The finer details of Habermas's analysis of language need not detain us; the emphasis falls upon his general characterisation of moral-practical learning.

Habermas (1979a) argues that Marx failed to appreciate the importance of the distinction between labour and interaction. For Marx, human labour is the key to historical development. The conquest of nature in the age of capitalist industrialisation had brought the human species to the threshold of a world free from material scarcity. Habermas argues that Marx failed to recognise the dangers which were inherent in the rise of unprecedented levels of technological power, and particularly the respects in which the state's capacity for dominating the lives of its citizens had been greatly augmented. For Habermas, human history revolves around interaction as well as labour. In the former domain, human beings determine the principles which make social order possible; in this sphere, they are involved in a process of moral-practical learning which differs from the realm of technical-instrumental learning in which human beings increase their mastery of nature. Moral-practical learning is the key to the development of free social relations.

Following Kohlberg's account of individual moral development, Habermas argues that there are three main stages of moral understanding: the pre-conventional, conventional and post-conventional (Habermas, 1979a; T. McCarthy, 1981, ch. 3 section 6). At the level of pre-conventional morality, subjects obey norms fearing that non-compliance will lead to sanctions imposed by a higher authority; at the level of conventional morality, they obey norms from a sense of loyalty to existing social groups or peers; at the level of post-conventional morality, subjects stand back from authority structures and group loyalties and ask whether they are complying with principles which have universal validity. Post-conventional ethical reasoning involves levels of critical disengagement from authority patterns or group norms and unqualified openness to the perspectives of others. For Habermas discourse ethics is the apex of post-conventional moral reasoning: it is the product of complex processes of moral learning.

Discourse ethics argues that norms cannot be valid unless they can command the consent of everyone whose interests stand to be affected by them (Habermas, 1989, pp. 82ff). It follows that a political community which has a commitment to discourse ethics will be deeply concerned about the damaging effects of its actions on outsiders. One of its central beliefs is that the validity of the principles on which it acts can only be determined through a dialogue which is in principle open to all human beings. A crucial point of contrast with Kant's writings is worth noting. In his critique of the miserable comforters, Grotius, Pufendorf and Vattel, Kant argued that political life ought to be organised in accordance with the fiction of a universal social contract. Kant argued that the ideal of freedom required political subjects to 'woo the consent of everyone else' (R. Bernstein, 1986, p. 229). All human beings and not only fellow-citizens had to proceed with regard for the politics of consent. Habermas's conception of discourse ethics has clear Kantian inclinations although one crucial difference separates the two perspectives. Kant believed that separate moral agents had a duty to ask if it was possible to universalise the maxim underlying any action. Judgements concerning universalisability involved a process of private ratiocination for individuals rather than any dialogic encounter with others. Habermas argues that the test of universalisability is found not in private reason but in associating with others in wider communities dedicated to open and unconstrained dialogue.

On this basis, Habermas is keen to define the procedures which are essential to authentic dialogue. These include the convention that no person and no moral position can be excluded from dialogue in advance, and the realisation that authentic dialogue requires a particular moral psychology. True dialogue is not a trial of strength between adversaries who are hell-bent on converting others to their cause; it only exists when human beings accept that there is no a priori certainty about who will learn from whom and when all are willing to engage in a process of reciprocal critique as a result (Habermas, 1990a, p. 26). Cooperation in dialogue requires that agents are prepared to question their own truth claims, respect the claims of others and anticipate that all points of departure will be modified in the course of dialogue. What guides participants is a commitment to be moved simply by the force of the better argument (Habermas, 1990a, pp. 66 and 89).[10]

Discourse ethics sets out the procedures to be followed so that individuals are equally free to express their moral claims, able to explore the prospects for resolving their moral differences and capable of reaching an appropriate compromise in the absence of consensus. It does not offer putative solutions to substantive moral debates, envisage historical end points or circulate political blueprints. What some may think is a profound weakness is for Habermas a significant strength. Discourse ethics establishes the procedural conditions under which human agents can explore the possibility or impossibility of moral agreement. All attempts to prejudge the outcome of dialogue or to supplant it with some notion of the higher authority of philosophical reasoning are abandoned. Discourse ethics supports a radical democratic ethos which is fundamentally at odds with the elitism which was central to much classical Marxism. Concrete decisions about substantive moral arguments are left to agents themselves (Habermas, 1993, p. 24).

Habermas argues that moral-practical learning involves the development of more sophisticated tests of the validity of moral claims. As the most sophisticated test of legitimacy, discourse ethics endorses a system of justification which stresses answerability to all human beings who stand to be affected by any action rather than accountability to the narrower circle of those with whom moral agents are linked by special ties and shared dispositions. Discourse ethics takes a critical stance towards all systems of exclusion and places the considerations which are decisive in pre-conventional and conventional moral reasoning in doubt. That is not to imply that all special ties and all modes of exclusion are suspect from the vantage-point of discourse ethics; all it suggests is that discourse ethics generates the concern that participants in any bounded association may not have been moral enough – in Bauman's words – because they may have failed to engage others as equals in a dialogue which considers the justice or injustice of the systems of exclusion which affect them. The aim of discourse ethics is to remove the modes of exclusion which obstruct the goal – which may never be realised – of global arrangements which rest upon the consent of each and every member of the human race. Discourse ethics is radically opposed, then, to any pretence to stand with absolute certainty on an exclusionary ground.

At this juncture it is important to return to feminist arguments that the universalist standpoint which discourse ethics attempts to recover risks perpetuating an exclusionary, male ethic. Habermas's claim that the ultimate end of dialogue is to discover which interests are generalisable has been assumed to imply the search for a universal consensus about the principles which should regulate the public domain of interaction between separate and autonomous strangers (Benhabib, 1993, p. 9; C. Brown, 1994).[11] As noted earlier, one of the most important contemporary critiques of the notion of generalisability in ethics argues that it is intertwined with gender-based exclusion. The universalistic claim that the higher levels of moral reasoning deal with abstract principles of justice has been judged guilty of devaluing the moral skills which are central to the ethic of care and responsibility for the concrete other which has traditionally defined the role of women as the primary carers for family members. Discourse ethics is implicated in preserving gender hierarchy, according to this line of argument, notwithstanding its inclination to bring all systems of exclusion into question.

Some feminist writers who make this criticism add that moral agents need to harmonise the two voices of 'individual integrity and autonomy, on the one hand, with that of care and connectedness on the other' (White, 1988, p. 84; Squires, 1996). For Benhabib, for example, one of the goals of feminism is to reach 'a more integrated vision of ourselves and of our fellow human beings as generalized as well as concrete others' (Benhabib and Cornell, 1987, p. 93). This raises intriguing questions about the relationship between the two ethics (see also Gilligan, 1993; O'Neill, 1989a).

O'Neill (1989a) identifies important linkages between them. The ethic of justice is largely concerned with public norms which omit consideration of the differences between persons, and the ethic of care and responsibility is mainly concerned with the welfare of particular others, but each should enter into the constitution of the other. Care needs to be principled to escape the risk of moral parochialism and selfishness, and considerations of justice need to take account of differences between persons, especially the striking inequalities of power and wealth which exist between them. O'Neill concludes that the legitimacy of political arrangements is in question if it lacks the consent of those who are constrained by public institutions and dominant social norms.[12] Answerability to universal norms and sensitivity to the specific differences of others require dialogic communities which assume that the legitimacy of social practices depends upon the consent of the traditional victims of unjust exclusion. Dialogue in such communities involves all members equally in a quest for universals which disregards the differences between persons where these are morally irrelevant, but also ensures that the enterprise of creating public norms and institutions is sensitive to salient social differences and committed to reducing debilitating material inequalities.[13]

Responding to Gilligan's critique of Kohlberg's stages of moral development, Habermas argues that discourse ethics is not a form of 'moral rigorism' which applies universal principles to social settings mechanically without regard for personal need and social context. At the level of practice, discourse ethics requires hermeneutic insights into the nuanced relationships between abstract moral principles, specific social contexts and particular human needs (Habermas, 1990a, pp. 176–80). Habermas argues that the ethic of care and responsibility complements the ethic of justice by bringing finely-tuned hermeneutic moral skills and interpersonal sensibilities to bear on the implementation of public norms. This formulation depicts the ethics of care and justice as two sides of the same moral coin.

In making these comments Habermas (1993, pp. 153–4) suggests that the ethic of care and responsibility enters the equation at the point where universal principles have to be applied to the vagaries of individual need and social context. Arguably, discourse ethics should be committed at a much earlier stage to engaging the hermeneutic skills associated with the ethic of care and responsibility, although Habermas does not always make this clear. The criticism that universality is always privileged over difference in Habermas's account of moral reasoning is understandable in consequence. The linkages between feminism and critical theory which are developed in recent work by Benhabib and Cornell (1987, ch. 4; Benhabib, 1993) explain how discourse ethics has to be sensitive to difference well before questions of applying abstract moral principles arise. Benhabib's stress on the need for deep engagement with otherness prior to issues of application reveals that the claim that discourse ethics is necessarily committed to absorbing all social differences within a universal consensus is misplaced.[14]

Benhabib's defence of 'post-conventional contextualism' explains how universality and difference are related in discourse ethics (Benhabib, 1993, pp. 151 and 163–4).[15] Post-conventional attachments to universal principles assume that similar individuals in similar circumstances should be governed by the same principles. Contextual considerations aim to overcome the limitations of earlier accounts of universalisability, including the Kantian categorical imperative, by affirming the need for dialogue between concrete others to ascertain which principles can be universalised. In the first place, Benhabib's contribution to the move beyond Kantian private ratiocination is that the question of whether agents are alike in relevant respects and therefore eligible to be governed by the same principles can only be answered by dialogue in which agents publicly examine the extent of their similarities and the moral importance of their differences (see also Young, 1987). Empathetic cooperation between individuals with all their particularities, and the search for mutual comprehension of their respective needs and contexts, is the starting-point of discourse ethics.[16] Post-conventional contextualism therefore indicates that the engagement with difference cannot be deferred until the moment at which decisions about applying universal principles to specific social contexts have to be made: engagement with the particularity of others is essential whenever agents become involved in any dialogue about whether there are any universal principles which ought to regulate their social interaction (see also Habermas, 1993, pp. 153–4).

Sensitivity to social context is therefore a primary feature of the more advanced approaches to generalisability in ethics. The search for agreement through open dialogue with concrete others guards against the danger of reaching a social consensus which obscures or neglects individual or cultural differences (Young, 1990).[17] With this in mind, some feminists agree with the communitarian argument that ethical universalists tend to overlook the part that communities play in the constitution of the moral self and underestimate the importance of community loyalties for individuals. But the agreement is far from total (Benhabib and Cornell, 1987, p. 12). Feminism takes issue with communitarianism when it defends traditional community loyalties and norms uncritically, without regard for the part they have played in the exclusion of women. Some feminists argue for 'dialogic communitarianism' as a result (Frazer and Lacey, 1993, pp. 203–12). Dialogic communitarianism overlaps with Rorty's position because it denies the existence of an Archimedean perspective and concludes, appropriately, that actors have no choice but to start from where they are. (See above, p. 77.) The accent falls on *dialogic* communitarianism since true dialogue permits the reconstitution of social norms and expectations and the development of new roles and possibilities for subaltern groups such as excluded women (Benhabib and Cornell, 1987, pp. 12–13). Only through critical dialogue – only when *Sittlichkeit* has been exposed to *Moralität* – can excluded groups begin to enjoy equal membership of the communities to which they belong, and with which they may identify even though they are unfairly excluded. Dialogue is not confined then to maximising consensus within the normative parameters which dominant groups take for granted. One of its key purposes is to widen social parameters by making it possible for individuals to expand the realm of admissible disagreements which political communities have often suppressed in the name of the totalising project.

The ideal of a dialogic community involves the pledge not to sacrifice 'unassimilated otherness' on the altar of a 'unified public' (Frazer and Lacey, 1993, p. 204; Young, 1990, p. 105). It requires the willingness to actively empower rather than simply tolerate otherness (White, 1991, p. 110). Dialogic encounters which promote greater diversity in this way may never come to an end, and no lasting resolution of the ethical differences between human subjects can ever be anticipated, as Habermas (1990a) has argued. The idea of moral progress retains its meaning but it is neither associated with the conviction that ultimate moral truths reside in any one culture nor linked with the Archimedean supposition that immutable universal moral principles are built into some conception of human rationality which transcends history. What moral progress refers to is the widening of the circle of those who have rights to participate in dialogue and the commitment that norms cannot be regarded as universally valid unless they have, or could command, the consent of all those who stand to be affected by them. Moral progress involves a movement beyond provincial forms of life to a thin universality in which discourse is the means which the radically different employ in their efforts to explore the possibility of an agreement about the principles of coexistence.[18]

The link between dialogue and consensus has been criticised by postmodernists such as Lyotard who are troubled by the threat which universality poses to difference. Lyotard (1984, p. 82) defends a plurality of incommensurable language games and urges others to 'activate the differences'. Plurality is incompatible with traditional conceptions of community in which 'the social bond' which ties the members of a society together allows one language game to trump all others (Lyotard, 1985, p. 93). Social bonds have to be reconstituted so that different language games cannot encroach upon each other. For Lyotard, the affirmation of radical otherness and the suspension of all efforts to bring differences within a unifying social consensus are the prerequisites of a society which is open to new expressions.

On this reasoning, a just society is one which 'recognises and allows all participants to have a voice, to narrate from their own perspective' (Haber, 1994, p. 30). The sovereignty of their different language games requires the adoption of the principle of mutual respect. In this context there is no place for forms of dialogue in which adversaries strive to win each other to their respective causes or participate in efforts to subsume differences within an over-arching consensus. Lyotard's position would therefore appear to be at odds with the Habermasian notion of discourse ethics. For Habermas, discourse is Socratic in the sense that moral subjects are steered by the force of the better argument towards a determinate normative consensus or to an appropriate compromise where moral disagreements remain unresolved. For Lyotard (1985, p. 4) 'dialectical discourse in the Platonic sense . . . is associated with power', and specifically with efforts to control 'the effects of the statements exchanged by the partners of the dialogue'. Lyotard (1984, p. 61) supports dialogue without dialectic in which nuances are explored and differences are enlarged on the understanding that '[c]onsensus is a horizon that is never reached'.[19]

Some interpretations of Lyotard's position suggest that he drives a curiously deep wedge between language games by claiming that they are sovereign and incommensurable (Weber, in Lyotard, 1985, p. 104). It has been argued that the goal of disrupting consensus and uprooting conformity has the peculiar effect of protecting the language games which underlie unjust systems of exclusion. Not only does this arbitrarily rule out dialogue with a dialectic which leads to 'genuine agreement'; it seems to discount the possibility of transcending language games which legitimate social and political domination (Haber, 1994, ch. 1). These include language games which defend patriarchy (Haber, 1994, p. 32) or which present gender, racial or ethnic inequalities as natural phenomena. The critique of such language games and the search for a new consensus which deepens the engagement with egalitarian norms are central features of modern political communities which are responsive to the force of the better argument. Illustrating the point with reference to the extension of the suffrage to women, Taylor (1985, p. 382) argues that the logic of the better argument in the first part of the twentieth century clearly required 'lifting . . . an indefensible restriction, grounded on a misguided view of the human potentialities of half the human race'. The evolving social consensus resolved to open one of the 'doors to otherness' which had previously been closed (Taylor, 1985, p. 383). From this perspective, dialogic encroachment upon the sovereign territory of language games which perpetuate social inequalities, and the search for a social consensus which opens doors to otherness, are essential for the realisation of Lyotard's own principle of openness to minorities (Lyotard, 1985, p. 95).[20]

Whether postmodernism and Frankfurt School critical theory provide incommensurable accounts of the relationship between dialogue and dialectic is a matter requiring far more detailed analysis than is possible here. Lyotard's comments in a recent Amnesty International lecture suggest that the gulf between critical theory and postmodernism is not as large as is sometimes thought. In his lecture, Lyotard (1993, pp. 140–1) argues that the right to speak, and the right of the different not to be excluded from the speech community, are fundamental rights. This being so, all human beings have an equal right to take part in dialogue and to 'establish their community by contract' using 'reason and debate' (Lyotard, 1993, p. 138). It is desirable 'to extend interlocution to any human individual whatsoever, regardless of national or natural idiom' (Lyotard, 1993, p. 139). In a formulation that is strikingly similar to the universalistic theme which is more typically associated with Frankfurt School critical social theory, Lyotard adds that 'civility may become universal in fact as it promises to do by right'. These remarks tend to support White's observation that there are striking parallels between Habermas's discourse ethics and Lyotard's thesis that social constraints should be determined by participants within free contractual arrangements (White, 1991, p. 136).

Frankfurt School critical theory and postmodernism support the ideal of communities of discourse in which there is a consensus about the need to universalise access to dialogue, and an agreement that decisions about the legitimacy of social and political arrangements should be open to all. As previously noted, discourse ethics sets out some of the preconditions of open dialogue. Postmodern thinkers such as Lyotard are similarly concerned about the nature of these preconditions but are troubled that the quest for social consensus can too easily fail to detect the subtle operation of power or to respond sympathetically to important differences – hence Lyotard's claim that in 'the game of the just' it is essential that 'one speaks only inasmuch as one listens' (Haber, 1994, p. 42). Shapcott (1994, p. 75) argues that similar considerations are central to philosophical hermeneutics, and particularly to Gadamer's notion of the 'fusion of horizons' which denies that perspectives are radically incommensurable. According to philosophical hermeneutics, human subjects can place themselves within an alien horizon and enlarge and transform their own world-views accordingly. The idea of conversation in Gadamer's hermeneutics allows for universal agreement 'through openness to the other's truth claims' (Shapcott, 1994, p. 75). Gadamer argues that agreement through conversation 'always involves the attainment of a higher universality that overcomes not only our particularity but also that of the other' (quoted by Shapcott, 1994, p. 75). Butler (1995), who approaches these issues from a feminist perspective, argues that very different cultures have generated notions of universality and some basic similarities do seem to exist between them. However, 'the task that cultural difference sets for us is the articulation of universality through a difficult labour of translation' (Butler, 1995, p. 130). Universal agreement is not ruled out but 'it may be that the universal is only partially articulated, and that we do not yet know what form it may take' (1995, p. 30).

The stress on the voice of the other highlights the difficulty (and ultimately the impossibility) of entering into pure dialogic relations in which only the force of the better argument prevails. Dialogic communities can never be confident that all the barriers to open discourse have been removed. An important contribution to democratic theory is inherent in this emphasis on the permanent danger of failures of comprehension between the members of different cultures or the exponents of radically different perspectives. For the most part, the main strands of democratic theory have reflected upon the structures and procedures which must be in place before a democratic polity can be said to exist, or they have stressed the social and economic resources which citizens must have at their disposal before their effective participation in an open society can be realised. More recent accounts of dialogic communities and deliberative politics shift the emphasis to the subtle and complex socio-psychological prerequisites of truly democratic encounters: they focus less on the public rules of the game or on the distribution of social resources than on the hermeneutic skills which are necessary for the radical extension of democratic forms of life.[21] By stressing the existence of imperceptible socio-psychological constraints upon unforced dialogue these approaches reveal that public agreements are necessarily precarious: they may not rest as much on the force of the better argument as satisfied actors suppose.

Habermas's argument that actors may consent to arrangements without being aware of a range of constraints upon their thought and behaviour is essential to a thin universality in which increasing numbers of human beings cooperate to eradicate unjust exclusion without assuming that they will ever converge around one universalisable conception of the good life. The crucial point which separates this account of universality from the one which seems to run through Marx's writings is that human beings cannot anticipate living in a condition in which they have overcome all constraints upon their freedom and in which there is, as a result, no further business to contemplate. Previously unknown constraints upon their freedom may await the discovery of permanently reflective agents. The endless scrutiny of agreements for evidence of hidden influences and constraints upon genuinely equal participation is a necessary commitment for any dialogic community. Very different approaches to dialogue exist in the current literature and it is essential not to underestimate the differences and divisions between them. But one common theme stands out, namely the desire to deepen democratic imperatives in the context of increasing cultural differentiation within modern states and world society.

Universalism Revisited

Rorty's observation that *we* have to start from where *we* are given the elusiveness of the Archimedean ideal has been central to the argument thus far. Of course, all statements which refer to collectivities in this all-inclusive manner are notoriously problematical since they risk aligning very different groups with purposes which they do not accept. One response to this challenge is to renew the quest for an Archimedean perspective which reveals that the whole of humanity might yet become orientated to one universalisable conception of the good life. The goods on this shelf are, at least, temporarily unavailable.[22] The doubts which immediately engulf any claim to speak on behalf of any collectivity, or any belief that particular purposes and value-commitments are shared by every member, invite a different starting-point which concerns the ethics of systems of exclusion.

This point of departure has the virtue of reflecting powerful moral and cultural trends which exist, to some degree, in all contemporary societies. No modern political community is immune from internal ethical debates about the exclusion of national or racial minorities, women, subordinate classes, migrants, gays and lesbians; and no modern political community can evade similar moral questions about the exclusion of outsiders – whether closure involves denying refugees entry into the society, exporting harms with total disregard for the well-being of non-nationals, or refusing outsiders representation and voice in national decisions which affect their vital interests. To start from where *we* are (where *we* includes all those who are sensitive to the ethics of exclusion) is already to be implicated in complex moral questions about the character of modern political community.[23] It is to be deeply troubled by the perennial questions about the distribution of membership, citizenship and global responsibilities which have resurfaced with particular urgency in the context of globalisation and fragmentation.

To start with these ethical sensitivities about the nature of bounded communities is not to assume that human beings can live without social boundaries, but rather to accept Derrida's claim that no practice of 'boundary-fixing', no practice of exclusion, is automatically beyond question and reproach (R. Bernstein, 1991, p. 184). The primary issue is whether, and by what criteria, *we* can justify the modes of exclusion which are integral to *our* social and political practices. This question arises in conjunction with the social divisions and barriers within the community, and in connection with the moral significance which the community attaches to national frontiers. Whether such systems of exclusion can be justified is essentially a question about the moral relevance of the human differences which have been thought to justify unequal treatment in the past. How modes of exclusion are best legitimated is largely about ensuring that decisions about the justice of exclusionary practices are not monopolised by dominant groups.

These issues are closely related. Many of the traditional appeals to natural hierarchies of class, race, nation or gender which have been used to justify regimes of exclusion have been problematised in the modern epoch. Ethical claims that racial differences justify enslavement, or that immutable gender distinctions vindicate the confinement of women to the domestic sphere, have been delegitimated. Stronger commitments to dialogic politics have emerged from the struggle to dismantle unjust exclusion. Heightened awareness of the spurious grounds for several modes of closure has encouraged recognition of the need to involve the systematically excluded in open dialogue about the harms committed in the past, about the best means of remedying historical wrongs and about the ideal future configuration of political institutions. Sensitivity to the ways in which societies wrongly imputed moral significance to a range of human differences necessitates the radical extension of dialogic relations. Past practices of unjust exclusion might not have developed (and future ones would be easier to prevent) if stronger attachments to communities of discourse had accumulated in the past.

On this reasoning, no conception of ethics is satisfactory if it endorses the systematic exclusion of any individual member of the human species, on a priori grounds, from a communication community which has the potential to become universal.[24] Universality here assumes neither the essentialism of natural law perspectives nor the teleology evident in the speculative philosophies of history associated with the Enlightenment. Universality takes the form of a responsibility to engage others, irrespective of their racial, national and other characteristics, in open dialogue about matters which impinge on their welfare.

These themes are crucial for the radical intensification of the democratic impulses which are inherent in modernity but frequently stifled or cancelled by competing logics of normalisation and control.[25] But whether these themes have any claim whatsoever on human beings elsewhere – that is, whether *they* are obliged to share these ethical sensibilities – is, for many, the central question. It is clear that Western ethical codes have been drawn towards debates about whether discriminatory practices are based on morally relevant differences between persons; and the movement beyond the modes of exclusion which did assume the moral relevance of differences of gender or race has been facilitated by arguments that these presuppositions are erroneous. But what counts as a compelling reason for resisting practices of exclusion in a Western society cannot be assumed to hold automatically for all forms of life. Transcultural validity can only be established by bringing judgements about good reasons for actions before a tribunal which is open to all others.

In some cases, the critique of unjust exclusion appears to rest on good arguments rather than on the normative considerations which happen to have most resonance in the West. Some arguments, including those made against slavery or apartheid, enjoy transcultural validity. Certain moral convictions, including the belief that justice ought to reign even in the midst of war, have the support of different cultures or civilisations. These instances of moral convergence do not rest on a consensus about the ontological primacy of the individual, or assume that all or most social roles and institutions can be renegotiated. There are sharp differences of opinion about these modernist claims in the contemporary world, and a good deal of evidence that disputes about such matters may be increasing. Even so, most cultures recognise that the differences between insiders and outsiders are not always morally decisive, and that there are duties to the other which require limitations on the use of force. Some notion of answerability to others, and some sense of an obligation to engage outsiders in dialogue about matters which concern them deeply, may not be universally accepted but they are widely supported across the world nonetheless. Critical and dialogic components of culture are evident in different societies, and the outlines of a cosmopolitan culture in which *Moralität* has brought a reflective orientation towards *Sittlichkeit* are already apparent. As a result, the issue of whether *they* are obliged to participate in universal discourse may be less important than debates about the nature of authentic dialogue and its legitimate sphere of operation.

Notions of dialogue and consultation exist in many different cultures but they may not have exactly the same meaning, and rival understandings deserve due recognition.[26] A broad consensus about the nature of openly dialogic relations may exist alongside profound disagreements about the range of social practices which should be exposed to radical critique. Some cultures are more prepared than others to open their borders to international scrutiny in order to increase protection for human rights. Others take the view that outsiders do not have a legitimate right to criticise their domestic practices. This standpoint warrants respect as long as internal practices do not violate international moral agreements which outlaw doctrines of racial supremacy, for example. Of course, difficult questions inevitably arise about who claims to speak for the society as a whole, and whose privileges are being safeguarded by efforts to shield domestic arrangements from international scrutiny.[27] But despite these complexities, the proposition that no individuals should be excluded by virtue of their class, nationality, ethnicity, sexual identity, gender or race from participating in decisions which impinge upon their welfare and interests is central to a modern cosmopolitan ethic. Debates about whether this commitment allows the strong to intervene in societies where certain practices contravene this principle inevitably arise at this point, but this is not the primary issue. Ensuring that the most powerful groups in international society honour this cosmopolitan principle in their own relations with the weak is a prior ethical consideration.[28]

As noted earlier, this approach to universality strives to overcome the criticisms levelled against natural law theory and the speculative philosophies of history. It aims to avoid the accusation which was directed at Enlightenment thinkers that their enthusiasm for a future cosmopolis devalued cultural diversity. It accepts many of the claims which have arisen in the contemporary critique of cosmopolitanism. The sociological observation that individuals acquire their identities within historical communities, and that moralities are social products, is not in doubt; the moral principle that individuals have the right to choose their associates and to expect that others will be respectful of their communal loyalties is not in question; the related contention that special obligations between family members or fellow-citizens may override general obligations to humanity is not in dispute. Particular social bonds (such as the ties of nationality) which unite the members of a group and set them apart from the rest of humanity will endure. The important point is to ensure that group membership does not clash with the ideal of a universal communication community.

A dialogic community which addresses actual or potential tensions between group norms and the communicative ideal will not claim the right to choose systems of inclusion and exclusion without involving those who may be adversely affected in open dialogue. National boundaries cannot be assumed to be so morally significant as to justify confining the right of access to unconstrained dialogue to members of the group. A dialogic community must therefore involve relevant outsiders in key decisions regarding the distribution of membership, citizenship and global responsibilities. Bonds between members have to be loosely formed to permit the evolution of wider communities of discourse which are in principle open to all others.

Answerability to others for the consequences of exclusion can take many forms. Some communities may opt for marginal involvement with the rest of the world, and engage in dialogue only insofar as they cause harm to others. Regarding the distribution of membership, vulnerable cultures have the greatest right to exercise the right of closure which Walzer defends in his account of communal self-determination. The claims of an indigenous people to refuse members of the dominant cultures the right to purchase property on its land seem compelling for the reasons set out by Kymlicka (1989). A state which fears for the survival of its culture is entitled to exercise similar rights. Whether states can exclude outsiders simply because they do not share the collective identity of those who are already citizens is a different matter (see Preuss, 1995). Advancing spurious reasons for the exclusion of outsiders leaves a society open to international condemnation, as Walzer (1995) points out in his comments on United States immigration policy, and reveals that the burden of proof may not fall entirely on refugees who solicit entry. Decisions about the distribution of membership need to be taken with regard for the circumstances of the victims of the acts of enclosure which have divided the world into separate sovereign states with the result that the victims of expulsion do not enjoy rights of entry elsewhere. This is especially important when affluent societies benefit from large-scale human movement from less affluent societies. An open-door policy on admissions can be criticised because it allows rich states to benefit from the global transfer of skills without adequate compensation for poorer societies.[29] The extent of answerability to others must vary considerably between societies; it cannot be the same for privileged states and weak indigenous peoples. Affluent societies have special duties to involve relevant outsiders in dialogue about the principles which should govern the distribution of membership and about global responses to the plight of the world's refugees. It is incumbent upon them to constitute themselves as world citizens and act as local agents of a world common good.[30]

What is true of the distribution of membership also holds for the distribution of citizenship: the right to lead a separate existence does not mean then that a community can make decisions about citizenship exactly as it pleases. If minority nations are denied citizenship rights, if their differences are ignored by members of the dominant culture, if they have good reason to fear for the survival of their own way of life, then the point may be reached where a political community forfeits the right to sovereign independence. Recent discussions of 'failed states' argue that humanitarian intervention can be justified where those who flee from human rights violations create intolerable strains on the societies in which they seek refuge (Helman and Ratner, 1992–3). Dialogic communities have a legitimate interest in protecting minority nations in other societies, and they have a right to protest against appeals to sovereignty which are designed to shelter governing elites from international accountability for the conduct of national policy (Jackson, 1990). The ethical credentials of the intervening states will be stronger if they have previously taken steps to protect ethnic and other minorities within their own borders. Group-differentiated notions of citizenship and the right of legal appeal to appropriate international authorities when accusations of unjust exclusion arise are two means by which dialogic communities can establish their credentials in matters concerning the distribution of citizenship.

Turning to global responsibilities, Rousseau argued in *A Discourse of Political Economy* (1968, p. 247) that citizenship has little value if non-citizens can claim the same legal and political rights as insiders. Special ties inevitably place limits on global responsibilities but, as previously noted, the distribution of membership and citizenship may raise issues of international concern. Some element of moral favouritism is an intrinsic feature of any separate way of life, but that does not justify a 'concentric-circle image of duty' in which obligations to fellow-citizens inevitably have priority over duties to the rest of humanity.[31] Shue's discussion of the export of hazards sets out the case for applying a universalisable principle in circumstances in which citizens and aliens must be deemed to have equal moral standing.[32] The main impetus for enlarging the sense of global moral responsibility arises in the context of increasing transnational harm.

Under such conditions, democratic societies have a special obligation to unite citizens and aliens as co-legislators in a wider political community. They have a moral duty to establish what David Held (1995, p. 232) describes as a cosmopolitan community of democratic societies in which citizens from different societies come to be associated as members of a transnational citizenry. One of the central problems of social contract theory is overcome by the idea of cosmopolitan democracy. According to many writers in the contractarian tradition, the citizens of different societies entered into separate agreements to create sovereign communities. The human race which had originally belonged to one universal society came to be fragmented through multiple social contracts. But the right of human beings to secede in this way was morally questionable. In a critique of social contract theory, Sir Robert Filmer pointed to a tension between the proposition that separate compacts could divide the species and the contractarian belief in the primordial unity of humankind. If, Filmer (1949, p. 285) argued, the contractarians were right that 'all mankind ... makes but one people', if they were right that all things were initially held in common, then no one could properly be made sovereign without the 'universal consent' of all humanity. Filmer's critique of social contract approaches is a useful reminder that political theorists have often failed to take the moral and political implications of the Stoic-Christian tradition seriously (Gallie, 1978, ch. 2).[33]

Kant drew the appropriate conclusion which was that progress in international relations involves the move from an international system to an international society of states, and the continuous evolution of that society to enlarge the domain of human interaction which is governed by dialogue and consent. As participants in a universal kingdom of ends, states would not act in ways which adversely affected other communities or human society as a whole – as if they were free from any obligation to woo the consent of the rest of humanity. The role which three different forms of international society can play in realising this end has already been noted (see above, pp. 7–8).

However, Kant's liberal notion of wooing the consent of the members of other communities needs to be further refined to stress the need to create the social and economic preconditions of an effective universal communication community. Horkheimer's observation that 'a materialist theory of society' was needed to progress 'beyond the utopian character of Kant's idea of a perfect constitution of humankind' conveys the essential point (Hoy and McCarthy, 1994, p. 56). Taking the discussion further, Offe has argued that no individual or group should 'be deprived of the material means of subsistence, of human and civil rights, or of opportunities for political and social participation' (1994, p. 56). Similar themes arise in conjunction with Habermas's notion of ideal speech. Progress towards the ideal of undistorted communication requires the critique of all modes of 'domination, violence and systematic inequality' which obstruct equal participation in dialogue (Cohen, 1980, pp. 71 and 100).[34] A commitment to the ideal of a universal communication community involves a neo-Marxist critique of all 'asymmetries' of power (Apel, 1980, p. 283). Here Kant's liberal vision of wooing the consent of humankind within a universal kingdom of ends is extended in the defence of the normative goal of a universal communication community in which all individuals are equally free from domination.[35] The dialogic ideal interlocks with a Marxian-inspired critique of alienation, estrangement and exploitation.[36] Collaboration across the frontiers to produce arrangements which are more universalistic, more sensitive to cultural differences and more committed to reducing social and economic inequalities than their predecessors is entailed by commitments to domination-free communication. A global narrative of universal emancipation which aims at this, the triple transformation of political community, is immanent within the dialogic ideal. The ethical foundations of political community in the post-Westphalian era should revolve around these convictions.

Conclusions

Modes of universalistic reasoning which presuppose the reality of an Archimedean perspective no longer enjoy much support, and the commitment to defining one universalisable conception of the good life has fallen into disrepute. The demise of traditional universalistic ethics does not justify the conclusion that anything goes in the era of post-metaphysical thinking. Indeed, the critique of universalistic ethics is part of a larger challenge to the systems of unjust exclusion which have existed in the West and which have underpinned the dominant attitudes and behaviour towards the non-Western world. Sensitivity to the ways in which the boundaries have been drawn between us and them, between insiders and outsiders, is pronounced in most recent social theory and radical politics. A new universality is evident in the widening critique of the grounds for many traditional modes of exclusion, and in the close scrutiny of what many actors assume to be morally significant human differences. The outcome of these developments is a thin conception of universality which defends the ideal that every human being has an equal right to participate in dialogue to determine the principles of inclusion and exclusion which govern global politics. Thick conceptions of universality have been criticised for advocating substantive visions of the good life which pose a threat to cultural diversity: the thin conception defends the ideal of a universal communication community which enlarges the range of differences which can be publicly expressed.

The preference for associating with those who have similar social predispositions and the ideal of a universal communication community exist in a state of potential conflict. Particularistic social bonds can be incompatible with participation in a wider community of discourse, and universalistic sentiments may clash with the special ties between the members of bounded communities. The tension is overcome when social bonds are reconstituted to ensure that systematically excluded groups enjoy rights of participation. A dialogic community in which members choose to live together because of their common allegiances but wish to ensure that their practices command the consent of internal subaltern groups already has the potential to become involved in wider universalities of discourse which ensure rights of participation for the victims of transnational harm.[37] Particular social bonds remain but they are reconstituted in the light of a normative commitment to engage the systematically excluded in open dialogue. These wider universalities of discourse necessarily take several different forms, given the variety of social systems with which a dialogic community has relations, but each of these wider dialogic frameworks involves communities in the project of striking appropriate balances between universality and difference. Collectively these wider frameworks enable a larger portion of humanity to challenge the forms of exclusion which prevent them from pursuing their legitimate ends and interests. Wider universalities of discourse which increase the range of permissible disagreements would represent a significant shift beyond the Westphalian era of classical sovereign states and their totalising projects.

4

The Modes of Exclusion
and the Boundaries
of Community

The question of the ethical justification for various systems of exclusion
is common to most strands of contemporary social and political theory.
Frankfurt School social theory, postmodernism and feminism exhibit a
similar concern with criticising the unjust practices of exclusion which
are built into social structures and their external relations. These
approaches reject the supposition that there is one conception of the
good life which ought to be universalised, but their resistance to
unjustified modes of exclusion is linked with a conception of the self and
society which values the expansion of the boundaries of dialogic forms
of life. Dialogue is the preferred means by which subjects should decide
whether systems of exclusion are justified.

A commitment to universality is integral to these approaches, and is
most clearly expressed by their conviction that the right to take part in
dialogue to influence decisions which affect them should be possessed by
all humanity. Restructuring social arrangements to promote the normative ideal of a universal dialogic community is a principal aim of critical
social theorists such as Habermas. Transcending state sovereignty which
remains the constitutive principle of modern political life is understood
as essential to promoting narratives of increasing cosmopolitanism.
Expanding the realm of dialogic commitments is regarded as necessitat-
ing measures to reduce or eradicate the asymmetries of power and wealth
which exist within sovereign states and in the global economic and
political system. Critical international theory defends the triple transformation of political community by advocating dialogic communities
which are cosmopolitan in orientation, respectful of cultural differences
and committed to reducing social and economic inequalities, nationally
and internationally.

Sensitivity to unjust forms of exclusion and the normative attachment to dialogue are historical products. Societies which question the moral significance of racial, cultural, ethnic and gender differences are the result of complex processes of social change which have been influenced by various forms of political struggle and resistance. Critical cultures which problematise the moral relevance of various social differences and favour dialogic means of conducting politics are not the historical norm; they are unevenly distributed across time and space, and they command unequal levels of support from the members of the political systems which proclaim their allegiance to the democratic process. No cunning of reason oversees the development of dialogic communities; no teleology has steered them to this point, guarantees their future development or underwrites their long-term survival. Dialogic principles govern limited areas of domestic social and political life in the Western societies with the most secure democratic traditions and hardly impinge at all on the conduct of foreign policy. Even those democracies may be doomed to decay if the right of participation is restricted to particular sectors of national societies which are increasingly at the mercy of 'worldwide systemic operations' (Habermas, 1994, p. 165).

To return to an earlier theme, critical theories which are sensitive to these issues need to develop philosophical, sociological and praxeological inquiries into how some human beings are included in, while others are excluded from, communities of discourse. Within this division of labour, philosophical inquiry has the task of defending the dialogic imperative and criticising the practice of unjustly excluding others from open dialogue. Sociological inquiry has the purpose of considering the forces which have shaped the origins, reproduction and transformation of dialogic communities.[1] Praxeological inquiry has the function of commenting on the possibility of enlarging the boundaries of communities of discourse and institutionalising loyalties to the ideal of a universal communication community.

Praxeological questions about how the ideal of the universal communication community can make progress in the contemporary system of states are deferred until chapter 6. The present chapter offers some reflections on the possibility of a sociology which seeks to understand the forces which have shaped (or hindered) the development of wider communities of discourse. There is as yet no adequate sociological account of these forces although a number of different perspectives can contribute to its development. It will be argued below that some of the fundamentals of such a sociology can be found in Weber's writings on the rationalisation of the world religions, in Nelson's approach to civilisational structures and inter-civilisational relations, in Habermas's account of moral-practical learning which stresses the achievements of

Occidental rationality and in Mann's recent analysis of the history of social power. All of these theorists have explored themes which ought to have been more central to the study of international relations: these include the ways in which different societies exclude outsiders from their respective conceptions of the moral community and the extent to which different societies have regarded outsiders as dialogic equals within a wider community of humankind. Laying the foundations for future work in this area is the principal aim of this chapter.

All of the authors mentioned in the last paragraph contribute important themes to the development of a post-Marxist sociology. They provide means of realising the emancipatory ambitions of the Marxist tradition. The great strength of Marxism was its profound insights into the systems of class exclusion which existed throughout human history and its striking analysis of the role that production had played in social evolution. Its main theoretical weakness was its failure to take account of forms of exclusion based on gender, ethnicity and race, and its neglect of the role that state-building, geopolitics and war, and moral-cultural developments have played in the construction of human societies. As argued elsewhere, Marxism was acutely aware of the importance of understanding the expansion and contraction of the boundaries of community in different historical epochs, but it ultimately failed to provide a satisfactory account of the development of the human capacity to engage others in wider communities of discourse (Linklater, 1990b). The Habermasian project of promoting the reconstruction of historical materialism endeavoured to solve these problems by arguing that all societies have the capacity to participate in a universal communication community. However, modernity is distinguished from other epochs by the greater depth of the commitment to this normative ideal.

There is little in Habermas's analysis which deals directly with encounters between societies. However, the writings of Nelson and Mann have explored lines of sociological inquiry which are alert to the historical importance of inter-civilisational and inter-state relations. These writings have been concerned with variations in the willingness to problematise the moral relevance of differences from other societies and with the uneven development of the capacity to become associated with outsiders in wider communities of discourse. They have addressed the extent to which the major civilisations, empires and states-systems have differed in these respects, and they have been keen to show how moral and cultural factors explain these variations. An analysis of these writings suggests the following proposition, which will receive more detailed discussion on another occasion. The key proposition is that empires have encouraged advances in universality yet simultaneously stood in the way of their further development. Societies of states, by contrast, permit more creative possibilities. The Greek city-state system was the site for the emergence of commitments to universality and dialogue which broke through the limitations of the early empires. These commitments have developed further in the modern society of states. More detailed analysis of this claim is one method of building on the strengths of Marxist sociology without repeating its fatal weaknesses.

This chapter is in four parts. Part one argues that the main task of critical theory is to understand how human beings learn to include some in and exclude others from their social arrangements. The main strengths and weaknesses of Marxist analyses of systems of exclusion are summarised, and the claim that the main challenge facing post-Marxist critical theory is how to develop a more comprehensive account of social exclusion is strongly endorsed (Murphy, 1988, pp. 61 and 101–2). Part two develops these themes in the context of Habermas's reconstruction of historical materialism. It was noted earlier that Habermas criticised Marx for placing technical-instrumental learning (the mode of learning which provides societies with increased mastery of their physical environment) at the heart of the empirical philosophy of history, and for neglecting the role of moral-practical learning in societal evolution. Part two also analyses the significance of Habermas's account of moral learning for a sociology of bounded communities and their unequal potentials for creating wider communities of discourse. Moral learning involves careful scrutiny of the moral relevance of the differences between persons and the commitment to institutionalise the ideal of a universal communication community.

Nelson's neglected analysis of civilisational structures and inter-civilisational relations, which reveals how the analysis of social learning can be applied to the study of international relations, is considered in part three. Nelson was principally interested in the extent to which different civilisations have been willing to broaden their moral horizons by participating in wider communities of discourse. Various themes from the sociology of civilisations which Nelson developed in his writings are important for the sociology of relations between states although Nelson was not concerned with tracing these connections. Part four brings Mann's analysis of the evolution of social power into the discussion as a means of bridging the gap between Nelson's account of civilisational dynamics and the comparative sociology of international states-systems (Wight, 1977). The next chapter will apply some of these considerations to the analysis of the modern state. It will endorse Habermas's claim that modernity has potentials for promoting the ideal of a universal communication community which were less developed in most other epochs. Particular emphasis will be placed on the moral resources provided by modern conceptions of citizenship. The final chapter will consider how these resources can be mobilised in order to make further progress in realising the ideal of a universal communication community.

The Critical Sociology of Inclusion and Exclusion

Many social theorists have observed that systems of inclusion and exclusion are constitutive of all forms of life and warrant a central place in social and political theory as a result. Three illustrations will suffice. Walzer argues that human beings do not confer loyalty on universalistic associations but identify closely with those with similar cultural traits. Debray's critique of socialist internationalism maintained that all human beings prefer to belong to bounded communities which are sharply differentiated from one another (Debray, 1977). Marxism, Debray argues and Walzer would agree, ignored the human need for social boundaries which clearly distinguish self from other, inside from outside, domestic from foreign. Walzer and Debray rework the Hegelian theme that systems of closure are a central dimension of the ontology of the social world, but there are other approaches to exclusion which avoid the conclusion that the human race is condemned forever to remain partitioned between bounded communities.[2] These approaches point to the manifold forms of exclusion which can be consulted in the annals of social organisation; they do so without issuing parallel claims of an ontological nature.

Foucault's writings are insightful on this point. Foucault (1989, ch. 6) was less interested in uncovering primordial modes of closure which might be universal features of social existence than with developing a sociology of the ways in which the unity of Western cultures has been grounded in the rituals of exclusion. Mainstream sociology had been preoccupied with explaining the elements of commonality and consensus which bind the members of a society together: Foucault's approach emphasised the extent to which the modern forms of social cohesion rested upon complex systems of exclusion practised against the members of subaltern groups who were deemed to lack the qualities of rationality, normality or responsibility already possessed by the supposedly competent members of the society. Debray and Walzer argued that the social bond is partly constituted by the rituals of exclusion which are pointed against other societies; Foucault was more inclined to stress the unifying effect of the systems of exclusion which are directed against the criminal and the insane within bounded commmunities. But these two dimensions are closely interwoven in many instances, with the result that social identities are secured through stark contrasts with the internal and external other.[3]

Systems of inclusion and exclusion are ubiquitous features of social life which extend from face-to-face encounters to the more distant contacts involving human collectivities such as territorial states, civilisations and empires. At the micro-social level, kinship groups, peer networks, local communities and voluntary associations weave their variations on the theme of exclusion. Principles of inclusion and exclusion are equally evident at more distant levels where independent political communities interact with one another. The standard of civilisation in the nineteenth century which set out the criteria which non-Western societies had to satisfy if they were to be received into the European-dominated society of states is a notable example (Gong, 1984).[4] Systems of inclusion and exclusion exist at all intermediate levels of social interaction which include relations within, and access to, occupational groups, political organisations and public institutions. Minimum criteria must be satisfied, and basic conditions must be met, before rights of access or participation are conferred.

The social principles which are used in defence of exclusionary regimes vary enormously and extend across a range of dialogic and non-dialogic modes of legitimation. Voluntary associations, occupational groupings, public institutions and societies of states often exclude outsiders because they lack sufficient competence or display insufficient merit. Whether they are justified in doing so need not detain us here. It is sufficient to note that the absence of sufficient merit or need is regarded as a legitimate defence of exclusion in many social contexts. Exclusion has been justified because of commitments to ascriptive criteria which convert differences of gender, class, religion, ethnicity and race into morally relevant features of social and political organisation. Judgements about the morality of systems of exclusion based on these differences clearly vary from place to place and alter over time. Societies have different moral criteria for defending the modes of exclusion around which they are organised. Leaving questions of justice aside, all social systems are constructed from the complex webs of inclusion and exclusion which stretch from face-to-face interaction to distant relationships conducted across vast expanses of space. Exclusion at each level influences the others, however indirectly, and is shaped by them in turn.

Not all social actors understand the connections between these modes of inclusion and exclusion to the same extent, but all are conscious of many of the respects in which systems of inclusion and exclusion impinge upon their daily lives. It seems reasonable to suppose that social actors at all times and places harbour ethical opinions about the justice or injustice of exclusionary practices, possess some sociological account of the reasons for their existence and make practical judgements about their meaning for the ways in which they lead their lives. In all societies, human beings make normative, sociological and praxeological judgements about the systems of inclusion and exclusion which shape the contexts in which they interact. To be immersed in these modes of inclusion and exclusion and to possess accounts of their significance for the self and for relations with others is a large part of what it means to belong to a form of life.

Social and political analysis proceeds from the assumption that it is possible to improve upon the explanations and understandings of the social world which exist at the level of everyday existence. One function of normative inquiry is to ask whether there are universally valid means of determining the justice of systems of inclusion and exclusion; one purpose of sociological analysis is to enlarge human understanding of the origins and development of the modes of inclusion and exclusion; one aim of praxeological inquiry is to ascertain how societies can best solve the moral and practical problems which their dominant modes of inclusion and exclusion generate. The social sciences aim for levels of comprehensiveness, reflectiveness and systematisation which elude actors in everyday life, and many are committed to promoting dialogic principles. But, as postmodernism has argued, social observers may be as immersed in systems of inclusion and exclusion as the subjects they endeavour to comprehend.[5] What is more, social analysis does not simply reflect on the supposedly external realm of human conduct but also shapes the nature of moral subjects. The critics of positivist social science have unravelled the myriad connections between theoretical inquiry and social structures, and they have shown how the former can confer legitimacy on unjust, but malleable, social practices. Marxism was the first perspective to integrate these themes in one comprehensive mode of social inquiry. The normative, sociological and praxeological analysis of class-based exclusion was developed within a highly reflective mode of social investigation which was acutely aware of the ideological power and unrealised critical potential of social inquiry.

Marxism, which was the paradigmatic critical social science in these respects, was long without peer, and settling accounts with the Marxist tradition has been important for those who believe that Marxism remains the starting-point for the development of critical theory.[6] Assessments of Marxism have noted that Marx's writings considered two axes of exclusion: the horizontal axis in which the dominant social class excludes subordinate groups from ownership of the instruments of production, and the vertical axis in which societies are closed to, or estranged from, each other. But class exclusion had pride of place in Marx's inquiry, and the transformation of the capitalist mode of production was held to be the key to eradicating intersocietal estrangement. Marx believed that the rising tide of proletarian internationalism more or less guaranteed the extension of political community beyond bounded nation-states. The analysis took too little account of national and cultural resistance to the movement beyond nation-states – and certainly insufficient account of the considerable unease or hostility which national movements have displayed towards class organisations which attached less value to cultural diversity than to emancipating exploited labour (see Linklater, 1990b, chs 2–3).

Marx's and Engels's comments on the national struggle in Europe, and Engels's observations about the role of war in history and the unprecedented destructiveness of the modern instruments of violence, began to recognise the limitations of the approach (Gallie, 1978, ch. 4). But their summaries of the central features of historical materialism invariably stressed the primacy of class conflict and the centrality of modes of production (Gallie, 1978, pp. 67–9). Later Marxist writings on nationalism underlined the tenacity of bounded political communities and sought to overcome the simplifications of class analysis. The main theories of imperialism, for example, pointed to the intensification of particularistic loyalties, and argued that predictions about the rise of cosmopolitan sentiments and the imminent widening of political community had been seriously premature. Even so, Lenin and Bukharin believed that the experience of major war would dissolve the national bonds between the members of the proletariat and the exploitative bourgeoisie. Marxism ossified around the normative vision of universal socialism, the sociology of the rise and fall of modes of production and a practice of class revolt which largely ignored the non-class-based modes of exclusion. Marxism failed as a critical theory because it believed that reconstructing property relations was tantamount to transforming political community.

Systems of exclusion which are grounded in nationalist or statist ideology, or which revolve around patterns of intersocietal estrangement, are clearly important for the critical project, and Marxism went some way towards recognising their significance. But many other forms of exclusion which are interconnected with, but hardly reducible to, class monopolies of power suffered terrible neglect. Systems of exclusion inherent in hierarchical conceptions of ethnicity, race and gender are three of the more frequently discussed examples of the larger reality of monopolisation and closure. What Marx and Marxism regarded as the central axis of exclusion was therefore just one instance of a broader phenomenon which Weber rightly called 'the closure of social relationships and the monopolization of opportunities' (Kalberg, 1994, pp. 120ff; Callinicos, 1995, pp. 110–11). Developing a more comprehensive account of the various modes of exclusion is one way of moving beyond the impasse of historical materialism.

Class analysis lacked the capacity to explain the various modes of monopolisation and exclusion which have shaped human history, and the related normative vision of universal socialism failed to offer a solution to the problems inherent in modernity. The great strength of Marxism was its concern with unlearning and dismantling class-based systems of exclusion, but it captured only one facet of modernity. Contemporary politics has witnessed sustained challenges to a greater range of modes of exclusion than ever before. The struggle against the closure of social relationships and the monopolisation of significant resources and opportunities revolves around ethnicity, race and gender as well as class. The critical theory of modern societies is now concerned with the ways in which subordinate classes, women, minority nations, migrants, gypsies, gays, lesbians and indigenous peoples are exposed to unjust forms of exclusion within their own national societies and within the larger world economic and political system. If the idea of progress has any meaning at all – and there has been no shortage of sceptics – it lies in their activity of questioning the rationale for the 'doors to otherness' which remain firmly closed (Taylor, 1985, p. 383).[7] Challenges to these modes of exclusion often stress one or more of the following themes: first, that social differences do not have the moral relevance which hegemonic groups have traditionally attached to them; second, that the public sphere fails to recognise important racial, cultural or gender differences; and third, that vulnerable groups cannot exercise their nominally equal rights without significant transfers of power and wealth from the privileged social strata.

What is striking about modernity is that the challenge to unjust exclusion is not simply confined to arrangements between members of the same society. Efforts to secure the triple transformation of political community also engage the world of international relations. The modern sovereign state may be one of the last bastions of exclusion to attract critical scrutiny (Murphy, 1988), but problematising the morality of bounded communities is one of the constitutive features of modernity. The central importance of unlearning the moral significance of political boundaries and national differences was stressed by Kant and Marx. This remains a key dimension of the unfinished project of modernity with its reflective orientation towards the modes of exclusion and the boundaries of community.

To summarise the argument thus far: all human subjects learn the specific rituals of inclusion and exclusion which enable them to function as competent members of their societies. They engage in moral discourse about the justice of these modes of exclusion, possess some understanding of the reasons for their existence and reflect on their significance for the conduct of everyday life. The purpose of social inquiry is to improve upon these commonplace understandings and everyday explanations while reflecting on the complex relations between knowledge and social practice. Normative, sociological and praxeological questions arise then for the analysts of systems of exclusion, as for social actors in general. Marxism was the most comprehensive account of the systems of exclusion to grapple with these questions but it failed as a critical theory of modernity. It imputed primacy to developments within the modes of production on the grounds that class-based exclusion was more fundamental than the other systems of exclusion which make up social life. The challenge facing post-Marxist critical theory has been to develop a deeper understanding of the diverse patterns of closure which run through social and political life. A parallel concern has been to identify the many determinants of social structure and historical change which cannot simply be reduced to logics of production.

In sociology, the efforts to transcend Marxism have identified several logics which interact to shape social and political structures and influence social change. State-building and war, culture, ideology and identity-formation have been added to the classical Marxist emphasis on production and exchange to create more complex accounts of the nature of social systems. Many of these developments in sociology have aimed to produce more satisfactory explanations of the modern state (Giddens, 1985) and the forms of social power (Mann, 1986). Studies of the origins, development and transformation of bounded communities remain in their infancy by comparison with sociologies of the state; however, it seems safe to argue that the various logics mentioned above shape the extent of their willingness to eradicate unjust modes of exclusion and to engage the previously excluded in wider communities of discourse. The need to understand the importance of cultural factors is suggested by an earlier observation about the central role that struggles against the doors to otherness play in modern societies. The sensitivity to unjust modes of exclusion which pervades contemporary societies reveals the potency of modern ethical conceptions of the freedom and equality of all individuals. It is impossible to understand the reasons for the development of these ethical themes without analysing the part that state-building, war and production played in their creation (see below, chapter 5). That said, the central point for present purposes is that just as human subjects can learn the rituals of exclusion which are based on hierarchical conceptions of class, ethnicity, gender or race, so can they unlearn them. These have been crucial themes in Habermas's project of reconstructing historical materialism, which focuses on how human subjects learn more complex means of assessing the legitimacy of their political arrangements. Habermas's account of social learning is an important starting-point for any analysis of the relations between societies which attempts to understand their capacity to associate with outsiders in wider communities of discourse. It is also important for the task of understanding just how far the promise of new forms of political community is already contained within the moral and cultural resources of modernity.

Social Learning and International Relations

The idea of social learning, which is an important theme in Habermas's thought, is not without its advocates within the study of International Relations. Karl Deutsch's work is especially important in this regard. In his analysis of the emergence of security communities, Deutsch (1970) referred to the learning processes in which the members of different societies develop a sense of 'we feeling' while their governments become committed to the peaceful resolution of international disputes. Embedded within this formulation is the notion that human subjects can unlearn the moral relevance of political boundaries and national differences, and learn to cooperate with outsiders in creating new communities of discourse which are authorised to resolve disputes peacefully.[8] Deutsch's emphasis on 'we feeling' indicated that human beings can unlearn systems of national exclusion as associates within wider international security communities.[9] Due importance was attached in this account to social and psychological factors involving the construction of national identity, the different levels of inter-cultural understanding and varying potentials for assuming novel international responsibilities and obligations. However, the study of international relations has failed to develop the core themes in Deutsch's analysis although, as noted, references to social learning have been important in the subsequent theories of international organisation and cooperation.[10] An analysis of social learning which offers one way of building on these approaches to international relations can be found in Habermas's project of reconstructing historical materialism.

The notion of 'communicative action' lies at the heart of Habermas's analysis of social learning. His pivotal observation is that human subjects make claims about the truth, rightfulness, sincerity and intelligibility of their views whenever they are involved in an attempt to arrive at an understanding with each other. A commitment to be guided by the unforced force of the better argument is made whenever subjects bring their respective views before the tribunal of open discussion and explore the prospects for an inter-subjective consensus. Habermas's account of the discourse theory of morality exalts features of communication which are universal in that they arise whenever human beings cooperate to reach an understanding. Their universality does not mean that all societies are equally committed to discourse as the means of establishing legitimate principles of association. Acceptance of tradition and authority restricts the opportunities for discourse in the most ostensibly democratic societies, and confines it to the margins of society in many forms of life. But the potential for enlarging the sphere of discourse so that it embraces wider realms of social and political life, including international relations, exists in all societies, albeit unequally, given their different commitments to public participation. This is why Habermas (1972, p. 314) claims that the very first speech act already anticipated the creation of a communication community which includes the whole of humankind. Moral-practical learning refers to the process of recognising the injustice of many of the social and political barriers to involvement in open dialogue, and to the practice of questioning the rituals of exclusion which prevent the features of communicative action from being more widely accepted as principles of international relations. For Habermas, all societies have these potentials but these normative commitments have only become central to social and political life following the passage to modernity.

Habermas argues that modernity reveals substantial progress not only in understanding the theoretical possibilities of discourse but also in overcoming some of the practical obstacles to its embodiment in actual political life. This controversial thesis is developed through an intricate critique of Weber's analysis of the rationalisation of modern society. Weber argued that the encroachment of increasingly rational techniques of administration upon all forms of social interaction was one of the unique features of the modern epoch. Marx had been wrong to suppose that freedom would be realised by socialising the means of production; in fact, for Weber the transformation of property relations in socialist societies would consolidate rather than disturb the deeper societal logic of rationalising the techniques of administration. The metaphor of the iron cage captured Weber's despairing belief that modernity is ultimately dedicated to intensifying social control.

Habermas accepts the Weberian claim that Marxists were naive to assume that the technological mastery of nature would prepare the way for the emancipation of the entire species.[11] Political applications of developments in the technical-instrumental sphere increased the potential for surveillance and control. Weber possessed deeper insights into the destructive capabilities of modernity. In a similar vein, Foucault provided detailed anatomies of the logics of normalisation and regulation in allegedly more free societies. That modern societies possess these logics is not in doubt; but whether they fully express the nature of modernity, and whether the Enlightenment project has to be abandoned as a result, are different questions. Habermas's answer reveals his intellectual debt to Kant and Marx. His response seeks to defend the emancipatory project from Weber's belief that modernity is reducible to advances in the technologies of administration and from the conviction, which Habermas imputes to Foucault, that developments in the normative sphere merely reconfigure the dominant forms of social and political power. Habermas emphasises the existence of a distinctive realm of moral-practical learning in his response to Weber and Foucault and in the course of reconstructing historical materialism.[12] Moral-practical learning refers to the development of more advanced tests of the legitimacy of social principles and political arrangements. The highest stages of moral-practical learning claim that rival conceptions of the nature of legitimate practices should be resolved by a post-conventional ethic which defends the prima facie moral responsibility of engaging the whole of humanity in open dialogue about matters of common interest. This is why Habermas's reconstruction of historical materialism emphasises the importance of developments in the moral-cultural sphere.

The idea of moral-practical learning resonates with a crucial theme in Weber's sociology of the major world religions, namely how far each developed an ethic of universalistic commitments (Habermas, 1984, p. 162). Weber argued that the rationalisation of the ethical code (the systematic analysis of the foundations of moral systems) was one of the distinctive features of Western civilisation, and maintained that the ethic of universal brotherhood was one of the major achievements of the modern age. The rise of Western capitalism had been profoundly shaped by the rationalisation of ethical life but, Weber argued, the very idea of the rational demonstration of ultimate ethical ends was undermined by the progress of the natural sciences. In the twentieth century, modernity was finally deprived of the ethical resources for mounting a reasoned moral challenge to the growing dominance of technical-instrumental rationality.

Contra Weber, Habermas argues that important, but flawed or incomplete, expressions of the dialogic potential which is inherent in communicative action can be glimpsed in the practices of liberal-democratic societies.[13] Logics of administration, commodification and economic competition which reveal the dominant place of power and money in modern societies restrict the opportunities for authentic discourse. But the modern West represents a major advance in the development of moral-practical rationality, and dialogic potentials are embodied in liberal-democratic institutions to an unusual extent. Despite all its ambiguities, modernity or Occidental rationality retains the potential for generating an improved social order out of itself which extends the critique of wrongful exclusion. The rule of law in bourgeois society and democratic processes institutionalise advancements in post-conventional moral reasoning. Capitalism extends intricate mechanisms of control throughout the social order, but it also disrupts fixed identities, stable roles and secure traditions and produces reflective agents who must construct the moral realm for themselves. Potentials for further moral advances cannot be closed off by capitalist rationalisation processes although social and political struggle is essential if these potentials are to be actualised. Modes of resistance that endeavour to preserve or widen dialogue in the context of intensifying systemic pressures which are increasingly global in character are evident in the politics of assorted social movements. Habermas maintains that in their efforts to halt and reverse the 'colonisation of the life world', these movements act as the custodians of a universalistic ethic and reveal the critical potential which exists in the practices of modernity.

According to Habermas, Weber explained the uniqueness of the West by stressing its initial affirmation of the ethic of brotherhood and by analysing its ensuing subjection to new technologies of social control. Habermas maintains that the uniqueness of the West is evident in its persistent ambiguities, and especially in the struggle between the logics of administration or regulation and enduring forms of resistance to totalising forces. The positive features of modernity are evident in continued sensitivity to the plight of the marginal (Habermas, 1992a, pp. 266–7) and in surviving uncertainties about the moral significance of national boundaries. Regarding the latter phenomenon, some European societies are already 'on the way to becoming post-national societies' (1992a, p. 240). Trends towards new forms of supranational organisation, increasing awareness of growing global interconnectedness and inequalities, and extended communication networks 'have heightened the world-wide *sensitivity* to violations of human rights, to exploitation, hunger, misery, and the demands of national liberation movements' (1992a, p. 240; italics in original). Modernity continues to raise the vital Kantian ethical question of how universal principles can be institutionalised in the international state of nature (1992a, p. 240). This problem is especially acute, it might be added, because elementary commitments to universality, dialogue and consent already exist in the international society of states. (See below, pp. 168–75.)

Liberal-democratic welfare states are evidence for Habermas that modernity has institutionalised some of the moral potentials which are inherent in communicative action. The capacity to develop these moral possibilities is present in all societies, but the West has embodied them in its social and political practices to an unusual degree. Habermas argues that technical-instrumental and strategic rationalisation are barriers to further moral-practical learning, and modernity remains an ambiguous phenomenon.[14] Deep logics of control prevent modern societies from realising their emancipatory potentials but the capacity to extend human sympathies and to eradicate unjust exclusion has not been extinguished. Habermas rejects Weber's image of the impending iron cage because it fails to register the significance of these cultural resources and moral potentials. The unfinished project of modernity has the task of releasing the prospects for wider communities of discourse from powerful systemic constraints.

Inclusion and Exclusion in World Civilisations

To explain the ambiguities of modernity Habermas reworks the Weberian analysis of the processes of rationalisation which are specific to the West, and develops a new account of the societal potentials which are immanent within communicative action. Various sectors of life within Western societies confront pressures to submit to the imperatives of technological-instrumental rationalisation, as Weber's metaphor of the encroaching iron cage vividly suggested, but for Habermas the achievements within the independent sphere of moral-practical learning have been neither squandered nor lost. Modernity retains its potential for critical dialogue amidst the pressures to enlarge the dominion of the logics of administration and control. Habermas's analysis of the ambiguities of modernity stresses the contribution which universalistic ethical orientations have made to the moral configuration of Western societies. Because of the influence of these ideas, modernity holds out the promise of a dialogic community which overcomes the division between citizens and aliens: the possibility of a universal communication community therefore remains part of its ambiguous legacy. The more advanced moral codes within the bounds of modernity deny that there are convincing prima facie reasons for denying any member of the human race the right to participate in dialogic arrangements which ensure that all interests and perspectives receive due consideration. By this reckoning, the nature of a just international society ought to be determined by universal dialogue which guarantees the inclusion of all marginal voices. Although the universal communication community may never be realised completely, it is an important ethical ideal which permits the critique of defective social arrangements and offers direction to the future course of events.

Benjamin Nelson's framework for the comparative analysis of the major civilisations and their external relations used Weberian themes for similar ends (Nelson, 1973). Rather like Habermas, Nelson assumed that potentials for following this path have existed in all societies, although modernity contains advances which are rarely encountered in non-Western civilisations (see below, p. 130). Nelson's framework is indebted to Weber's observation that the peculiar identity of each civilisation is revealed by the dominant patterns of rationalisation (Weber, 1930, pp. 26ff). Weber argued that rationalisation involves the application of reflective and systematic thought to the various modes of human experience (Gerth and Mills, 1948, p. 293; Kalberg, 1980). According to this definition, every realm of human activity including the mystical or religious, the artistic and the erotic can be subjected to the process of rationalisation (Habermas, 1994, pp. 168–9). Weber argued that the development of systematic, reflective knowledge in the spheres of science, technology and economic action, and similar patterns of rationalisation in the domains of morality, law and politics, gave Western civilisation its unique identity. Nelson (1949, p. vii) cites Weber's emphasis on the rationalisation of the legal and moral domain as evidence that he did not explain the differences between civilisations simply in terms of their unequal commitments to the technical-instrumental rationalisation of the forces of production. Weber's exploration of the West's unique path of capitalist development and the supremacy of technical-instrumental rationalisation belonged to a larger comparative analysis of the economic ethics of the major world religions and their degree of tolerance for universalistic orientations to moral behaviour.

Conventional interpretations of Weber's explanation of the West's path to capitalist development stress the role which the Calvinist ethic played in fostering a methodical way of life. Weber believed that there were important affinities between the religious rationalisation of everyday conduct and the formation of capitalist subjects who sought prosperity by refining the techniques of rational economic action. However, there is an additional dimension to Weber's account of modern capitalism which Nelson was especially keen to explore. Weber suggested that there were links between the Christian ethic of universal brotherhood and the rise of industrial capitalism. Habermas emphasises this dimension of Weber's work to analyse the ambiguities of modernity and to show how stronger attachments to dialogue can emerge within post-nationalist societies. Nelson stressed this theme to show how Weber began to concentrate towards the end of his life on a comparative analysis of the world religions and civilisations which focused upon their unequal commitments to universalistic and dialogic orientations. Weber was inclined to treat civilisations as if they were discrete entities, whereas Nelson argued for a new framework of analysis which revealed how civilisational structures were shaped by the nature of their inter-civilisational relations. Nelson was specifically concerned with showing that a more sophisticated account of the rise of the West could be developed in this way. But by extending the Weberian framework to embrace inter-civilisational contacts he also raised important themes for a broader sociology of systems of inclusion and exclusion in international relations. Nelson's focus on the extent to which different civilisations have been prepared to participate in wider communities of discourse is instructive for any attempt to apply Habermasian notions of social learning to the sociology of international relations.

Weber's observation that unusually high levels of fraternisation developed in the Occidental city was central to Nelson's approach. Weber believed that the transcendence of 'restrictive particularisms' between the members of Christian groups, the eradication of barriers to 'wider *commercium*, *connubium* and *commensalism*', and the rise of 'wider universalities, new communities, new communications, new communions' were the hallmarks of the medieval Occidental city (Nelson, 1976, p. 120). Overcoming 'invidious dualisms' between insiders and alien outsiders was a central factor in the emergence of a distinctively Western form of civilisation (1976, pp. 116–17).[15] Such patterns of social change did not occur at all, or did not develop as far, in many other civilisations. Confucian principles which stressed the centrality of five particularistic social relations obstructed the rise of ethical universality in China (1976, p. 122). The caste-system ruled out high levels of fraternisation across the social divisions in India (1976, p. 125). In China and India, the dominant conceptions of authority and tradition prevented the development of wider networks of social cooperation and more inclusive solidarities.[16] The crucial social bonds were deeply exclusionary.

Weber believed that the distinctive nature of Occidental rationality was influenced by developments in the religious-ethical sphere which encouraged the widening of the boundaries of moral communities. The exercise of trying to understand the unique qualities of Western modernity involved Weber in analysing the impact of the economic ethics of different world religions on the development of non-Western civilisations. Nelson argued that Weber's account of the cultural logics which swept across traditional social boundaries marked the emergence of a new stage in sociological thought in which the largest human collectivities – civilisations – began to replace national societies as the principal object of analysis. He also maintained that the later writings of Durkheim inclined in a similar direction (Nelson, 1971). Enlarging this focus to include the neglected dimension of inter-civilisational relations was

Nelson's way of building on the convergence on civilisational analysis which occurs in Weber and Durkheim's last writings.

Nelson regarded one theme in an essay by Durkheim and Mauss as central to the enterprise of creating new understandings of the relationship between civilisational identities and inter-civilisational contacts. In their short commentary on the value of civilisational analysis, Durkheim and Mauss referred to the importance of understanding the 'unequal coefficient of expansion and internationalisation' (Nelson, 1971, p. 812). They observed that certain social and political phenomena display a remarkable tendency to spread rapidly and extensively across societal boundaries, while others remain stubbornly tied to their place of origin. Some phenomena are more likely to be internationalised, some forces are more inclined to be universalised, than others. By way of illustration, Durkheim and Mauss maintained that political institutions have been less prone to internationalisation than religion, myth, technology and commerce.

To put this another way, some phenomena cross societal frontiers with relative ease because they do not threaten important values or because they facilitate existing projects; others make the passage with great difficulty, or fail to penetrate borders at all, because they threaten core concerns or because they are unintelligible or alien. In any event, entirely self-contained cultures have been extremely rare. Most cultures have borrowed from their neighbours, and most societal boundaries have been sufficiently porous that their character cannot be understood in isolation from their inter-societal relations. Durkheim and Mauss coined the phrase 'the unequal coefficient of expansion and internationalisation' to refer to varying levels of societal receptiveness or resistance to external phenomena. To relate this theme to other concerns: some societies have been more prepared than others to problematise the moral relevance of social differences and to enter into wider communities of discourse. Nelson developed this point by arguing that the different levels of tolerance which medieval Europe and the Islamic world displayed towards extra-societal influences was an important reason for their subsequent fate, and especially for the rise of a hegemonic Western civilisation.

The crux of Nelson's argument was that the development of rational theology in the Islamic world provided the impetus for the intellectual revolution in twelfth-century Europe. Several accounts of this period of Islamic history have maintained that the jurists promoted the rationalisation of the different religious traditions or *hadiths* which flourished after Mohammed's death. The exercise of independent judgement, or *ijtihad*, was encouraged in the expectation that a more coherent and systematic interpretation of the prophet's teachings and their subsequent explications would evolve. The philosophical claim that the Koran was a metaphor for the moral truths which could be grasped by unaided human reason was a startling development within Islamic theology but, in the fourteenth century, the gate to *ijtihad* was closed because of a fear of the social consequences of allowing greater freedom to the philosophical imagination.[17] But profound intellectual changes were set in motion in the West as a result of its encounter with the rationalisation of Islamic theology.

Western intellectual elites were very receptive to these developments in Islamic thought, and they were powerfully inclined to import the scientific and technical achievements of Chinese civilisation. Nelson's conclusion was that the rise of the Western natural sciences has to be understood against the background of an extraordinary movement of religious ideas and scientific inventions across the boundaries between the major world civilisations. Western civilisation outpaced other civilisations in the spheres of technological innovation and economic growth because of an eagerness to borrow ruthlessly from Islam and China. These non-Western civilisations were overtaken by the West in these domains because they were less disposed to look beyond the civilisational boundary for scientific and technological developments which were worthy of imitation or which could be imported to their material advantage.[18] Thus did the unequal coefficient of expansion and internationalisation vary between the major civilisations.

Nelson's observations about the Western encounter with Islam in the twelfth and thirteenth centuries maintained that there was a small step from the development of rational theology to the emergence of the Western natural sciences (Nelson, 1973, p. 97). Building on this encounter, various groups challenged all suppositions that truths about social organisation or the physical world could be grounded in unreflective appeals to higher authority or received tradition; they argued that all claims to truth, virtue and legality should be made answerable to new philosophical 'rationales' which were distrustful of authority and convention. These societal pressures to expand the domain of these new rationales across all of the domains of human experience were decisive elements in the Western path to modernity, as Weber had argued in his account of the unique patterns of Western rationalisation. Nelson argued that Weber's account of the development of Western modernity was deeply flawed but suggestive of new lines of sociological analysis. His emphasis on developments in the realms of science, technology and economics recognised that these were anchored in larger processes of cultural transformation. Weber emphasised that the diverse levels of fraternisation which the main world religions had encouraged had been a powerful factor in the subsequent development of very different civilisations (see Gerth and Mills, 1948, pp. 329–30). Yet Weber wrote as if these diverse cultural variations and potentialities unfolded separately within civilisations which had very little contact with one another. Nelson sought to build on Weber's analysis by showing that their different historical trajectories (including variations in their willingness to fraternise with outsiders and to import significant achievements) had been moulded by their inter-civilisational encounters. No account of different civilisational structures and their constitutive rationalisation processes would be complete without analysing the impact of inter-civilisational relations upon their separate paths of development (Nelson, 1973, p. 85). No account would suffice without due regard for Durkheim and Mauss's concern with the unequal coefficients of expansion and internationalisation. No account would succeed without analysing different inclinations to reflect on the moral relevance of differences from outsiders and to contemplate associating with others in wider communities of discourse.

Nelson attempted to broaden Weber's analysis of the rationalisation of different ways of life; he envisaged a sociology of civilisations which explored different levels of resistance and receptiveness to external influences including religious ideas, scientific perspectives and developments in technology. But he was not only interested in civilisations as modes of inclusion and exclusion which differed in their enthusiasm for appropriating modes of understanding which might contribute to their economic and technological success. Nelson was also interested in how the unequal coefficients, to which Durkheim and Mauss had referred, were evident in different civilisational propensities for developing what Weber called fraternisation, or what Sir Henry Maine called the 'extensions of the boundaries of the moral and political communities' in human history (Nelson, 1973, p. 87). Different civilisations possessed contrasting accounts of the moral and political relevance of their 'symbolic frontiers' and cultural differences from others. They varied in their willingness to break down invidious dualisms between insiders and outsiders, and in the extent of their commitments to be bound by a universalistic ethic when dealing with other societies. Nelson envisaged an inquiry into the moral grammar of different civilisations which would analyse the extent to which universals of language, logic and consciousness developed in different civilisations and shaped their decisions about the possibility or impossibility of widening the realm of interaction governed less by power and force than by dialogue and consent.

Durkheim and Mauss's passing comment on the law of nations helps to relate Nelson's themes directly to mainstream concerns in the study of international relations. In their essay on civilisations, Durkheim and Mauss cited the law of nations as evidence of the extension of the moral boundaries of political community. One of the main principles underlying the modern law of nations, namely the idea of the equality of states, was alien to most non-Western civilisations until recent times, as the contributors to Bull and Watson (1984) reveal in great detail. The passage of this principle across the frontiers of different civilisations, and its current acceptance in virtually all parts of the world, is a striking illustration of the impact of Western ideas on Chinese, Japanese, Hindu and Islamic civilisations which once subscribed to hegemonial conceptions of international relations. The advent of a diplomatic dialogue between independent political systems in the modern world, and in previous societies of states, is evidence of what Nelson described as the widening of the 'community of discourse'.[19] One of the central aims of Nelson's proposed sociology of civilisations was to understand the extent to which different civilisations possessed the moral and cultural resources for participating in wider universalities of discourse such as the diplomatic dialogue between equals which exists, however qualified, in societies of states (see Wight, 1977, ch. 1). A related aim was to defend universal discourse as a normative ideal.

Whereas the first of these purposes invites comparison with the Grotian project of accounting for the expansion of international society, the second involves certain parallels with Habermas's discourse theory of morality. Post-conventionalist themes are evident in Nelson's remarks about breakthroughs 'in the moralities of thought and in the logics of decision' which made progress towards 'wider universalities of discourse, and participation in the confirmation of improved *rationales*' possible (Nelson, 1973, p. 96). In a formulation which echoes themes which were considered in earlier chapters, Nelson supported efforts to build upon past experiments in fraternisation by granting 'rights of dialogue and citizenship' to the 'hitherto excluded'.[20] Ideally, increases in 'the range of permissible expressions and disagreements' would result from the widening of the boundaries of community (1973, p. 96). Wider communities of discourse would encourage a more 'open future' in which diversity could flourish along with measures to undo the 'undesirable privileges and prerogatives of the past' (1973, p. 102). The normative defence of dialogue which is evident in Nelson's writings shares the commitment to the triple transformation of political community required by the discourse theory of morality.

In a response to Habermas's interpretation of his work, Nelson (in Huff, 1981, p. 11) denied that the historical analysis of societal potentials for universality required either 'transcendental' or 'evolutionary' foundations of the kind which underpin the Habermasian notion of unconstrained communication. Nelson was keen to stress that this 'universalistic potential' is not peculiar to the West but is embedded in the world images which emerged in China, India, Greece and Israel in the period between 800 BC and 300 BC (Huff, 1981, p. 11).[21] In a more transcendental moment, he added that all peoples may have the potential for universalising commitments to dialogue but, thus far, few societies have gone far 'in articulating and institutionalizing universalities in the spheres of social relations and cultural designs' (1981, p. 11). Nelson was less concerned than Habermas with anchoring the normative defence of universal discourse in transcendental foundations than with observing that, while all of the major civilisations had the potential to strike out in this direction, none had granted the ideal of a universal communication community vigorous institutional support. But Habermas and Nelson appear to be agreed that anxieties about failures to realise this ideal are constitutive features of modernity.

The ambiguities of modernity figure prominently in the writings of Weber and Habermas, and they reappear in Nelson's writings which comment briefly upon their increasingly global effects. Modernity, for Nelson, includes the demise of pre-scientific epistemologies, the globalisation of logics of administration and control and various political struggles to promote social justice and equal participation. Modernity also involves growing reflectiveness as the members of different societies reconsider their identities in the light of intrusive global forces (Nelson, 1973, p. 80). The decision to place key elements of Western rationality on trial in many parts of the world was one of the paradoxical consequences of the triumph of modernity. European Fascism was the first major reversal faced by the modes of political consciousness which were enthusiastic about realising the normative ideal of universal communication. The growing strength of collectivist and exclusionary ideologies in the non-European world in more recent times led Nelson to the conclusion that the new rationales had reached their zenith in the period between 1890 and 1920 (1973, p. 101). Nelson believed it was highly unlikely that further progress in widening the communities of discourse would occur in the immediate future (1973, p. 102).[22]

Nelson's fears about the prospects for greater universalities of discourse inevitably raise the question of whether he regarded the cultural revolt against the West as incompatible with the cosmopolitan principles of the Enlightenment and with the normative foundations of the international society which first emerged in Europe and now embraces the entire world.[23] His enthusiasm for universalities of discourse which would widen the range of admissible expressions and disagreements reveals tolerance for the concerns of the radically different. But the belief that the West is the leading, and increasingly threatened, custodian of allegiances to universal dialogue is pronounced in his writings, notwithstanding his conviction that most peoples have a similar potentiality for taking part in wider communities of discourse. The whole question of otherness was less important in the period in which Nelson was writing than it is now. But more recent discussions of the rights of the culturally different invite the judgement that there may have been a tension in Nelson's thought between his celebration of Western modernity and his enthusiasm for extending the range of permissible expressions and disagreements. Be that as it may, an ethical defence of open communities of discourse necessarily requires the tolerance of points of view which may lack much support in the West. Not least, it requires efforts to understand why there cannot be a modern Requirement (see above, p. 65).

Habermas's defence of an ethical universalism which affirms the value of multiculturalism clarifies the nature of the moral issue which is at stake in this discussion, and suggests future directions for a sociology of civilisational complexes and inter-civilisational relations which overcomes this possible tension in Nelson's writings. Nelson posed the important question of how far different civilisations had developed the potential for including alien outsiders in wider communities of discourse. The question of whether these civilisations were prepared to dismantle the modes of exclusion encountered by groups within their midst, and willing to engage internal subaltern groups in open dialogue, was less important in his work. Herein lies one key to developing a post-Marxist sociology of the modes of inclusion and exclusion in international relations. It was noted earlier that Marx considered two axes of social and political exclusion: the primary horizontal axis, which was narrowly conceived as involving relations between social classes, and the vertical axis comprising bounded communities which received rather less attention from those working within the Marxist tradition. An appraisal of Nelson's innovative analysis of civilisational logics reveals that a post-Marxist sociology can overcome these weaknesses by focusing on the larger realm of systems of inclusion and exclusion and the forms of social learning which lead to their contestation. Analysing different societal potentials for enlarging the boundaries of moral and political community so that subaltern groups and aliens can engage in open dialogue is, then, one of the central purposes of a post-Marxist sociology of systems of inclusion and exclusion. This involves precisely that analysis of cultural frameworks and their potentials which Marxism with its stress on the primacy of production was unable to carry out.

Towards a Sociology of Bounded Communities

The questions which are posed by Nelson's work on civilisations and their symbolic frontiers are relevant to other forms of international relations. The extent to which interaction between egocentric civilisations such as the West, China and Islam has been shaped by conceptions of human equality and reciprocity is one of three possible areas of sociological inquiry. A second concerns the ways in which the ruling strata of states, empires and civilisations assimilated or segregated the different cultures which they incorporated within their respective jurisdictions. A third area of investigation concerns the patterns of inclusion and exclusion which the members of international states-systems have practised in their dealings with one another.[24] One central question in this discussion is whether different forms of world political organisation such as empires and states-systems exhibit marked variations in their capacity for widening the boundaries of association and for creating communities of discourse which respect the differences of others. Such questions are suggested by the stress on the dialogic potentials of modernity which is evident in the writings of Nelson and Habermas. The dominant form of world political organisation in the modern world is the international states-system in which there is an important commitment to dialogue between the constituent parts. Whether the potential for enlarging the realm of social interaction which is governed by dialogue rather than by force is greater in states-systems than in empires is an important question. No less important is the issue of whether societies of states differ from one another in this respect. This section offers tentative conclusions to these questions. Above all else, it seeks to establish the need for further research in these areas.

Nelson's civilisational perspective observed how developments in the ideational realm of language, culture and consciousness made extensions of community possible, but it also recognised that economic and political factors are powerful determinants of cultural change in their own right. Developments in historical sociology during the past decade have been especially concerned with refining these themes, invariably as part of the critique of historical materialism. Designing systems of explanation which move beyond single-logic accounts of social structure and historical change, as in the case of classical Marxist analyses of the centrality of production and realist forms of geopolitical determinism, has been a primary objective (Giddens, 1985; Mann, 1986, 1994; Tilly, 1992a). Mann's account of the sources of social power is the most insightful example as far as the sociology of bounded communities is concerned.[25]

His analysis of the rise of the first empires and societies of states explains how multiple forces shape the moral and political boundaries of communities, and the pattern of social and political development more generally.

Explaining the development of the human capacity to organise and control peoples, materials and territories across history is Mann's principal objective (Mann, 1986, pp. 2–3). Important distinctions between different forms of social power (extensive, intensive, authoritative and diffuse) are employed to this end.[26] The conceptual framework which Mann brings to the analysis of social power is an important means of developing various sociological themes explored in the writings of Habermas and Nelson.[27] The differing potentials for tightening the social bond within bounded communities and for exercising control over more extensive forms of political organisation are key elements of Mann's inquiry into the development of social power over the past five millennia.[28] His analysis of the complex relationships between territorial concentrations of power and the spread of universalistic ideas in states, empires and civilisations in the three millennia between the rise of Mesopotamian civilisation and the ascent of Rome extends several themes which exist in Nelson's writings. More specifically, Mann's account of the origins of bounded societies and the evolution of the first empires reveals that the governing classes invariably lacked the capacity to promote the totalising project. The earliest imperial elites governed through intermediaries and presided over social systems which were locked into wider economic, political and cultural spheres of interaction which elites were unable to control. They were incapable of securing the closure of tightly-bound communities and they relied on universalistic ideologies in their efforts to extend their power over social relations. Universalistic ideologies were promoted by the governing classes in the first empires. The fate of these world-views as ruling elites increased their power over society and acquired the means to initiate totalising projects is an important feature of Mann's inquiry. In Rome, especially, counter-hegemonic groups converted universalistic ideologies of administration into egalitarian visions of a Christian community. But they were forced into a series of accommodations with Roman imperial power (see Mann, 1986, pp. 326ff).

Mann develops these points within a conceptual framework which takes issue with the foundational concept in sociology, namely the idea of society which implies the existence of intimate ties between the members of a bounded community and which assumes that most interaction occurs within the clearly defined boundaries of autonomous forms of life. The earliest forms of social organisation lacked these characteristics (Mann, 1986, p. 39). The 'looseness' of the social bond, the greater permeability of boundaries and the continuing possibility of 'escape from the social cage' are three factors which distinguished the 'pre-civilised' from more 'civilised' social systems. The capacity to trap human beings in bounded societies emerged with the formation of small city-states in Mesopotamia, following the introduction of alluvial agriculture in the third millennium BC. At first, states could wield authoritative power within a few square kilometres. Poor communications and low levels of literacy meant that there were few opportunities for the emergence of diffuse forms of power of the kind which operate through international trading networks and the spread of religious ideas. Not that the first city-states were totally closed off from one another. City-states were loosely integrated within a larger civilisation in which a common stock of religious beliefs served as the main factor of cohesion (1986, pp. 89–90). But none of the city-states had sufficient intensive and extensive power to be able to absorb this larger social space within its exclusive territorial jurisdiction. In the third millennium BC Mesopotamia was a 'multi-actor federal civilisation' – an international society of states.

Endemic geopolitical struggle produced greater concentrations of military power which culminated in the first major empire of Sargon of Akkad in 2300 BC. Increases in authoritative and extensive power occurred in the subsequent Assyrian and Persian empires. The governing elites in these empires were capable of retaining control over the peoples and territories which they had united by force, but intensive power remained limited, and elites lacked the capacity to regulate daily life. Ruling strata secured their power by coopting subjugated elites and by promoting their allegiance to a common ideology. The Akkadian conquerors encouraged loyalty by granting the local deities of subjugated groups a place in the religious pantheon (1986, p. 91). The Assyrian empire from 1200 BC disseminated an elite nationalism throughout the core but lacked the power to create a national culture or to instil mass loyalty (1986, p. 231). Growing fraternisation and cosmopolitanism in the Middle East from the start of the sixth century BC permitted the further development of extensive power within the Persian empire. The linguistic unification of the empire, intermarriage amongst members of the ruling elite and a common education for the children of dominant and conquered groups facilitated the dissemination of a more universalistic ruling class ideology which held 'local particularism' in check (1986, pp. 239–41). The limited power resources of the dominant groups did not permit centralised control of a homogeneous people within clearly defined and monitored national boundaries. Governing elites were not in a position to create nation-states, and the capacity to initiate totalising projects remained well beyond their reach, but they were capable of drawing larger numbers of human beings into the widening sphere of social and economic interaction.

Mann (1986, p. 170) cites Weber's observation that the dominant elites in the first empires began to realise that particularistic, aristocratic rule could not be legitimised. Imperial elites therefore 'rationalised the symbolic sphere' to ensure that subjugated groups freely identified with a more universalistic ethos. The cultural symbols which were most frequently employed for this purpose invited those groups to subordinate their religious particularism to universal structures which were in harmony with the cosmic order. Despite such advances in organisational power, early empires remained incapable of tightening the social bonds and the capacity to enclose their subjects within sealed boundaries continued to elude them. Increasing cosmopolitanism in the Middle East facilitated the spread of the dominant imperial ideology but it also meant that emergent salvation religions were free to circulate in the 'interstices' of the wider networks of social and economic interaction which evolved in this period.[29] Salvation religions expressed a new moral vision of how human beings could be organised. They challenged imperial class divisions with a new egalitarian image of how all humanity could be united by allegiance to one God (1986, p. 241). By virtue of rationalising the symbolic sphere, the first empires generated a basic contradiction between immanent ideologies, which were designed to hold the ruling strata together, and transcendent ideologies, which set visions of a universal and egalitarian social order against the dominant asymmetries of power.[30] The possibility of resisting increases in state power was created by the very symbolic tools which the governing elites used to consolidate their rule.

The contradiction between immanent and transcendent ideologies became most acute in the Roman empire. The empire represented a dramatic increase in the level of intensive and extensive power (1986, p. 260). Of all the societies in the ancient world, Rome came closest to being a unitary, closed society. Deep class inequalities developed in tandem with the Romanisation of elites and the gradual extension of citizenship rights to the members of conquered groups (1986, p. 262). The Roman empire possessed higher levels of ideological, economic, political and military power than any other form of social and political organisation yet encountered (with the possible exception of Han China) but failed to engender the popular loyalties and attachments which the long-term reproduction of the social order required (1986, p. 293). Rival and more cosmopolitan normative commitments developed (1986, p. 307) because Roman institutions lacked mass support.[31] Discontent with systematic exclusion from economic success, coupled with the absence of meaningful involvement in shared institutions, bred widespread demands for new forms of solidarity and community (1986, pp. 323–4). The Christian world-view emerged as a principal determinant of social change in the context of increasing alienation. To the members of the excluded groups, Christianity promised a human society which was free from class and ethnic divisions, and united by profound attachments to a universal ethic rather than by the threat of force (1986, p. 326).

Mann's analysis of early empires intersects with Nelson's discussion of the process of fraternisation in which divisions between insiders and outsiders are overcome, and with Habermas's notion of moral-practical learning which includes the evolution of post-conventional moral codes. Weber's observations about the rationalisation of the symbolic sphere is an important link between these approaches. Establishing more universalistic symbolic systems in the first empires was meant to solve the legitimation problem which occurred as particularistic and aristocratic conceptions of government clashed with the exigencies of administering diverse, multi-ethnic orders. These symbolic structures removed or moderated some of the dualisms between insiders and outsiders, especially at the elite level, in order to legitimate the extension of rule over new peoples and territories. But imperial governing classes lacked the intensive power to monitor daily life in the more remote outposts of the empires, and high levels of tolerance for radically different groups (such as the Jews in the Persian empire) existed alongside the elementary forms of fraternisation.[32] Universalising ideologies were immanent ideologies which were designed to cement imperial rule in circumstances where ruling groups lacked the capacity to unleash totalising projects on their populations. The growth of intensive power generated forms of resistance powered by subaltern groups which were committed to transcendent ideologies within the 'interstices' of empires. In Rome, which was the first empire to display many of the features of a bounded, homogeneous society, a powerful religious longing for membership of a universal community emerged in opposition to an immanent ideology of imperial rule which underpinned increased social exclusion.

Mann's approach is an important reminder that universal moralities can only emerge under particular material conditions although they can become powerful determinants of social change in their own right. Normative images of a universal community in the ancient world would have been impossible but for the prior development of various universalising processes involving the expansion of trade, the revolution in transport and communications and the diffusion of literacy (1986, pp. 363–4). Transcendent world-views could not have emerged unless imperial structures had already created unprecedented forms of economic, political, ideological and military integration. Counter-hegemonic groups embodying visions of alternative conceptions of community formed in response to the powerful state structures which had created the larger social world in which their organisation became possible. States in the ancient world, as in later epochs, feared these movements which cut across 'official channels and boundaries' and eluded the official mechanisms of control (1986, p. 522). They were suspicious of the salvation religions which supported the establishment of new forms of solidarity across all social boundaries and which came into conflict with imperial authorities as a result. In Rome and China, central authorities blocked all efforts to rally support for images of human community which challenged the state-building project. These empires or world civilisations simultaneously encouraged the formation of universalistic structures of consciousness and frustrated the realisation of the egalitarian visions of community which were made possible by the prior development of these cultural universals (1986, p. 367).[33]

Rival visions of ultimate obligations and responsibilities first appeared in the early empires. They have also been a recurrent feature of societies of states and a powerful brake upon totalising projects. Separate states resemble empires in their efforts to create immanent ruling ideologies and to ensure that universalistic ethical commitments do not clash with societal objectives, as they conceive them. All past states-systems ended in empire but, while they survived, their constituent parts had to respond to moral claims made on behalf of two wider communities – the international society of states and the imagined community of humankind which no one state could control. The existence of these wider conceptions of community frustrated national efforts to tighten the social bond and close off the moral community. As already noted, the visions of human solidarity which appeared in the first empires were defeated by the holders of state power. But this is impossible in societies of states where no single power has dominance and where appeals beyond the state to the principles of international society or some universalistic ethic cannot be eradicated (see Mann, 1986, pp. 223–7). Whereas empires can capture or contain universalistic ideals, the members of a multi-state system confront 'transnational' ethical belief-systems which none of them can expect to control. Separate states may compete with one another in struggles over the nature of the true universalism (as the superpowers often did during the Cold War). An intriguing question is whether societies of states in which there is some commitment to a diplomatic dialogue between the constituent parts provide an environment in which notions of a universal communication community can more easily develop. The evidence suggests that a commitment to a dialogue between equal states did not appear until late in the history of the Hellenic states-system, and that visions of a universal communication community which included each individual member of humankind clashed with the dominant beliefs about the superiority of Hellenic culture. Contrasts with modern international society will be considered in the next chapter.

Wight (1977, ch. 1) explained the existence of rival accounts of community in states-systems by arguing that the three recorded examples (the Chinese, the Graeco-Roman and the modern European) appeared within a region which had already been united by a common culture or civilisation. The constituent parts established their shared identity through a series of sharp contrasts with allegedly inferior peoples in the world beyond the society of states, but answerability to the other members of that society checked tendencies to promote the closure of the moral community.[34] Conceptions of a universal community of humankind acted as a similar counterweight to such predispositions, and questioned the exclusionary nature of international society itself.[35] Geopolitical rivalry and war ensured that separate political associations were not dissolved in either of these wider conceptions of the human community. Competition between these different images of moral and political community has been common to all states-systems as a result.[36]

The city-state system which developed in ancient Greece provides ample evidence of these tensions between different conceptions of community and obligation. Mann (1986) and Wight (1977, ch. 2) both emphasise the tensions between three conceptions of society anchored respectively in the polis; in Hellas, which was united by a common religion, ethnicity and language, and by a profound sense of cultural difference from non-Hellenic peoples; and in 'a partial and hesitant conception of humanity as whole' (Mann, 1986, p. 190). Much of the dynamism of ancient Greece resulted from the tensions and contradictions between these rival images of society whose boundaries did not coincide (1986, pp. 211 and 227). Conceptions of Hellas and human reason ensured that fraternisation extended beyond the boundaries of particularistic city-states, but the depth of loyalties to the polis obstructed wider solidarities anchored in the identification with Hellas or in the cosmopolitan commitment involving what Nelson called greater answerability to universal rationales.

Conceptions of Hellas nevertheless ensured that the social bonds between citizens and the symbolic frontiers of the polis were less exclusionary than would otherwise have been the case. The rudimentary society of states which existed in the Greek world owed much of its coherence to perceptions of the cultural distance between Hellas and the rest of the human race.[37] The exclusion of the supposedly barbaric peoples from the religious institutions and festivals of Olympia and Delphi gave expression to Hellenic ideals. Hellenic perceptions of superiority to the Carthaginians, whom Erastothenes deemed inferior because they denied assistance to the shipwrecked, were further means by which the Greeks established their symbolic frontiers (Wight, 1977, p. 103).

Persia posed the deepest challenge to Greek modes of thought. Before the Persian Wars, *barbaros* did not connote racial inferiority but simply described the non-Greek-speaking peoples. No sharp boundary ever came between the worlds of Greece and Persia notwithstanding the increased use of the term *barbaros* during the Persian Wars to character-ise the Persians as an uncivilised people. The practice of medising (going over to, or fighting for, Persia) subverted efforts to seal the boundaries of the Hellenic society of states (Wight, 1977, p. 80). The King's Peace of 387–386 BC, in which Persia agreed not to intervene in mainland Greece as long as none of the Greek city-states sought hegemony in the Aegean, revealed that Greece and Persia were being drawn into a wider international society (Ryder, 1965, p. 29). Wight (1977, p. 87) inter-preted Alexander's observation that 'among Greeks there are many worthless characters, and many highly civilised are to be found amongst the barbarians' as evidence that the Greek city-state system had been dissolved, albeit temporarily, in a wider international society.

Unprecedented developments in promoting the rationalisation of the moral code occurred in ancient Greece.[38] Ethical rationalisation involved the systematic investigation of the structure of moral language and the elaboration of more sophisticated tests of the legitimacy of beliefs and practices. Questioning the moral relevance of the differences between Hellenes and non-Hellenes was a central theme in various philosophical efforts to rationalise Greek modes of consciousness and to create more reflective forms of life. Unease about the grounds for refusing equal moral status to the members of different cultures created the environ-ment in which universalistic ideas could flourish. Sophists such as Antiphon, a contemporary of Socrates, prescribed *homonoia* (harmony) between all peoples, and his follower Hippias of Elis advocated 'the universality of human sympathy' (Wagar, 1971, p. 95). Critical analysis of the rationale for the exclusion of aliens and slaves from the world of rational human beings emerged as an independent force in the Greek city-state system, and came to exert significant influence on the pattern of social and political change (Mann, 1986, pp. 211–16). Greater reflectiveness about the ways in which Greeks conceptualised their relations with the non-Greek world was testimony to the importance of the rationalisation of the moral code. Abundant illustrations of fraterni-sation not only in the relations between Greeks but in their relations with Persia exist, but there is no evidence of any strong commitment to modern notions of a universal communication community.

It is important to ask why the extension of 'the rights of dialogue and citizenship' to the members of previously excluded groups rarely occurred in ancient Greece despite the role that fraternisation played in widening the boundaries of the moral community.[39] There appear to be three main answers to this question. First, citizenship rights were restricted to adult males in the most participatory city-states. Women, slaves, resident aliens and foreigners were denied political rights because of their assumed inferiority (Manville, 1990). Second, the idea of citizenship was intimately linked with communitarian sentiments which held that active membership of the separate polis was the supreme political good. The majority of Greeks would have been bewildered by the argument that citizenship could be separated from the polis and attached to membership of some wider dialogic community.[40] The sense of the unity of Hellenic culture was simply too weak to encourage experiments in enlarging the boundaries of political community. Third, there was no strong commitment to the principle of human equality in ancient Greece which could be used to break down social divisions within the polis and to support visions of a wider political community which might embrace all Greeks and even, at some time in the future, the whole human race. The absence of any counterpart to modern notions of world public opinion indicates the weakness of 'answerability to universal rationales', to use Nelson's phrase (Wight, 1977, pp. 67–72). Not only was there no Grotius or Vitoria to define the principles of an international society of states in the ancient world (Wight, 1977, p. 52); there was no Kant to defend a vision of political community in which the citizens of different states might come together as members of a universal kingdom of ends.

The Greek ideal of active citizenship was incompatible therefore with any project of creating wider communities of discourse which would confer rights of participation on the members of previously excluded groups. The historical evidence suggests that the most enthusiastic exponents of democratic communities in the ancient world would have been mystified, and even disturbed, by modern commitments to the radical democratisation of social and political life so that aliens and subaltern groups can participate in any decision-making processes which affect their well-being. Modern convictions that societies have a duty to redistribute power and wealth to the most vulnerable of their citizens seem to have been alien in ancient Greece (Resnick, 1992). Conceptions of the triple transformation of political community are a specifically modern ideal. Democratic episodes were infrequent and short-lived in any case. Given the precarious existence of democracy in the ancient world, it would have seemed fanciful to envisage experiments in creating a transnational democracy. This is perhaps one of the respects in which the modern states-system differs radically from its Hellenic counterpart. Democratic cultures are firmly embedded in the modern society of states, and the absence of any obvious threat to the survival of this multi-state system creates opportunities for internationalising the politics of dialogue and consent which may well be unique in the history of international relations. Modern international society has been a more fertile ground on which to develop notions of a universal communication community and to imagine close cooperation in building a transnational democracy among societies which have similar commitments to citizenship (see chapter 5).

Striking advances in the widening of the moral and political boundaries of communities did take place, however, in the Hellenistic states-system which succeeded Alexander's empire.[41] Constraints on the use of force were strengthened; reliance on international arbitration became widespread; and closer social and economic interdependence led to the universalisation of legal principles (Tarn, 1930, pp. 80–92; Wallbank, 1981, pp. 144–5). New constructions of citizenship which no longer assumed individual membership of an exclusionary city-state also emerged in the post-Alexandrine world. *Proxenia*, the granting of citizenship to individuals in other states (and to entire populations at times) and *sympoliteia*, the creation of a single state from different communities, were two important innovations (Wallbank, 1981, pp. 148 and 151). Ventures in federal government occurred in Aetolia and Achaea, where the city-state had traditionally lacked strong roots (1981, p. 153). Alternative conceptions of community and citizenship which built upon previous experiments in widening the boundaries of association began to appear late in the Hellenistic period. This is one of the few periods in the history of ancient Greece in which citizenship appeared to acquire meaning apart from the polis, and in which some form of dialogic community wider than the polis could have become possible.

New conceptions of community and citizenship which overcame divisions between insiders and alien others appear in the Hellenistic world but the common assumption seems to have been that these would remain exclusive to Greeks. Hellenic assumptions about the superiority of Greek culture have already been noted, along with the reluctance to confer full citizenship rights on metics.[42] Following the conquest of Persia, Alexander the Great seemed committed to the belief that 'the cultural framework for the proposed racial fusion' of Greeks and Persians would remain 'Hellenic' (Toynbee, 1978, p. 205). Exactly the same point has been made about the Hellenistic kingdoms which existed in the period between the collapse of Alexander's empire and the rise of the Roman empire (Wallbank, 1981, p. 65). Yet it seems that private religious associations in many of the new Hellenistic cities brought

'Greeks and barbarians, free men and slaves, men and women' together in ways which public institutions did not allow (1981, pp. 64–5). An intriguing question is whether these developments in loosening the social bond and widening the boundaries of moral community would have progressed further but for the ascent of Rome (1981, p. 157). Perhaps societies of states rather than empires provide the more likely environment in which commitments to dialogue can develop. Speculations about how the Hellenistic world might have developed must recall that efforts to widen community and to rationalise the moral code promoted advances in universality without corresponding developments in recognising the equality of the radically different. In the Hellenic and Hellenistic worlds, social learning produced significant, yet limited, advances in the imagination and creation of dialogic communities. Radical visions of a universal communication community only make their appearance with the rise of modernity.

Conclusions

All modes of exclusion invite the ethical question of whether they are guilty of assuming the moral relevance of certain social differences and unjust in depriving others of the right of participation in decision-making processes which affect their vital interests. Some of the impetus for thinking about modes of exclusion in this way is derived from the writings of Kant, but Marxism was the first social theory to raise key normative, sociological and praxeological questions about social exclusion. Marxism regarded class exclusion as the central mode of exclusion in history, and assumed that the analysis of human production would reveal how social arrangements which were dedicated to the abolition of class exclusion could be created. Habermas's project of reconstructing historical materialism has stressed the importance of the moral-cultural sphere. For Habermas, the role of communicative action in social existence makes the establishment of a universal communication community possible. The implications for critical theory are threefold. The normative task of critical theory is to defend the ideal of universal communities of discourse; the sociological dimension of critical inquiry ought to investigate the forms of social learning which are capable of turning ideals into reality (and specifically the forms of learning which highlight morally irrelevant social differences and remove barriers to the development of wider communities of discourse); the praxeological function of critical theory is to reflect on the moral and political resources which can be exploited in order to make progress towards a universal communication community. Habermas's writings combine a complex account of social learning with an assessment of modernity and its potentials which is designed to repudiate Weber's vision of the impending iron cage. But these writings make very few references to the international domain, and it is necessary to turn to other writings to reflect on how important themes within them can be used to develop a sociology of international relations.

Interestingly, many of Habermas's themes are replicated in Nelson's analysis of civilisational structures and inter-civilisational relations. Nelson explored the extent to which different civilisations problematised the moral relevance of social differences and valued participation in wider communities of discourse. Along with Habermas, Nelson acknowledges the dark side of modernity – which includes its tendency to generate new forms of social control – while stressing its unique resources which may yet permit significant progress towards a universal communication community. Complex questions arise at this point. These include the issue of whether modernity has unique possibilities because it takes the form of a society of states which is committed to some form of diplomatic dialogue. Whether modes of social learning which problematise the moral relevance of social differences and enable richer forms of dialogue to develop are more likely to occur in societies of states than in empires is a matter which requires further analysis. No clear answer to this question is possible without a more detailed discussion of how societies of states differ from empires and from each other. Some provisional observations about what that analysis might discover are suggested by Mann's inquiry into the evolution of the different forms of social power.

According to Mann, the first empires broke down some of the invidious dualisms between the self and other, and rationalised the symbolic sphere so that more extensive political organisations could be better administered. But imperial concentrations of power limited the extent to which universalistic moralities and religions could govern social life. Universalistic themes had a greater capacity to shape human existence in the Hellenic society of states, since no state could bring these ideas under its control, but few experiments in devising communities of discourse which went beyond the polis seem to have occurred. Some movement in this direction may have occurred in the Hellenistic society of states. New visions of political community and citizenship which broke with the insularity of the classical polis emerged in Greece in the Hellenistic age. Some rough parallels with more recent explorations of the nature and possibility of a post-Westphalian European international society suggest themselves although it would undoubtedly be unwise to press this point too far. If these parallels are exaggerated, then modernity may be unique in possessing the resources with which a universal communication community can be created. This proposition deserves more serious investigation.

Questions of uniqueness aside, modernity has been the site for movement along three separate axes: first, the moral relevance of many social differences has been questioned and frequently been found to be wanting; second, the value of creating the same rights for all members of society without ensuring that they have the resources to exercise these rights has been called into question; and, third, the practice of treating all citizens as if they were identical (as if they did not have different cultures and rights to cultural integrity) has been brought into disrepute. Visions of community and citizenship which take up these concerns are not testimony to the greater intrinsic rationality of modern societies. The dark side of modernity stands in the way of that judgement. A brief overview of the differences between early empires or societies of states and modern forms of political organisation captures the essential point. Extraordinary advances in the capacity to organise large numbers of human beings took place in the first three millennia BC, as Mann reveals, but these developments seem slight when they are compared with the forms of social control and surveillance which states have acquired during the last two centuries. Modern forms of government have unleashed totalising potentials which would have been unimaginable in most parts of the ancient world. The members of modern states have been exposed not only to these massive extensions of state power but also to the destructive effects of capitalism and industrialisation. The three axes of development mentioned above occurred within this context. They are the result of popular resistance to distinctively modern forms of power and inequality. If modernity has the potential to make significant progress towards a universal communication community, it is because of the resources provided by the modern conceptions of citizenship which have been formed in the struggle against power and inequality. The next two chapters consider the nature and significance of these resources in more detail.

5
State Power, Modernity and its Potentials

Early empires lacked the intensive power with which to administer their territories from a central point. Most governing elites had to rule through intermediaries and tolerate local cultural differences as a result. Numerous universalising processes in the ancient world produced higher levels of social integration which the state with its monopolies of power was best placed to control. The Roman governing class, for example, was able to project its monopoly powers across vast expanses of territory and to homogenise society to a far greater extent than any of its predecessors. Even so, the capacity to eradicate alternative images of human community remained elusive in all of the early empires. Similar characteristics are evident in the traditional states which prevailed in Europe between the sixteenth and the late eighteenth centuries, and in modern states which emerged alongside the process of capitalist industrialisation.

One of the main differences between traditional and modern states has been summarised in the following terms: traditional states exercised low levels of intensive power within ill-defined *frontiers*; modern states enjoy high levels of intensive power within clearly demarcated *boundaries* (Giddens, 1985, pp. 49–53). Capitalist industrialisation is one reason for this crucial difference. Remarkable advances in technology, communication and literacy made unusually high levels of linguistic unity and cultural homogeneity possible in modern industrial states (Giddens, 1985, p. 270). Nationalism emerged in this context as the primary determinant of the social bond which unites peoples and simultaneously drives them apart. National ideology made unprecedented levels of social and political mobilisation possible. No previous form of political organisation has ever enjoyed the modern state's capacity to regulate social interaction within its territory (Bauman, 1993, pp. 138–9); no earlier form of political community acquired its extra-ordinary capacity to administer a world empire or to oversee informal mechanisms of global control from a central administrative site (Model-ski, 1978).

The modern state is a monument to the radical extension of the capacity to pacify, monitor and regulate society which was fuelled by the rise of industrial capitalism. But, despite the dramatic extension of their power over the past two centuries, modern states have been unable to prevent the diffusion of ideologies across national boundaries or block the emergence of images of political community which run counter to the dominant tendency in which sovereignty, territoriality, citizenship and nationality have been fused together. Wight's observation that the periods of transnational revolution have been approximately equal to the periods of international stability in the modern states-system is worth recalling at this point (see above, p. 23). One of the ambiguities of the modern state is that although it has amassed considerable power it has been highly susceptible to forms of civil unrest and political disturbance which have often possessed a transnational dimension (Wight, 1977; Halliday, 1994; Armstrong, 1993). These last two developments are closely related. The struggle for legal, political and social rights developed in response to the growing intrusion of state power into the everyday lives of citizens (Hintze, 1975; Mann, 1994). War and industri-alisation gave the modern state an unusual capacity to mould political community but they did not equip it with the ability to tighten the social bond and to close off the moral community entirely, much as the totalitarian regimes of the twentieth century laboured to achieve these ends. National boundaries have been highly permeable and social bonds have displayed limited and precarious coherence in most of the territories governed by modern states.

State-building, geopolitical rivalry and war, and capitalist industrialis-ation are three forces which have interacted to lend modern political communities their peculiar identities, and recent historical sociology has produced several sophisticated analyses of their complex interaction (Skocpol, 1979; Giddens, 1985, 1993; Mann, 1986, 1994; Tilly, 1992a). Few of these accounts attach as much importance, at least explicitly, to the role played by the rationalisation of the moral code in modern societies. Yet these societies have been the site for unique experiments in rationalising the ethical criteria which states and their citizens have used to evaluate the legitimacy of the dominant modes of inclusion and exclusion. Reference was made earlier to the ambiguities of modernity. These ambiguities reveal themselves in the strange paradox of the modern state: on the one hand, it is the site on which radical intensifications of social control have been established but, on the other hand, it has been the setting for unprecedented efforts to eradicate the tyranny of unjust exclusion.

The paradoxical nature of the modern state is the starting-point for the argument of this chapter. The analysis is in four parts. Part one argues that the modern state has stood at the intersection of several rationalisation processes. Some of these have promoted the intensification of social control and the contraction of moral and political community, while others have checked the extension of state power and encouraged the widening of the boundaries of association. The interplay between these different logics explains the paradoxes of the modern state and its role in balancing competing political principles. Part two develops this theme further by considering Hegel's argument that the modern state succeeded because it struck the correct balance between individual rights and loyalties to the community, the market economy and social welfare, state sovereignty and international order. Part two also considers E. H. Carr's argument that the crisis of the modern state in the first part of this century occurred as these balances (and particularly the balance between nationalism and internationalism) collapsed.

Carr believed that the progressive side of modernity contained the ethical resources with which to invent new forms of political community. Part three builds on Carr's argument for state structures which break with traditional systems of exclusion and widen the boundaries of moral and political community. The argument is that new governmental structures can overcome the paradoxical character of the modern state by freeing the potential for reducing unjustified exclusion from the logics which support intensifications of social control and favour the closure or contraction of moral community. Part four considers the respects in which the positive side of modernity – specifically the critique of unjustified forms of exclusion and the notion of answerability to universal rationales – might be embodied in new state structures. It suggests that the modern states-system contains moral possibilities which exceed those which existed in the Hellenic society of states and in the first empires. The logic of this part of the inquiry invites consideration of new forms of community and citizenship. This will be the subject of the concluding chapter.

Origins of the Paradoxes of the Modern State

The sovereign state is one of the main pillars of exclusion in the modern world. States exercise exclusive jurisdiction over their respective national territories, and invariably resist any pressures to internationalise or decentralise authority which threaten their territorial power or challenge the principles of association and disassociation to which they are committed. Various systems of exclusion which are confronted by subordinate classes, women, racial minorities and sub-national groups are interwoven with the practices of state exclusion. How far the state is the source of these modes of exclusion or the innocent site on which they have been established is a complex question which need not delay the discussion here.[1] Suffice it to note that many different kinds of social and political movement have resisted the forms of social closure which exist within modern states. The majority of these movements have sought to reduce or eradicate the forms of exclusion which constrain subordinate groups within the community, but efforts to check extensions of state power have also prompted the emergence of transnational movements which argue for widening the boundaries of the community so that the rights of outsiders are properly recognised. Such demands for extending the rights of citizenship and dialogue to members of excluded groups have clashed with the efforts of sectional interests to monopolise crucial resources and opportunities. The paradoxical nature of the modern state is the result of the tension between the forces which have encouraged, and the forces which have resisted, the development of wider communities of discourse.

Recent sociologies of the modern state break with Marxism by arguing that the sphere of production and exchange is only one of the domains which generate the dominant forms of social and political power and provoke the emergence of movements which aim to alter the course of social change. In the course of making this point, Giddens (1985; 1993, ch. 2) argues that increased surveillance, capitalist enterprise, industrial modes of production and the consolidation of the centralised control of the instruments of violence are the chief determinants of modernity. Four types of social movement which are committed in turn to protecting civil liberties, combating class inequalities, reversing environmental degradation and checking threats to peace have emerged in response to these forces (Giddens, 1985, p. 314; 1993, pp. 158–63). Other political groups which have organised to advance gender equality, ethnic rights and national self-determination are further instances of the 'tendencies and pressures towards democratic participation' which have emerged alongside the expanding 'dialectic of control' (1985, p. 314). Mann stresses the same theme (1994, p. 20). In early modern Europe, most peoples were governed by local power elites and the transnational Church as much as by the emerging national governments, and they felt little compulsion to struggle for the rights of citizenship. The growth of state power after the wars of the eighteenth century heightened their experience of the increasingly restrictive and demanding character of national political institutions. The struggle for greater representation developed in response to the intrusion of capitalist economic relations, the effects of the centralisation of national power and the destructive consequences of emergent militarism (Mann, 1994, p. 81).

These analyses of the competing forces at work within modern states are relevant for any inquiry into the possibility of wider communities of discourse. Three inter-related points need to be made at this stage in the argument. First, as Giddens and Mann have indicated, multiple logics which include strategic rivalry, state-building and capitalist industrialis-ation have interacted to shape the constitution of modern political communities. The inclusion of geopolitics and war in modern sociological analyses of the nature of modernity is important because it marks a significant break with mainstream accounts of the state in the nineteenth century which emphasised the primary causal role of domestic factors and overlooked the massive impact of geopolitical rivalry and war on the configuration of modern societies. The stress on geopolitical factors corrects this oversight but it is only part of the larger move which has to be made. Recent sociologies of the state which seek to forge links with the theory of international relations rely too heavily on realist analyses of strategic interaction, and neglect rationalist accounts of the ways in which sovereign states belong to a distinctive form of international society. Consideration of the legal and moral principles which link sovereign states within an international society ought to figure more prominently in contemporary sociological analysis, not least as a means of transcending the mechanistic accounts of international relations which have been favoured by realism and Marxism.[2] Rationalism is an import-ant perspective in this context because it calls attention to the elements of dialogue and consent which are built into modernity organised as an international system of states. The autonomous role of the moral and cultural dimensions of international politics has not gone unnoticed in recent sociology, but this domain has yet to be accorded its appropriate place within sociologies of traditional and modern states.[3] The praxeo-logical significance of this move will be considered later in this chapter and developed further in the concluding discussion.

The second point is that this emphasis on the legal and moral dimensions of international relations inevitably brings the process of moral-practical learning or rationalisation to the centre of the analysis. Moral-practical rationalisation has two dimensions. First, the moral-practical realm includes principles of coordination which mediate between the traditions and interests of different individuals, groups and cultures (T. McCarthy, 1981, ch. 2, section 3). The principles of coordination which bring states together within modern international society have this mediating role although a significant number of states protest against those principles which privilege order over justice. Protests against the injustice of principles of coordination are the key to the second dimension of moral-practical learning, which involves the development of more complex tests of the legitimacy of the principles of coordination which the systematically excluded regard as unnecessarily restrictive or unjust. Moral-practical rationalisation in this second sense has played an important role in the transformation of national political communities and the evolution of international society. Its effect within the modern state is evident in decisions to subject the exclusion of subordinate classes, women, ethnic and racial minorities from the public realm to more rigorous moral tests, and in the very real advances which have taken place in extending and deepening the rights of modern citizens. The impact of moral-practical learning on the society of states is exemplified by challenges to past rationales for denying non-Western peoples equal membership of the society of states, and by the ongoing practice of subjecting the principles of the Western-dominated international order to more demanding moral tests which address the plight of excluded groups including the global poor, the world's refugees and indigenous peoples.[4]

An analysis of modern political communities and their prospects for creating wider universalities of discourse should therefore consider the interplay between state-building, geopolitical rivalry, capitalist industrialisation and the process of moral-practical learning which includes the development of principles of social coordination and the evolution of more complex moral assessments of the legitimacy of systems of exclusion.[5] The third point is that the purpose of the analysis is to examine the relationship between societal potentials for extending citizenship rights to all members of the modern state and the potential for recognising the rights of the members of all other communities. The relationship between these two aspects of moral-practical rationalisation is complex and has changed dramatically over time. As Carr (1945) argued, the extension of citizenship within European states in the first part of the twentieth century eroded loyalties to the international community. Demands for welfare citizenship encouraged the development of more powerful states which intensified national sentiments and increased estrangement between societies. However, intensifications of control within the modern state have not closed off the notion of a dialogic community between free and equal citizens; and conceptions of the political community as an association of free and equal citizens have not ruled out commitments to a universal community which includes all human beings. Totalising projects have not been so successful as to erode the sense of moral anxiety when duties to fellow-citizens clash with duties to the rest of humankind. Ethical particularism remains strong in modern states but, as recent discussions of cosmopolitan democracy suggest, there are encouraging signs that the pressures for greater representation and participation within modern states may become more closely connected with the commitment to extending rights of dialogue and citizenship to outsiders (Held, 1995). As previously noted, there were few pressures of this kind in the Hellenic system of states. One crucial question for a sociology of community which is geared to praxeological ends is to understand how citizenship might come to be separated from the sovereign state and embedded in the practices of a more powerful international society. How to develop new forms of citizenship and community which release the potential for wider universalities of discourse which is already immanent within the modern state and international society is the central praxeological question. It is important first to make some observations about the process of state-formation in Europe.

State-formation in early modern Europe was marked by the intensification of social closure. Charles Tilly's aphorism that the state made war while war made the state summarises the essential point (Tilly, 1992a). In his work on Renaissance diplomacy, Mattingly (1955) argued that small city-states and sprawling empires were poorly adapted for the organisation of war. The territorial state prevailed in the struggle between different types of political organisation because it was sufficiently compact to be administered from a central administrative point and sufficiently large to withstand external attack. What Hintze (1975) called the rationalisation of state operations led to the creation of new axes of vertical and horizontal exclusion. The use of force to pacify and control the domestic realm, the exclusion of religious groups whose political allegiance could not be guaranteed and the development of a centralised bureaucracy for extracting wealth from peasant classes furthered the process of horizontal exclusion. The establishment of sovereign control over clearly defined boundaries, the concurrent assault on the religious and political authority of the transnational Church and the destruction of local political institutions installed new systems of vertical exclusion. The five monopolies of the modern state were the result of this transformation of the principles of association and the modes of exclusion. (On these monopolies, see p. 28.)

Tilly (1975, pp. 36–7) has argued that in the early stages of European state-formation 'the builders of states worked to stamp out or absorb existing rights, not to extend them'; they were involved in 'abridging, destroying or absorbing rights previously lodged in other political units', including the local manors and provinces. The external counterpart to this assault on traditional intra-state rights was the challenge to the principles of a Christian international society which was undertaken in the name of state sovereignty. The erosion of international society was gradual but incomplete. The sense of belonging to an exclusively European (as opposed to Christian) international society placed some constraints on the exercise of state sovereignty, and only in the late nineteenth and early twentieth century did the positivistic idea that sovereigns could break international legal obligations at will briefly prevail (Hinsley, 1994, ch. 5). The earlier Christian notion that the rights of individuals were morally prior to the rights of states was gradually stripped away with the rise of European international society but never entirely suppressed.[6]

Traditional political rights were cancelled as states emerged in the context of systemic war and struggled with internal and external competitors for monopoly control of the instruments of violence. State-formation was a totalising project (Corrigan and Sayer, 1985, p. 4) in which governing elites endeavoured to subsume subjects within the 'illusory community', to which Marx referred, and manufactured crude distinctions between insiders and aliens to encourage popular identification with national societies. Emerging states lacked the intensive power to be able to complete political community by ensuring that loyalty to the state or nation displaced all others. Governing elites also depended heavily upon the resources which national economic actors acquired through their participation in the wider global economy. The economic environment in which state-formation occurred, with the impossibility of confining social and economic interaction within national boundaries, was one of the main brakes upon the totalising project.

Tilly's work on the interplay between coercive capability and capitalist development in the formation of modern territorial states considers these themes in more detail. All governing elites in Europe in the period beginning in AD 990 had the problem of extracting sufficient wealth from their subjects in order to accumulate sufficient military and administrative power to resist adversaries. Three different types of political organisation existed in Europe in AD 990, and none seemed certain to prevail even five centuries later (Tilly, 1992a, p. 43). They were tribute-based empires, systems of fragmented sovereignty (city-states and urban federations) and emerging national-territorial states. Tribute-based empires possessed high coercive capability but failed to encourage high levels of capital accumulation; systems of fragmented sovereignty were leading centres of capital development but possessed low levels of coercive power; emerging national states struck the right balance between capital accumulation and the development of coercive power and came to dominate other forms of political organisation during the sixteenth and seventeenth centuries (Tilly, 1992a, pp. 30–1).

Britain and France were the pre-eminent examples of the new form of the territorial state which commanded powerful standing armies (1992a, p. 159).

In the relationship between capital and coercion, cities 'shaped the destinies of states' as the principal 'containers and distribution points for capital' (1992a, p. 30). One of the distinctive features of emerging national states was the relatively equal position of the governing class, which controlled the instruments of violence, and the urban elite, which owned significant reserves of capital (1992a, p. 51). Urban elites partici- pated in long-distance trade relations from which states benefited but which they were unable to control (1992a, p. 52). Alliances with the holders of capital placed constraints on the state's power to subdue society and acted as a counterweight to the totalising project (1992a, p. 90).

Many sociologists from Weber on have argued that war and state- formation provided the main impetus for the development of modern capitalism which spread extensively beyond national frontiers and eluded governmental control. In earlier states-systems, universalising forces such as the widening circle of commercial exchange and the dissemination of religious beliefs created a transnational economic and social domain which, initially, no individual state could hope to overpower. The increase of coercive power and the gradual elimination of competitors in warfare led to the point where a single hegemonic state could bring the wider transnational society within its jurisdiction (Mann, 1986; Wight 1978). This two-step pattern of development which occurred in earlier international systems has not been repeated in the modern world for at least two reasons: the balance of power has held the ambitions of aspiring imperial powers in check, and the spread of capitalism over the last two centuries has counterbalanced the development of greater national coercive power. War and state-formation were major driving forces behind the internationalisation of capitalism; but the spread of capitalism has been a major reason for the reproduction of the modern international system of states (Chase-Dunn, 1981). As a result, the modern system of states may avoid the fate of earlier international societies (which was to be absorbed within an empire). Conceptions of a universal communication community may yet come to make an unpre- cedented impression upon political life.

War and state-formation in Europe produced the dual structure of a multi-state system and a capitalist world economy rather than a single empire. The European states were engaged in an incessant struggle for power and prestige which required an ongoing commitment to 'the consolidation and rationalization of state operations' (namely making improvements in administration and control) and to promoting the economic and political measures which would rationalise the process of capitalist accumulation (Hintze, 1975, pp. 308–9 and 434). Rationalisation in these domains was accompanied by efforts to rationalise the principles of coordination in international relations. Hintze (1975, pp. 432–3) believed that 'the true character of modern political life' was demonstrated by the shared predisposition to round off and consolidate the control of territory rather than by the struggle for the unlimited expansion of national power. States were influenced at first by the belief that they should not infringe the principles of 'the ecclesiastical and religious cultural community' and later by the commitment to 'the civilized society of states sustained by international law' (1975, p. 346). The great powers gradually came to share the responsibility for creating and maintaining the balance of power and for preserving the international society of states.

Hintze (1975, pp. 346 and 433) maintained that this sense of the common responsibility for governing international society was the secular equivalent and historical legacy of the religious and cultural unity which Roman Catholicism bequeathed to the modern West. The debt which the principles of the modern society of states owe to medieval political ideas such as constitutional government was also stressed by Wight (1977, pp. 131–2) and Bull (Bull et al., 1990, pp. 73–4), who developed Hintze's themes in two ways. First, Bull and Wight analysed the rationalisation of the principles of international relations in considerable detail by tracing the development of modern concepts of sovereign equality, non-intervention, international law, diplomacy, the balance of power and the notion of the special responsibilities of the great powers. Second, they stressed that one dimension of the 'true character of modern political life' is the coexistence of three conceptions of moral and political community centred on the sovereign state, the society of states and a potential community of humankind. This conception of the state, the society of states and human society is the modern equivalent of the 'triple power network' in ancient Greece (Mann, 1986, pp. 223–7) and one reason why questions about the legitimacy of exclusionary social bonds and the moral significance of national boundaries arose consistently during both epochs. That they feature more prominently in the modern society of states is largely the legacy of medieval constitutionalism.

As noted earlier, the rise of industrial capitalism made it possible for states to homogenise populations and to instil the conviction that obligations to co-nationals have priority over other political obligations. Although industrial capitalism greatly increased the state's ability to create national political communities which could be quickly mobilised during international crises, two cross-cutting pressures in addition to those which have already been discussed foiled the totalising project. In the first place, during the latter part of the eighteenth century, the globalisation of capitalist relations of production and exchange greatly enlarged the sociological horizon by making modern populations aware of their involvement in the lengthy chains of cause and effect which tied different societies together (Tronto, 1993, p. 188). The extension of sociological horizons encouraged the widening of moral horizons, with the result that the idea of universal humanity regained some of the importance which it had lost during the seventeenth century. In the second place, the greater the burden which states imposed on their populations in the form of increased taxation and national conscription, the more inclined their subjects were to organise to secure compensating legal and political rights (Hintze, 1975, p. 211; D. Held, 1995, pp. 57–9). Modern forms of representative democracy in which subjects transformed themselves into citizens emerged in the cauldron of state-building, geopolitical rivalry and frequent war, and rapid capitalist development. Demands for limited government grew out of popular resistance to the intensifications of power promoted by dominant elites. Notions of human equality and commitments to conferring citizenship rights on all members of society have been uniquely influential in the modern international society of states.

Multiple logics therefore interacted to create modern state structures wielding monopoly powers over bounded national communities. According to the prevailing discourse of legitimacy, the authority of the sovereign was ultimately derived from the antecedent liberties of free and equal citizens. In the bond between sovereign and citizen, Bodin (1967, p. 21) argued, loyalty and obedience were exchanged for justice and protection. Political community was exclusionary since the special ties between the sovereign and the citizen emphatically excluded aliens. Sovereign states claimed absolute rights to determine matters concerning the distribution of membership, citizenship and global responsibilities in their own way but they accepted that wider, though less morally demanding, international communities existed alongside the territorial state. The question of how the international state of nature could be made more responsive to universal moral principles has been a recurrent issue in the modern society of states because the boundaries of the political community have not coincided with the boundaries of the moral community, and because duties to fellow-citizens have not marked the outer limits of moral obligation. The vexed question of how the rights of outsiders are best protected has arisen because modern societies have problematised their systems of exclusion.

The denial of the rights of subaltern groups is an additional feature of the problem of modern political community. Demands for the extension of citizenship rights which widen access to the public sphere have been a central feature of the politics of modern states. Multiple forces have encouraged these demands. State-building and war generated these claims by imposing new military and political burdens on the mass citizenry. Capitalist industrialisation, as Tocqueville argued, played its part by undermining traditional aristocratic class responsibilities to the poor and by compelling subordinate groups to turn to the state for protection (Bendix, 1964, ch. 3). Marx maintained that the dominant mode of legitimation in capitalist society fostered political resistance: the contradiction between the dominant ideology which stressed the freedom and equality of citizens and the profound material inequalities engendered by the capitalist mode of production created demands for new social and economic rights. Marshall (1973) provided an account of the extension of rights in Britain which suggested that the language of citizenship possessed its own dialectical development: legal rights came to be regarded as incomplete without the right to participate in the enterprise of law-making, and rights of participation were deemed merely formal where citizens lacked the social and economic capacity to exercise them fully. For these reasons, citizenship came to mean rights of participation in the political process and entitlements to social welfare as well as the right of protection under the law. In general terms, important cultural developments in modern societies have shifted the burden of proof onto those who deny others access to the legal, political and social rights which they already enjoy.

The dominant mode of legitimation in modern societies has been an effective counterweight to efforts to tighten the social bond and to contract the moral community so that the interests of citizens are all that matter. Modern societies have developed moral potentials for transcending the modes of exclusion experienced by subordinate insider groups and alien outsiders. As Kant and Marx argued, the progress of these communities has involved the reduction and eradication of the dual system of exclusion. Both thinkers believed that the dismantling of domestic structures of exclusion would prepare the way for less exclusionary patterns of international relations. After all, the same moral and political principles affirming the right of the human subject to lead a free life were at stake in each domain. It is possible that the longer the modern states-system survives, and the stronger the constraints on totalising projects become, the more likely it is that the struggle against the tyranny of unjust exclusion will make further headway, but progress towards eradicating unjust exclusion in domestic politics has not always generated simultaneous pressures to end unjust exclusion within international society. The extension of citizenship in the early part of the twentieth century had the paradoxical effect of weakening the moral foundations of international society. The totalising project reached its peak in the first part of the twentieth century, and progressivist interpretations of the modern state looked increasingly hollow. Progressivist approaches to the state which celebrated its contribution to the enlargement of freedom were challenged by liberal and Marxist positions which argued for the transformation of political community in order to secure human autonomy (MacMillan and Linklater, 1995). The crucial issues are revealed by contrasting Hegel's defence of the modern state, which maintained that it alone secures the conditions for the enjoyment of a free life, with E. H. Carr's critique of the structure of modern political life and anticipation of new forms of political community.

On the Ambiguities of State Power

The tension between intensifications of social control and demands for more open political communities has recurred while state-building, war, international society, capitalist industrialisation and the struggle to eradicate systems of exclusion which fail the more sophisticated tests of legitimacy have continued to shape modernity. Some states are more concerned than others with the plight of the systematically excluded, indicating that national responses to the tensions within modernity vary considerably. Most states are incapable of suppressing the demands that they should dismantle pernicious systems of exclusion, although their power to thwart aspirations for social change should not be underestimated. The state remains the principal site on which the conflict between efforts to monopolise the control of significant resources and opportunities and struggles to create less exclusionary political communities is worked out. Whether or not most states make a positive contribution to resolving the tensions within modernity is a keenly contested issue (Wheeler, 1996). Much of the history of modern political thought has been divided between a progressivist interpretation, which stresses the state's essential role in creating a more ethical political community, and a geopolitical narrative, which argues that states are primarily concerned with accumulating power, increasing the surveillance of society, controlling challengers and outmanoeuvring adversaries (MacMillan and Linklater, 1995, pp. 5–8).

Hegel's political philosophy offers the most elaborate defence of the achievements of the modern state while recognising the depth of these ambiguities. Revolutionary terror and the forces of reaction had found expression in modern societies, Hegel argued, but the more advanced states had succeeded in realising their promise to secure the conditions in which citizens could lead free lives. Reconciling the competing principles of individualism and community, market and welfare, sovereignty and international responsibility was the principal accomplishment of the modern state. Its achievements allowed national citizens to feel at home in the world of modernity (Hardimon, 1994).

Balancing the principles which came into opposition in the context of modernity occurred in the following way. First, the modern state made it possible for citizens to feel that they belonged to a cohesive community, thereby recapturing the social solidarity which had existed, so Hegel believed, in the ancient polis. But unlike the polis, the modern state satisfied the modern subject's demand for personal freedom. Ethical life (*Sittlichkeit*) was reconciled with the demand for individual autonomy (*Moralität*) in the social and political institutions of the modern world. Second, the pursuit of economic self-interest and the play of market forces were released from state control but the poverty which civil society created was partially alleviated by state provision for the poor. Third, modern states necessarily came into conflict with one another since the sovereign principle ruled out all higher courts of appeal and limited international law to statements of 'what ought to be' (Hegel, 1952, para. 333). Nevertheless, states belonged to the European society of states.[7] As members of an international society, they had responsibilities to one another to control the use of force and to avoid committing acts of violence against private persons (Hegel, 1952, para. 338).

The very existence of European international society revealed that a loose political association could develop beyond the water's edge. Hegel denied that international society could secure perpetual peace, and he rejected any notion that its arrangements revealed progress towards the eventual unification of the human race. Violent conflicts arose in the relations between sovereign states because there was no shared moral discourse to ensure the peaceful resolution of fundamental political differences. Recurrent international conflicts proved that the modern state was still the most effective form of close political cooperation. By carefully striking the correct balance between the most cherished principles of modernity, the state could count on the loyalty of its citizens in crisis and war. The crucial difference between traditional and modern European states was that the latter did not demand the unconditional political obedience of their citizens. This was the key to their unprecedented ability to project their power globally, but it was also the reason why the state was without peer in creating the patterns of social cooperation which were most conducive to leading a free life.

The weaknesses in Hegel's position were exposed by the Young Hegelians and especially by Marx. Most of the Young Hegelians welcomed the social revolutions of 1830 and argued for the extension of civil, political and religious freedoms within the modern state. Marx's famous critique of Hegel's political philosophy stressed the failure of the modern state to satisfy the basic material needs of the subordinate classes. Some of the Young Hegelians argued for the absorption of the state within a religious community which would extend to the whole of humankind, a theme which was reworked in a secular form in Marx's vision of socialised humanity (see Toews, 1980). But not only was the modern state structurally incapable of satisfying the economic and social needs of its own population: one of the measures taken to reduce poverty, namely colonisation, clearly sacrificed the rights of human beings elsewhere. Whereas Hegel celebrated the achievements of the modern state, his critics pointed to its oppressive role which engendered profound social conflicts. The Young Hegelians argued that the central purpose of philosophy was critique, and that analysing the possibilities of higher forms of freedom and rationality which were immanent within modern societies was its principal rationale. Marx's critical project contained a double commitment to ending the exploitation of the proletariat and to promoting greater cosmopolitanism. His critique of the capitalist state was combined with a progressivist interpretation of the future socialist state which failed to realise the potential conflict between those two social objectives.[8] Hegel's attempt to reveal that the modern citizen ought to feel at home in the world, and Marx's proposed remedy for the forms of alienation and exploitation which dashed human aspirations to lead a free life, failed to recognise the ethical limitations of the modern form of political community.

The conflict between measures to reduce social inequality and the goal of universal solidarity was a central theme in E. H. Carr's writings. Carr (1945, part 1) argued that the crisis of the modern state in the early twentieth century occurred because the balance between nationalism and internationalism which had existed for much of the preceding century had dramatically broken down. Working-class demands for the enlargement of citizenship rights to include welfare provision led to the deepening of national rivalries. Social bonds were tightened and the sense of a moral community wider than the sovereign state was weakened as governments responded to working-class demands for more inclusive societies. In addition to explaining this development, Carr sought to explain the possibility of new state structures which would strike a new balance between respect for national differences and cosmopolitan sentiments.

Carr described three principal stages in the evolution of modern state structures. In the first phase, the mercantilist epoch, which reached its apex in the eighteenth century, absolutist states competed with one another for economic and military power. The dissolution of the mercantilist marriage of national economic and military power which occurred during the nineteenth century marked the second phase of development. New liberal state structures supported the free movement of goods and opened their borders to migrant labour in the belief that close commercial ties between peoples would replace mercantilist rivalry with international concord. The new national states which appeared in this period as a result of national secession and political unification were incorporated as equal members of the society of states without any serious disturbance to world peace. Nationalism and internationalism were balanced as a result for the greater part of the nineteenth century.

The destruction of this balance marked the third phase of development. Early indications of its impending collapse appeared in the 1870s, but the true magnitude of the crisis was most clearly revealed in the period between 1914 and 1939. Three phenomena, the socialisation of the nation, the nationalisation of economic policy and the geographical extension of nationalism, destroyed the liberal conception of the coming peace. The socialisation of the nation occurred as the subordinate classes enthusiastically embraced nationalism. More powerful working-class organisations used their new-found political strength in the aftermath of the extension of the male suffrage to protect themselves from the vagaries of the world market and from the unsolicited competition of migrant labour. The nationalisation of economic policy resulted from pressure on the state to adopt policies which would protect national wages and safeguard employment. Laissez-faire principles were abandoned as state structures engaged in a neo-mercantilist struggle for economic and political power. Mounting economic nationalism undermined the open world economy. The geographical extension of nationalism because of reunification and secession meant that the number of sovereign states virtually doubled in the period between 1871 and 1924. New nation-states could no longer be so easily absorbed within international society with the rise of economic nationalism, the escalation of international political rivalries and the decline of Britain's hegemonic, but stabilising, global role.

Measures to include the members of previously excluded groups within national frameworks triggered the closure of community. Economic nationalism created pressures to end large-scale immigration, and all major powers began to close their frontiers in the period beginning in 1919 (Carr, 1945, p. 22). After a lull of one hundred and twenty-five years, Europe once again witnessed the practice of deporting peoples to tidy up the national frontiers (1945, p. 33). Nationalism after the First World War encouraged total warfare, and popular hatred blurred the vital distinction between military and civilian targets. A more nationalistic stance on the distribution of membership was accompanied by increasingly particularistic orientations to the distribution of global responsibilities. The First World War was the first international conflict to embroil whole nations, and the first to decline into total war. The twenty years' crisis which was characterised by the growth of totalitarian power and the descent into unrestrained warfare revealed the final bankruptcy of the Western nation-state.

Carr's position was clearly at odds with the progressivist interpretation of the modern state which is illustrated by Hegel's political philosophy. Hegel believed that the modern state used its powers to create social and political arrangements which institutionalised the remarkable ethical advances of modernity. Carr described the collapse of the moral equilibrium which lay at the heart of Hegel's progressivist account of the modern state. Fine balances between the individual and the community, economic self-interest and welfare provision, national sovereignty and international legal responsibilities were destroyed by the state's sudden lurch towards exclusionary practices which were directed against minority groups and aliens. Similar themes emerged in the Marxist theories of imperialism, although Carr rejected their explanation of the principal dynamics at work in the emergence of highly particularistic modes of legitimation. These themes included the dramatic extension of the power of the state over society, the development of increasingly militarised social orders, and the sharpening of national divisions between peoples. They provided the basis for Carr's account of the climax of the totalising project and the emergence of the era in which the destructive potential of the state was most tragically revealed as states became more tightly bound internally and more sharply divided from one another. This was the period in which the state's monopoly control of the instruments of violence, its economic powers and its ability to make national identity the highest political identity were remarkably unchecked, as were its status as the highest court of legal appeal, its exclusive right of representation in international organisations and its assumed sole right to bind the whole community in international law. The fusion of territoriality, sovereignty, citizenship and nationality reached its zenith in this period.[9] This was the epoch, Carr believed, in which the sovereign nation-state with its monopoly powers lost its claim to be the authoritative means of organising human beings.

On the Possibility of New State Structures

Carr recognised that the moral and political boundaries of community are far from fixed and that the rights and duties of associations can be defined in very different ways, some more exclusionary than others. Similar points were registered by the Marxist theories of imperialism as they reflected on the ways in which nationalism and militarism dashed earlier expectations of the relentless advance of cosmopolitanism. With few exceptions, the mainstream literature in Political Science and International Relations has failed to build on these analyses of the diverse ways in which the boundaries of communities have been constructed.[10] The intellectual division of labour between Political Science, Sociology and International Relations rested on the false premise that domestic and international politics were clearly separated. Intriguing issues about how communities come to be bounded and distinct from one another, and about how boundedness and separateness change over time, were despatched to the margins of social and political analysis. These were central issues in Carr's account of the transformation of state structures over two centuries.

Mercantilist ruling elites which promoted the nationalisation of economic and social life and assumed a zero-sum conception of international relations formed a distinctive combination of state structures.[11] Relatively closed forms of political community prevailed in this epoch. Liberal governing classes which encouraged the domestic and international expansion of civil society presided over new configurations of state power which favoured more open conceptions of political community. Nationalist and militaristic forces produced the rise of new state structures which intensified the totalising project and promoted the closure and contraction of political community. Carr was not alone in analysing the contraction of the boundaries of moral and political community although he drew unusual conclusions. More than twenty years earlier, Lenin and Bukharin commented on the massive growth of state power, the nationalisation of communities which ought to have fragmented along class lines, and deepening estrangement between national communities. Their main conclusion was that the revival of class warfare would soon destroy the totalising project along with the states which had initiated it. Horkheimer and Adorno argued in the 1930s that the events of the inter-war period destroyed any hope of an international socialist revolution and concluded that the idea of historical progress was completely exhausted. Carr drew different conclusions. He stressed the possibility of a new configuration of post-nationalist or post-Westphalian state structures which would relinquish much of their power over human society, retreat from the supposition that national loyalties are always overriding and jettison the morally irrelevant differences between insiders and outsiders. Carr envisaged new state structures which were committed to the triple transformation of political community.

His central point was that the 'exclusive solution' to the problem of modern political community which allowed sectional interests ('white men, landowners, propertied classes and so forth') to monopolise rights had lost its legitimacy (Carr, 1945, p. 42). Practical steps to dismantle the primary modes of exclusion were essential if political communities were to command popular consent. What applied to domestic politics also held for relations between states. An international community which catered exclusively for the interests of the great powers could neither be justified nor reproduced indefinitely. But progress towards a less exclusionary international society would necessarily be uneven. Carr stressed the impossibility of 'creating an international community out of units so fantastically disparate . . . as China and Albania, Norway and Brazil', but stoutly defended international planning to promote not the equality of sovereign states but the equality of individual men and women (1945, p. 43). The most promising opportunities for remaking political community so that it embodied an ethic of welfare internationalism existed in the advanced industrial societies of Europe – the heartland of modernity.[12]

Sovereignty would endure yet relinquish much of its classical significance in the new configuration of state structures. The substance of national policy would contain powerful internationalist dimensions. Britain would enlarge the boundaries of moral and political community so that the interests of the people of Düsseldorf, Lodz and Lille would possess many of the rights enjoyed by the inhabitants of Oldham and Jarrow. Widening the boundaries of association would ensure that the citizens of one society did not establish their rights to employment, freedom from material deprivation and access to meaningful opportunities through the act of exporting harms to outsiders. Carr (1946, p. 230) was aware of the possibility that the enlargement of the boundaries of political community could provoke the 'recrudescence of disintegrating tendencies'. International planning organisations, he added, would not command popular support unless they displayed respect for cultural differences. As with the most successful domestic societies, international organisations would have to 'admit something of the same multiplicity of authorities and diversity of loyalties' (Carr, 1945, p. 49).[13] Nations would continue to be important in the new structures of cooperation, but the connection between nation and sovereign statehood would be severed. The new configuration of state structures would be more cosmopolitan, more respectful of multiple identities and more strenuously involved in combating economic inequality than any of its predecessors.

A crucial question is whether Carr's congenial vision of the post-nationalist state can be reconciled with his reputed support for political realism. Also important is the issue of whether his vision of a new configuration of state structures which would cooperate to promote the triple transformation of community is purely utopian. Carr's writings are instructive on these themes. Although he has long been credited with having coined the distinction between realism and utopianism, and with developing a robust defence of political realism, he was explicitly critical of both extremes. The characteristic fault of idealism, Carr (1946, p. 12) argued, was naivety; the parallel affliction of realism was sterility. The nature of Carr's alternative path is difficult to establish although the concept of immanent critique in Marxian critical theory comes very close to his own point of view. Starting from where *we* are, to use Rorty's formulation, immanent critique combines the utopian task of defending the higher possibilities in existing social orders with a realistic assessment of the ways in which the dominant structures constrain their realisation. It avoids realist resignation to fate and utopian normative commitments which are unlikely to be institutionalised by articulating visions of the future which stand more directly in the line of the most recent social and political advance.[14]

The tension between modes of legitimation which stress the freedom and equality of subjects and various asymmetries of power and wealth creates the objective possibility of far-reaching structural change, and the social and political movements which organise in the face of such contradictions are often in the line of the most recent advance. Progressive social movements frequently turn modern notions of citizenship which embody strong claims about freedom and equality against modes of unjust exclusion. Carr's somewhat nebulous alternative to realism and utopianism can be understood in these terms. In the manner of immanent critique, Carr's third path explores the latent potentialities which are inherent within the modern forms of citizenship which have developed in response to intensifications of social and political control.[15] Immanent criticism which investigates the respects in which the idea of citizenship can be used for the purpose of imagining new state structures relies on these three claims: first, much of the moral capital which has been accumulated in the course of resistance to the growth of state power and the rise of capitalism is invested in modern conceptions of citizenship; second, the idea of citizenship is a crucial moral resource which political actors can draw upon as they struggle to create forms of political community which overcome unjust systems of exclusion; third, increasing transnational harm in the modern world creates the moral imperative to use these resources to create new post-nationalist social and political arrangements. To put this another way, the state's totalising practices provoked a series of political challenges which led to the elaboration of a complex system of citizenship rights. It is the important forms of moral-practical learning which occurred within the cultural sphere which make the further transformation of state structures and progress towards a universal communication community possible. This is the key to understanding the progressive dimensions of modernity.

The objective possibility of the post-Westphalian state rests then on past achievements in deepening the meaning and significance of national citizenship.[16] Post-nationalist states in Carr's writings take on global moral responsibilities which resonate with their previous accomplishments in progressing beyond exclusionary solutions to the problem of community. The commitment to equality finds its outward expression in the vision of an international order which promotes the welfare of individual men and women rather than the interests of the dominant powers. The recognition that individuals cannot make use of their legal and political rights unless they possess sufficient social and economic powers demands support for welfare internationalism. The realisation that the members of a national community do not have the right to impose the dominant culture and beliefs on minority groups requires international recognition of the diversity of human loyalties. It is these national commitments to the principle of human equality, welfare rights and respect for cultural differences which make the triple transformation of political community possible.

Carr's vision of new state structures was an exercise in the domestic analogy because it assumed that the principles and procedures which contributed to intra-state order could be applied in the relations between states (Suganami, 1989). Important methodological issues separate Carr's 'utopian realism' (Booth, 1991) from the neo-realism of Kenneth Waltz. As noted earlier, Waltz (1959) distinguished between three images of the causes of war: the first image which believes that human nature causes war, and concludes that war cannot be eradicated without modifying human behaviour; the second image which holds that particular kinds of regime cause war, and argues that war can be abolished by creating new forms of government within existing states; and the third image which believes that war is inherent in international anarchy, and contends that the incidence of violence in the relations between states can be reduced, but not eradicated, by maintaining a balance of power. (See pp. 14–15 above.) Whereas Waltz was interested in accounting for the phenomenon of warfare, Carr was concerned with understanding the factors which had increased the probability of war in the first part of the twentieth century. The way in which the contraction of moral community had made violence acceptable was more central to Carr's inquiry than the role played by recklessness, serious miscalculation or aggressive foreign policy in the outbreak of war.[17] The important inference which Carr drew from this observation was that the creation of new forms of political community was necessary if the violence which dominated the first part of the century was not to be repeated. The transformation of European international society could only be achieved by reconstituting its exclusionary national parts.[18]

Carr's third path, which sought to escape the sterility of realism and the naivety of utopianism was not explicated in detail. Its strength lay in its implicit recognition that the struggle against the growth of state power and advancing capitalism created impressive moral reserves which could be harnessed to the task of reconstructing the European society of states. Considerable scepticism about any effort to universalise this project is evident from Carr's observation about the impossibility of creating an international community from societies as diverse as China, Albania, Norway and Brazil. Attempts to promote the triple transformation of political community within Europe would be unlikely to command world-wide support. Like-minded European states which shared similar conceptions of citizenship had a special obligation to develop new patterns of international cooperation under conditions of increasing transnational harm (Czempiel, 1974, pp. 748–9).[19] They had a duty to one another to sacrifice important elements of national sovereignty or to break with the habits which are associated with its possession.[20] They were obliged to establish different frameworks of political action when dealing with those societies which did not share their normative preferences.

Defining the nature of these alternative frameworks was not one of Carr's priorities.[21] It is possible to build upon his analysis by developing some earlier remarks about the three ideal-typical frameworks of action that are available to states which are committed to enlarging the boundaries of moral and political community and to cooperating with others to eradicate unjust modes of exclusion.[22] First, where states have deeply dissimilar political and economic systems that reflect differences of culture and morality, the appropriate framework of political action is a pluralist society of states in which the constitutive principles aim to preserve respect for the freedom and equality of independent political communities. Members of the Grotian tradition have described this framework as pluralist because the principles of association are designed to ensure that different societies coexist as peacefully as possible rather than collaborate to realise shared moral goals. A second framework of action is possible between states which have reached an agreement about a range of moral principles such as individual human rights, minority rights, responsibilities for nature and duties to other species which they believe they should promote together. Members of the Grotian tradition have described this political framework as solidarist because there is some consensus about the substantive moral purposes which the whole society of states has a duty to uphold. Third, a post-Westphalian framework can develop where like-minded societies are keen to establish closer forms of political cooperation to integrate shared ethical norms into the structure of social and political life. Post-Westphalian arrangements differ from a solidarist international society by virtue of the fact that states do not only break with the traditional habits associated with state sovereignty but also relinquish many of their sovereign powers entirely. The principles of international governance which are integral to this framework of action no longer presuppose the commitment to sovereignty, territoriality, nationality and citizenship which differentiates the modern form of political community from all previous forms of human organisation. Carr's vision of a configuration of states which are united to promote welfare internationalism, and recent notions of a cosmopolitan community of democratic societies, are two ways of conceptualising international society in the post-Westphalian era.

Each of these political frameworks widens the boundaries of community to ensure due consideration for the interests of others; each moves beyond the supposition that the difference of the other is a good reason for privileging the interests of insiders; and each involves a commitment to internationalising the politics of dialogue and consent. Yet these are distinct forms of international political association which reflect the varieties of solidarity or fraternisation which exist in the society of states. By promoting, in turn, the autonomy of sovereign associations, respect for individual or group rights and a reduction of the modes of exclusion which the members of a post-Westphalian order deem to be unjust, all three conceptions of international society contribute to the creation of a universal communication community. A post-Westphalian state can participate in all three frameworks simultaneously by virtue of the very different forms of international relations in which it is involved. A state which recognises the heterogeneity of international society will not assume that post-Westphalian arrangements are the most advanced system of cooperation or the destination which all other communities should strive to reach. The hermeneutic skills which are a necessary component of open dialogue with the radically different can be as complex as, and even more demanding than, the aptitudes involved in promoting welfare internationalism in the affairs of like-minded states. The observation that post-Westphalian arrangements are not inherently superior to the pluralist and solidarist forms of international society acknowledges that groups can enjoy the right to a separate existence which exempts them from the duty to cooperate closely with others.[23] A state can simultaneously be accused of failing to respect the rights of culturally different societies and of neglecting to promote solidarist or post-Westphalian arrangements with states with similar normative commitments.

Although these three forms of international society differ in important respects they have one quality in common: each involves progress beyond one type of unjustified exclusion. A pluralist international society embodies movement beyond egocentric social systems which deny the rights of outsiders; a solidarist international society breaks with the practice of excluding individuals, minority nations and indigenous peoples as subjects of international law; and a post-Westphalian order overcomes the role which sovereignty, territoriality and national citizenship has played in obstructing international political action to reduce transnational harm. The contention that post-Westphalian communities have a duty to recognise that other human beings may not wish to become entangled in their arrangements reflects the belief that universalising ethical systems may be as exclusionary as the forms of life which they protest against. The post-Westphalian state must be alert to the danger that the bonds which unite each of the three conceptions of international society can be as exclusionary as the bonds which unite the members of separate national societies. Each of the three communities of discourse is necessary to secure the form of autonomy and dialogue which is appropriate to the communities concerned. One of the main tasks of the post-Westphalian state is to determine the appropriate framework of action for each of the relationships in which it is involved, and to do so through a process of open dialogue with others. In so doing, the post-Westphalian state can help to institutionalise the unique possibilities inherent in modernity, including the ideal of the universal communication community.

The Post-Exclusionary State: Answerability to Universal Rationales

The modern state has been the site on which unique methods of social control and radical opposition to the constraints on human autonomy have developed. Various possibilities for extending the boundaries of community so that the members of systematically excluded groups can enjoy greater autonomy have long been immanent within the dominant ideologies of modern states. Earlier systems of states ended in empire (Wight, 1977, ch. 1); the modern states-system is the first states-system which might be transformed by peace rather than by war. This invites the question of whether it is possible to recover the levels of cultural diversity which existed before the age of consolidated states without returning to imperial rule or incessant war (Tilly, 1992b, p. 717).

Carr's analysis of post-nationalist societies sheds light on the moral and political resources which make the peaceful transformation of the modern states-system conceivable. The very possibility of Carr's post-Westphalian arrangements exists as long as a majority of nation-states or the most powerful among them are committed to constitutional rule, deliberative politics, social welfare and universalistic moral beliefs which value radical cultural differences. The moral capital on which modern societies can draw for the purpose of creating post-Westphalian arrangements largely consists of these normative orientations. These are the qualities of modernity which make the unit-driven peaceful transformation of the international system possible.[24]

As noted earlier, the post-Westphalian order is one of three ways in which the moral and political boundaries of communities can be extended. It is therefore important to develop Carr's analysis by considering the ethical resources which have facilitated participation within the pluralist, solidarist and post-Westphalian forms of world political organisation. The remainder of this chapter considers three dimensions of the moral capital which has been accumulated in the history of organised resistance to increasing state power and embodied in more complex notions of citizenship. These are constitutionalism, the extension of democratic possibilities and the evolution of more sophisticated understandings of the social and economic preconditions of dialogic communities. The claim that the peaceful transformation of international society can be achieved by the general practice of extending the boundaries of moral and political associations is tenable where member states possess these moral resources. These are resources which distinguish modern international society from earlier societies of states.

To begin with constitutionalism, which has been a crucial resource in the struggle against the growth of state power: as McIlwain (1947, p. 22) argued in his important work on the subject, constitutionalism stands for the rule of law as opposed to despotic and arbitrary government. It was used in criticism of 'reasons of state' which were employed to defend royal prerogatives and exceptional powers in England in the seventeenth century (McIlwain, 1947, pp. 125–6). In the words of Thomas Paine, 'power without right' was the danger which constitutionalism was intended to overcome (McIlwain, 1947, pp. 2–9). In recent times, the idea of constitutionalism has become linked with political liberalism and with the democratic principle that responsible government involves public accountability to citizens. But constitutionalism in the Middle Ages did not presuppose modern conceptions of individual freedoms and democratic rights, and indeed there have been many circumstances in which democratic government and constitutionalism have been in conflict (McIlwain, 1947, pp. 145–6). Constitutionalism predates modern conceptions of liberal democracy, and can exist in societies which are far from liberal democratic in the Western sense. The Grotian tradition echoes this theme by observing that different political systems (liberal and non-liberal) have been able to agree on the need for the rule of law in international society.

Constitutionalism is not a purely domestic factor which lacks relevance for world politics. Fears that war would permit dangerous increases in executive power have often provoked efforts to make the holders of state power answerable to the domestic and international rule of law. Martin Wight suggested that England and the Netherlands, two powers which were at the centre of the struggle against absolutism in the eighteenth and nineteenth centuries, made the greatest contribution to the development of the balance of power (Wight, 1973, pp. 96–7). The constitutive principles of European international society were explicitly connected, Wight believed, with 'the political philosophy of constitutional government'; the multiple balance of power was the 'international counterpart' of 'liberal constitutionalism' (1973, p. 111).[25] The importance which states have attached to the practices of an international society reveal that 'some of the categories of constitutionalism' have been transferred from the domestic to the international domain (Wight, 1991, p. 103).

It is possible to develop Wight's argument by distinguishing between four forms of constitutionalism which can be transferred from the domestic to the international arena to create one or more of the conceptions of international society discussed above. The first form of constitutionalism, which is central to Wight's analysis, is collective action to maintain a balance of power against any state which attempts to become predominant in international society. The emergence of the modern European pluralist society of states in which there is an expectation of collective military or political action to prevent imperial concentrations of power is indebted to medieval notions of constitutional rule. A willingness to resort to arbitration and adjudication to settle inter-state disputes is a second illustration of the transfer of constitutional principles from the domestic to the international domain. The members of a pluralist international society insist on their sovereign right to choose when to bring disputes before international courts of law. Reduced insistence on sovereign prerogatives about such matters may be said to symbolise the development of a more solidarist construction of international society. A third means of transferring constitutional principles from the domestic sphere is evident in the development of international legal standards which governments are expected to meet in the area of individual human rights and minority rights. Recognition that individuals and minorities as well as states are entitled to be subjects of international law is evidence of a movement towards a more solidarist form of world political organisation. A fourth approach to internationalising the achievements of constitutionalism enforces respect for human rights by punishing serious violations. Extending the rule of law so that all individuals including fellow-nationals can be brought before international courts of law when they are suspected of human rights violations marks the transition from a solidarist conception of world politics, in which states retain the form if not the substance of sovereignty, to a post-Westphalian global order in which significant national powers are transferred to international legal authorities.

Constitutionalism was a crucial resource in the struggle against absolutism in the period when most European societies were still feudal in character, but the rule of law acquired vigorous support from members of the emergent bourgeoisie with the rise of modern capitalism. New patterns of political development occurred as the bourgeoisie 'gradually replaced a public sphere in which the ruler's power was merely represented *before* the people with a sphere in which public authority was publicly monitored through informed and critical discourse *by* the people' (T. McCarthy, in Habermas, 1992b, p. xi). Popular protest against taxation without representation revealed how increased state demands on citizens created pressures for the establishment of a more democratic public sphere. The state's assumption of the right to conscript its citizens engendered demands for the public recognition of the citizen's moral entitlement to political participation (Hintze, 1975, p. 211; D. Held, 1995, p. 57). The radical contention that sovereignty was located in the people, and not in the state or in the person of the monarch, accompanied popular demands for the creation of a more democratic public sphere (D. Held, 1995, p. 42).

Citizens mobilised to create a public domain which embodied the principles of publicity, consultation and representation so that rulers could no longer ignore larger political considerations which clashed with their sectional interests. Ensuring that the conduct of foreign policy was not shrouded in secrecy was a crucial means of ensuring that executive power was constrained by popular sovereignty. The prospects for extending democratic accountability beyond national frontiers have been extremely low because of recurrent international rivalries, but in the contemporary world it has become reasonable to suppose that constitutionally secure, democratic states in the core of the world economy may be witnessing the end of geopolitics (Richardson, 1993). Be that as it may, the tension between the principles espoused within the public sphere in democratic states and the realist principles which inform foreign policy has been a central theme in liberal thought for more than two centuries (D. Held, 1995, p. 73). The absence of moral consistency between the two realms was at the heart of Kant's argument that liberal states had special obligations to one another to create an international public sphere. Kant argued that 'in all matters concerning universal human duties, each individual requires to be convinced by reason that the coercion that prevails is lawful, otherwise he would be in contradiction with himself' (Reiss, 1970, p. 85). What was true in the lives of individuals also applied to sovereign states. To make force and fraud central to foreign policy would be to reveal that they were not the liberal societies they conceived themselves to be (Brewin, 1988, p. 326). Liberal states had to imagine themselves as co-legislators in a universal kingdom of ends in which publicising the principles underlying their actions was an obligation to the rest of humanity which had to be honoured to ensure moral consistency.

Commitments to publicity, consultation and representation underpin each of the three conceptions of international society under discussion. The principle that regular consultation between the great powers is essential for the maintenance of international order was a key feature of the pluralist conception of the society of states which emerged after the Napoleonic wars (Clark, 1989, ch. 6). The veto power enjoyed by the permanent members of the United Nations Security Council institutionalises the principle that legitimate international action requires the consent of the great powers. Modern international society has introduced a modicum of parliamentary diplomacy by endorsing Vattel's principle that small states are as sovereign as the most powerful kingdoms. International recognition of the idea of sovereign equality does not suspend enmity and suspicion between states, but their equal membership of the United Nations General Assembly is an important reminder that states now belong to a pluralist international society which first emerged in Europe and now embraces the entire world (Bull and Watson, 1984).

In their reflections on the transition from a European to a universal society of states, Bull and Watson (1984) asked whether the principles which had underpinned the European order commanded the support of the majority of non-European peoples. Nationalist elites in the anti-colonial period turned European principles of freedom and equality against the doctrines of racial and cultural supremacy which had been used to justify their exclusion from a Western-dominated international society. The language employed in the struggle against empire suggested that all societies across the world had embarked on a similar pattern of economic, political and cultural development which can be described as the path to modernity. Claims that growing inequalities of power and wealth negated the achievement of sovereignty introduced new moral themes into the diplomatic language of international society. Third World states began to argue for the reconstruction of the world economy and for the redistribution of the world's wealth (Jackson, 1990). The language of distributive justice in which Third World demands were couched was far from alien to the West, but what has been described as the cultural revolt against the West poses a more profound challenge to Western values. The relatively recent claim that the societies which are committed to these values do not have the right to question or criticise the practices of non-Western ways of life suggests that while states in the modern world can agree on the principles of a pluralist international society, they do not exhibit a common desire to establish more solidarist arrangements.[26]

Third World demands for the international recognition of the virtues of non-Western forms of life resonate with Western intellectual developments which have been critical of demeaning representations of other cultures (Said, 1978; Todorov, 1992). The emergence of the first global society of states requires the engagement with social principles and cultural perspectives which are unfamiliar, and even alien, to many in the West (C. Brown, 1988; Shapcott, 1994). The commitment to dialogue which was evident in the rise of the Concert System after the Napoleonic Wars did not require the depth of engagement with the wildly different which is imperative in the contemporary universal society of states. On one interpretation, dialogue in the context of added diversity is unlikely to result in a global moral consensus but may yield minimum agreement about the principles of international coexistence (C. Brown, 1988; 1995). A second approach inclines to the different and perhaps more 'optimistic' view that, for the first time in human history, very different societies are involved in 'consciously working out . . . a set of transcultural values and ethical standards' (Watson, 1987, p. 152). Support for this vision of a more solidarist future can be derived from the universal consensus on the evils of apartheid which developed in the 1970s and 1980s and from more recent trends to apply pressure to national governments which fail to comply with global normative expectations concerning human rights (Vincent and Wilson, 1993, pp. 128–9). The expanding international law of the rights of minorities, indigenous peoples, women and children offers further support for the belief that radical dialogue between diverse societies might yet result in limited progress towards a more solidarist version of international society.

Which conception of international society will ultimately prevail is impossible to predict, and it may be wise to suppose that the pluralist and solidarist conceptions of international relations will continue to coexist within their respective domains. But as liberal accounts of the liberal zone of peace observe, important pockets of solidarism already exist within the wider pluralist society of states. Doyle (1982, 1986) argues that shared respect for societies which are based on consent has encouraged the abolition of war in the relations between liberal states. Liberal states have replaced the competition for security and power with novel experiments in joint rule by drawing on domestic preferences for the politics of publicity, dialogue and consent (Brewin, 1988, pp. 330–1). A solidarist conception of international society involving liberal states has developed within a universal society of states in which the majority of states prefer pluralist principles of global governance.

The mechanisms of joint rule in the liberal zone of peace can take two forms. The first was described in Kant's political writings. Kant argued that human beings have 'a natural vocation' to communicate with one another 'especially in matters affecting mankind as a whole' (Reiss, 1970, pp. 85–6). Heads of state had a special duty to establish wider communities of discourse which would eradicate the tension between state practice and natural right (Kant, 1970b, pp. 228–9). Imagining ways in which individuals could come together as world citizens who participated in joint rule was not one of Kant's concerns (Archibugi, 1995), and it has hardly been central to the subsequent political theory of the inter-liberal peace. But just as pockets of solidarism can emerge within the broader framework of a pluralist international society, so can closer forms of political cooperation which embody a second conception of joint rule develop inside the framework of the solidarist zone of peace. Radical images of joint rule which envisage a transnational citizenry are central to the political theory of cosmopolitan democracy. David Held (1995, pp. 223 and 233) argues that a system of 'cosmo-political governance' in which citizens come together as participants in trans-national networks of joint rule has become essential now that citizenship rights can no longer be 'sustained simply within the framework which brought them into being' – the framework of the sovereign nation-state. States cannot expect to monopolise decisions about membership, citizen-ship and global responsibilities in either of the two mechanisms of joint rule mentioned above; but in the second version dialogue about these matters involves all members of the transnational citizenry rather than the narrower realm of Kant's heads of state. New patterns of state-formation have to be imagined at this point, where the emergence of an intricate system of transnational rule marks the transition from a solidarist to a post-Westphalian society of states. Sophisticated under-standings of the social and economic preconditions of dialogic com-munities need to be embodied in post-Westphalian frameworks of cooperation to complete the transition.

Ensuring that the members of excluded groups enjoy equal rights of access to the public domain has been one of the central ambitions of radical political movements. Efforts to equalise protection under the law and rights of political participation remain important but they are seldom regarded as adequate unless accompanied by attempts to remove social and economic barriers to truly dialogic communities. Socialist organisations have concentrated on the respects in which class inequalities bar the development of full participation; feminist movements have challenged the constraining role of traditional conceptions of gender roles; identity politics, more generally, has resisted the patterns of language and culture which thwart the aspirations of minority cultures. Counter-hegemonic movements have struggled to equalise rights of access to the public domain, but most have wanted to do more than extend rights of participation within the existing rules of the game. Greatly increasing the range of permissible disagreements within the political community, and superseding the nationalist premise that all citizens should rally behind some dominant conception of collective identity, have also been principal elements of the ongoing struggle against systems of unjust exclusion.

Universalistic conceptions of ethics have been influential in equalising rights of access to the public sphere within sovereign states, and they have been important in resisting the tendency to confine the moral community to fellow-citizens. Constitutionalism, democratic commitments and recognition of the various constraints upon the development of dialogic communities have made their impression upon the modern society of states in which universalistic norms continue to create anxieties about wrongful exclusion in many of the constituent national parts. Membership of a pluralist or solidarist international society rests upon a prior decision to widen the boundaries of the moral community in order to do justice to the interests of outsiders. Participation within a post-Westphalian international society rests upon the commitment to widen the boundaries of the political community so that insiders and outsiders can be associated as the equal members of a transnational citizenry. Post-Westphalian arrangements break the nexus between sovereignty and citizenship and internationalise the struggle against wrongful exclusion. Instances of transnational harm confront nation-states which are committed to ending unjust exclusion within their boundaries with an obligation to cooperate with like-minded states in ventures which secure the autonomy of their citizens. Progressive state structures are those which deploy their powers to realise such objectives (Elshtain, 1994; Lawler, 1994; Tickner, 1995; Wheeler, 1996). States which block these developments are not as enlightened as they may claim to be since they fail to contribute to the unfinished project of modernity.

Conclusions

Resistance to the new monopolies of power which occurred because of state-building took the form of a long battle for legal and political rights in Europe; and opposition to the increasing material inequalities which occurred because of capitalist industrialisation has involved a similarly laborious struggle to secure and maintain economic rights. Early pressures for legal and political rights which involved the rising bourgeoisie turned into a larger contest in which a range of systematically excluded groups organised to acquire appropriate rights. The struggle to gain access to the social and economic resources which would enable these groups to exercise their legal and political rights became the principal dynamic in the widening dispute. The dispute has widened further as citizens have become as concerned with the impact of moral-cultural constraints on their lives as with the pressures of state-building and capitalist industrialisation. Resistance to the different axes of exclusion has generated sophisticated critiques of the dominant modes of legitimation within modern societies. The notion of a dialogic community in which equals are free to decide the principles of inclusion and exclusion which regulate their lives is the highest normative ideal to emerge from the tension between intensifications of control and democratising tendencies which is inherent within modernity.

The development of more complex measurements of the legitimacy of social and political arrangements is not just a domestic matter for nation-states. The formation of wider communities of political discourse is an essential step for societies which have reworked those features of the ties between citizens which violate higher ethical ideals. The critique of exclusion within sovereign states has been influential in generating three broader frameworks of political action which ensure that their separateness from the rest of the world does not turn into excessive particularism. Each of these political frameworks widens the boundaries of community in the light of universalistic commitments but each strikes the balance between the universal and the particular in a distinctive way. A pluralist international society strikes a balance between the principle of state sovereignty and universal principles of order and peaceful coexistence. A solidarist international society endorses the principle of state sovereignty but strives to balance it with a commitment to universal moral principles which address the injustices suffered by the victims of human rights violations, whether these be solitary individuals, indigenous peoples, or ethnic and other minority groups. A post-Westphalian society promotes greater universality and diversity by striving to balance demands for the recognition of deep diversity with the ideal of transnational citizenship.

Each of these frameworks releases, in Nelson's language, societal potentials for participating in wider communities of discourse and enlarging answerability to universal rationales which are already inherent in modern societies with their commitments to citizenship rights. Each framework reveals how the progressive side of modernity, which Hegel stressed in his account of the role of the state in harmonising potentially competing ethical principles, can prevail over the dark side of modernity, which Carr highlighted in his analysis of how the equilibrium between nationalism and internationalism was destroyed earlier in the twentieth century.

National commitments to citizenship make participation within these widened communities possible and necessary. Constitutionalist notions of limited government have been important in shaping the evolution of a pluralist conception of international society. Democratic ideals and commitments to the principle of national self-determination have been crucial elements in the politics of resisting exclusionary conceptions of international society which confined membership to European states and privileged the rights of sovereign states over the rights of minority nations, indigenous peoples and individuals. More recent conceptions of the social and economic rights of national citizens have encouraged approaches to international society which declare that affluent societies have moral obligations to the global poor and maintain that hegemonic cultures have duties to repair the damage caused to subjugated forms of life. These sentiments have had an important impact upon the pluralist and solidarist conceptions of the society of states. Post-Westphalian states which surrender their monopoly powers regarding decisions about the distribution of membership, citizenship and wider global responsibilities take the more radical step of breaking with the supposition that the sovereign nation-state is the only legitimate form of political community. The feasibility of such states poses a challenge to the neo-realist claim that states are bound to be functionally similar given the constraints within international anarchy.[27] The appropriate rejoinder to neo-realism is that the post-Westphalian state is a new kind of state which internationalises the struggle against the tyranny of unjust exclusion. The post-Westphalian state transforms the dominant principles of association and disassociation which declare that citizenship only has meaning within the boundaries of the territorial state.

Hegel argued that the boundaries of the modern state divided the harmonious realm of relations between fellow-citizens from the conflictual domain of relations between sovereign states and also marked the outer limits of effective close political cooperation. But the idea of citizenship which stands as one of the main achievements of modernity provides the moral resources with which to build still wider frameworks of cooperation, such as the pluralist and solidarist forms of international society. The moral capital which has accumulated in the struggle to extend and deepen the rights of citizens is a resource that can be used to envisage new conceptions of community and citizenship which are freed from the constraints of national sovereignty.

6
Community and Citizenship in the Post-Westphalian Era

With the rise of the nation-state, one identity was singled out and made central to modern political life. Shared national identity was deemed to be the crucial social bond which links citizens together in the ideal political community (Beetham, 1984, p. 220). Fascist states claimed that all other loyalties and identities were devoid of political significance, but most states have denied that the boundaries of the moral and political community are co-extensive. Cosmopolitan sentiments have checked the tendency to limit membership of the moral community to co-nationals or fellow-citizens. The members of modern states have had a dual identity as citizens and as human beings, and some have constructed themselves as world citizens as well as national citizens because of the continuing appeal of cosmopolitan convictions. But whatever their stance on cosmopolitanism, most have belonged to communities which have been willing to preserve an international society of states.

Notions of world citizenship usually refer to compassion for the rest of humanity; alternatively, they have been used to defend the creation of post-sovereign arrangements in which the whole human race owes its allegiance to global political institutions. The dominant traditions of political theory have often criticised efforts to enlist citizenship in support of these aspirations. They have argued that the civic ideal of active participation in politics can only be realised in the arrangements which bind co-nationals within a common way of life. They have stressed that there is no equivalent in the world of international relations. Some branches of political theory defend Hegel's claim that it is foolish to turn conceptions of world citizenship against the nation-state since it remains the only mode of political organisation which is capable of concretising the civic ideal (Miller, 1995). Some reiterate Rousseau's observation that citizens have special obligations to one another which they cannot extend to aliens without eroding the delicate foundations of their own community (Miller, forthcoming). Several influential strands of political thought over the past two centuries have fused citizenship with sovereignty, nationality and territoriality, and they have been quick to observe that citizenship, properly so-called, loses all meaning when detached from the nation-state.

The dominant strands of modern political theory may be sceptical or critical of the notion of world citizenship but most argue that citizens have duties to the members of other political communities which they have to reconcile with their obligations to one another. Hegel is a key representative of the tradition which maintains that harmonising the spheres of universal and particular obligations is one of the great achievements of the modern state. Universal morality influenced the state through its participation in a pluralist international society. Kant is the foremost analyst of the failure of the modern state to comply with the laws of world citizenship which require the avoidance of hostility and harm to foreigners (Williams and Booth, 1996, p. 91). In Kant's view, observance of the duties of cosmopolitan citizenship need not entail the surrender of sovereignty but rather a broadening of the moral purposes which its exercise should seek to realise. Membership of a solidarist international society made it possible for liberal states to progress in this direction. Kant's argument that the modern state had yet to harmonise the claims of universality and difference was extended further in the writings of E. H. Carr, who envisaged new forms of political association which made deeper inroads into the principle of state sovereignty. Carr recognised that claims to national sovereignty did not prevent states from acknowledging that citizens and aliens belonged to a wider moral community; nor did they rule out respect for the principles of an international society of states. From Carr's perspective, what was troubling about national sovereignty was its role in preventing citizens and aliens from associating as equals within a wider international political community. Carr's conception of forms of political organisation in which the union of sovereignty, nationality, territoriality and citizenship was dissolved, and replaced by a new European transnational citizenry, was a major advance upon Kantian critical theory. His analysis indicated that a commitment to the post-Westphalian experiment involves closer cooperation than either the pluralist or the solidarist international society requires of its constituent parts.

Carr assumed that loyalties to traditional state structures would remain important in future European institutions but he was emphatic that they would have to coexist with wider internationalist sentiments and with loyalties to the minority nations which had been marginalised or suppressed in the course of state-formation. The new form of political community which overcame invidious dualisms between citizens and aliens, and between hegemonic and subaltern groups, would remain bounded by virtue of being confined to Europe. There would be no requirement that the members of that community should share one dominant national identity or recognise the supremacy of a single political authority. Breaking with the classical nation-state, post-Westphalian communities would promote a transnational citizenry with multiple political allegiances and without the need for submission to a central sovereign power. This condition of diverse loyalties and multiple authorities would be an unlikely breeding ground for the re-emergence of the totalising project.

Critical international theory defends the normative ideal of forms of political community which release societal potentials for achieving levels of universality and difference. Casting light on the prospects for advancing in this direction is one of the primary sociological aims of critical theory. Reflecting on how modern societies can use the moral and political resources which were accumulated in the struggle against exclusion to secure these objectives is a central goal of praxeological inquiry. The evolution of national conceptions of citizenship is especially important in this regard because it creates the possibility of more radical trajectories of political development in which higher levels of universality and difference unfold simultaneously and the prospects for totalising projects are greatly eroded. States which are wedded to modern conceptions of citizenship are obliged by these convictions to participate in each of the three modes of international society mentioned earlier. They are obligated to cooperate with radically different states to establish and maintain a pluralist international society; they have an obligation to collaborate with states which have similar conceptions of human rights to create a solidarist international society; and they have the more far-reaching obligation when dealing with like-minded states which expose one another to high levels of transnational harm to join them in designing post-Westphalian arrangements. There are important differences between the pluralist or solidarist forms of international society and a post-Westphalian configuration of states. Striking an appropriate balance between universality and difference within pluralist and solidarist arrangements does not involve serious encroachment on the principle of national sovereignty, nor does it require efforts to create a transnational citizenship. Within post-Westphalian arrangements, on the other hand, the enterprise of realising societal potentials for deeper commitments to universality and difference does entail significant inroads into state sovereignty and the concurrent development of a transnational citizenry.

Like-minded states which are exposed to high levels of transnational harm have an obligation to replace state monopoly powers over decisions concerning the distribution of membership, citizenship and global responsibilities with bold democratic experiments in transnational rule.

This chapter defends the ideal of a post-Westphalian society of states in which like-minded states are vulnerable to significant levels of transnational harm. It then explores the nature of their obligation to enter into pluralist or solidarist arrangements with societies outside their ranks. The argument is in five parts. Part one considers Marshall's account of the role which citizenship has played in modern systems of inclusion and exclusion. Marshall observed that dominant groups have sought to maintain their privileges by restricting legal and political rights whereas subordinate groups have attempted to create more inclusive societies by increasing access to these and other rights. Part two observes that the political actors which have pressed for the extension of citizenship rights have tended to accept the legitimacy of the sovereign state. As noted in the previous chapter, the emergence of social citizenship in the first part of the twentieth century led to the intensification of wrongful exclusion. Since then, citizenship has remained one of the principal devices through which separate states have monopolised control of valuable resources and meaningful opportunities. Part two proceeds to argue that it is increasingly unlikely, in the context of rising instances of, and opportunities for, transnational harm, that the civic ideal will be preserved if citizens rely exclusively on national political institutions. Under these conditions, the ideals of citizenship clash with the sovereign nation-state in which they were first developed. The praxeological task is to use the moral resources which have been deposited in the idea of citizenship to imagine forms of political community which harmonise the claims of universality and difference by despatching state powers to stronger local and transnational political authorities.

Part three considers Bull's analysis of the possibilities for moving beyond the nation-state in Western Europe in the 1970s. Bull's observations about the feasibility of a neo-medieval political framework in that region reveal how one might build upon Carr's account of alternatives to the modern sovereign state. The central theme in Bull's analysis is the possibility of new relationships between sub-state, national and transnational authorities and solidarities. Part four develops Bull's approach by arguing that movement towards a neo-medieval or post-Westphalian European international society is necessary to protect and extend the achievements of national citizenship, and that the commitment to citizenship generates obligations to move in this direction.

An inquiry into the nature of post-Westphalian citizenship would be incomplete without some comments on the principles which should inform the relations between post-Westphalian states and the rest of the world. Part five turns to the issue of how states which are in the process of dissolving the union between sovereignty, territoriality, nationality and citizenship should conduct their relations with other societies which do not find the vision of a post-Westphalian community especially congenial. In these circumstances the pluralist and solidarist conceptions of international society are the appropriate communities of discourse. They can complement post-Westphalian arrangements by ensuring that global governance is based on the consent of an increasing proportion of the human race, especially its most excluded members. Cosmopolitan citizenship refers to the commitment to perfecting these mechanisms for wooing the consent of others; it refers to the conviction that strengthening these arrangements is an important means of realising the ideal of a universal communication community.

One question which inevitably arises is whether any combination of states or particular region provides the model for post-Westphalian international society. As Falk (1994, p. 136) argues, there is some evidence that Europe has embarked on 'the most significant political innovation' since the modern territorial state emerged in the seventeenth century. Efforts to formulate conceptions of European citizenship within the European Union, and the measures which members of the Council of Europe and the Organisation for Security and Cooperation in Europe have taken to safeguard individual and minority rights, may remain weak but they are encouraging legal and moral innovations from which more extensive developments may grow. The role which more reformist states, such as the Scandinavian states, play in international society is also significant for praxeological inquiry (Tickner, 1995, pp. 135–6; Lawler, 1994, forthcoming). Although these developments influence the analysis which follows, the aim is not to develop an empirical inquiry into how Europe will evolve if current trends continue. What follows is an exercise in immanent critique which highlights the possibilities for realising the higher levels of political autonomy which are already promised by the idea of citizenship.[1] The central task is to set out some of the primary duties and responsibilities of the post-Westphalian state, recognising that, although existing states in Europe and elsewhere often encourage these trends, they can also frustrate them in various ways.

Citizenship and its Development

Above all else, citizenship refers to the right of political participation, duties to other citizens and the responsibility for the welfare of the community as a whole. These themes were central to Aristotle's claim that citizens are 'those who are able and willing to rule and be ruled with a view to attaining a way of life according to goodness' (Aristotle, 1960, Book III, xiii, section 12). Active citizenship was the exclusive preserve of adult males in the ancient Greek polis; slavery and the subordination of women and metics comprised the other side of the civic ideal. The extension of citizenship rights in the Roman empire abandoned the commitment to public participation which had been integral to the idea of the citizen in Athens' democratic phase. Citizenship was narrowed to mean the right of protection under the law. These legal rights had little significance for the mass of the population which lacked real economic and political power.[2] While Rome universalised citizenship, it also reduced its meaning and diminished its role in political life.

During the last two centuries states have come under enormous pressure to grant citizenship to all members of the community, and to ensure that the sense of sharing in the government of society regains some of its classical meaning. Modern citizenship failed to embrace participatory ideals in the early stages of its development since the rising bourgeoisie was principally concerned with extracting the right to enjoy the rule of law from repressive absolutist regimes. Later claims for representative government aimed to secure a broad framework of legal *and* political rights for subordinate groups. But granting citizenship rights to an increasing proportion of the adult population in societies which experienced growing class inequalities bred new claims for deepening the meaning of citizenship. The crucial argument was that the mass of the population could not make effective use of their legal and political rights unless they commanded the requisite economic and social resources. As a result of subordinate class pressures, citizenship in the early part of the twentieth century came to mean rights to social welfare and, as a corollary, duties on the part of the strong to assist the weaker members of society. The development of citizenship rights has involved a series of struggles to dismantle the modes of exclusion which prevented marginal groups from enjoying fully-fledged membership of the political community. Struggles to universalise citizenship rights, and to create the social and economic conditions which ensure that their possession makes a significant difference to the life-chances of individual members, remain at the centre of radical politics in modern states.

A certain dialectic guided the development of citizenship in the modern European state. T. H. Marshall (1973, pp. 71ff) offered this interpretation in his influential study of the evolution of citizenship rights in Britain over the last two centuries. Citizenship in Britain evolved through three stages, beginning with civil rights, to which political and social rights were subsequently added. Eighteenth-century demands for civil rights which revolved around access to the courts of law opened the first phase in the development of the modern idea of citizenship. The meaning of citizenship was broadened in the nineteenth century to include rights of participation 'in the exercise of political power' which were met through greater access to the parliamentary process. Citizenship was extended further in the twentieth century to include the right to welfare, and 'the right to share to the full in the social heritage' which required universal participation in the educational system.

Marshall has been accused of 'evolutionism' (Mann, 1987). Be that as it may, he was correct to argue that the idea of citizenship has possessed its own forward momentum. The eighteenth-century claim that citizens should possess certain basic legal rights came under significant 'developmental pressure' because it was no more than a partial victory for human autonomy (Honneth, 1995, p. 115). The right of protection under the law was deemed to be incomplete without the additional right of participation in the law-making process. Rights of political participation came under similar challenge on the grounds that 'the formal recognition of an equal capacity for rights [is] not enough' (Marshall, 1973, p. 91). Efforts to reduce inequalities of power and wealth were required to ensure respect for the principle that all citizens have an equal right to be fully-fledged members of the political community.

The systematic reconsideration of the moral significance of the differences between members of the same society has been central to the development of citizenship rights. As Honneth (1995, p. 118) has argued, the expanding consensus that there are 'no longer any convincing arguments with which to oppose the demands of excluded groups for equality' has been a critical factor in the universalisation of citizenship rights. The extension of rights to the members of previously excluded groups occurred as the differences of class, gender, ethnicity or race, which had legitimated the denial of citizenship, lost their moral relevance. But, as Marshall argued, efforts to discount the differences between citizens were flawed unless they were accompanied by measures to ensure that the weaker members of society could fully exercise their civic rights. Recognition of the need for 'sensitivity to difference' (Honneth, 1995, p. 118) has meant that the practice of universalising rights has been accompanied by specific strategies which try to ensure that citizenship rights are more than formal rights for the least powerful groups in society. On the one hand, then, the extension of citizenship has been associated with the development of an ethical point of view which argues that various social differences no longer possess moral relevance; but on the other hand, the expansion of citizenship rights to include social and economic entitlements has occurred because social differences clearly have profound political relevance for commitments to the free society.

Societies which have covered this much ground invariably face two further developmental pressures in the age of globalisation and fragmentation. They confront pressures to make adjustments to citizenship to ensure due recognition of cultural differences within the nation-state, and many are invited to explore the possibility of creating transnational citizenship rights which overcome invidious dualisms between insiders and outsiders. Each development continues the dialectical advance of citizenship which Marshall analysed, and each involves societies in additional sensitivities to difference. Consideration of the second of these pressures is deferred until the next section.

The first developmental pressure exists because societies are more aware than they were when Marshall's influential essay was first published of how modes of exclusion anchored in hierarchical conceptions of gender, culture and race deny large sections of the population full membership of the political community. An important critique of Marshall reveals the nature of recent demands for the further transformation of citizenship. The critical point is that Marshall's emphasis on social rights highlighted the economic constraints to which large numbers of the white male population were exposed under capitalism, but it neglected the axes of exclusion and domination faced by large numbers of women and by the members of ethnic and racial minorities (Vogel, 1991; Walby, 1994, p. 388; Fraser and Gordon, 1994, p. 93). At first glance, the emphasis on these forms of exclusion contributes to the developmental logic which is set out in Marshall's framework. The essential point is that racial, cultural and gender differences do not justify the practice of denying subaltern groups the rights which the dominant strata already enjoy. Denying the moral relevance of these distinctions has contributed to the process of universalising rights. More deeply, however, simply universalising the existing rights of citizens is not enough to reduce the forms of exclusion regularly encountered by those who belong to subordinate groups. As already noted, Marshall was emphatic that extending legal and political rights across society may make very little substantive difference to the lives of the most vulnerable members of the political community, and on this basis he argued for greater sensitivity to class differences within society. But sensitivity to class differences and sensitivity to racial, cultural and gender differences do not have exactly the same implications for the theory and practice of citizenship.

Phillips (1991, pp. 81–3; 1993) explains the nature of the contrast by arguing there is a short step between acknowledging that all citizens are equal despite their differences to concluding that racial, gender and cultural differences do not matter at all. In short, to invite different groups to transcend their particularity and to work for the greater good is to issue a summons to submit to the hegemonic culture. One of the limitations of abstract, universalistic notions of citizenship is that they drive 'particularity and difference' into the private domain (Mouffe, 1993, p. 81). Social rights which endeavour to correct inequalities of wealth may fail to address many issues which deeply concern many women along with the members of culturally marginal groups. Welfare citizenship promises to improve the position of the most economically vulnerable social strata so that they can make effective use of legal and political rights. But this response to inequalities of power and wealth is perfectly compatible with the determination to preserve the dominant conceptions of culture and identity within the community. Although the politics of recognition is far from unconcerned with the redistribution of wealth, it is essentially preoccupied with transforming the forms of cultural hegemony which mean that subject cultures do not feel at home in the political community.

Feminist movements, national minorities and indigenous peoples' organisations illustrate the point because they do not strive to be incorporated within the community on the same terms as everyone else. They are not simply concerned with universalising citizenship rights or with ensuring that these rights are substantive rather than formal. They are emphatic that abstract notions of citizenship which affirm the equality of all members of the community despite their differences should yield to 'group-differentiated' citizenship which bestows public recognition upon the special interests and needs of subaltern cultural groups (Young, 1990).[3] The public acknowledgement of cultural diversity which admits an array of group-specific rights is a significant advance beyond Marshall's analysis. The politics of recognition demands new expressions of sensitivity to difference and new possibilities for expanding the range of permissible disagreements within political communities.

What remains valid in Marshall's account is the argument that the original claims for citizenship in the eighteenth century provoked demands for a more comprehensive understanding of what it means to be a full member of a political community. Each re-articulation of the idea of citizenship has been associated with struggles to enlarge the circle of those who are entitled to participate as equals in public deliberations about the nature of the collectivity; and each has involved efforts to deepen the meaning and expand the significance of citizenship for the members of excluded groups. Of course, the notion that citizenship has been subject to specific developmental pressures is different from the claim that the politics of the last two centuries reveals the gradual but inevitable ascent from rudimentary to advanced conceptions of the rights of citizens. Exclusionary distinctions between full members of the political community and those who belong to what might be called the lumpen-citizenry exist in all societies, albeit to differing degrees.[4] Even so, societies in which citizenship has been influential in constituting the social bond have become involved in peculiar tensions and contradictions which arise less starkly, when they surface at all, in societies where political claims are not couched in the language of citizenship. Demands for dismantling unjust systems of exclusion inevitably result, invoking the progressive side of modernity; and pressures to further rationalise the moral code, and to take its political implications seriously, ensue with equal inevitability but without the guarantee of success. The possibility of further modifications of social and political life which give expression to more radical formulations of citizenship is immanent within these developments.

To recapitulate and extend the argument: there have been three main phases in the development of citizenship, and at each stage social actors have challenged past assumptions about the moral and political significance of the differences which exist between them. In the first phase, the conviction that various class, gender and other differences are morally relevant was questioned, and the belief that all members of society should have exactly the same legal and political rights gained ground. The second phase involved greater sensitivity to social differences and the introduction of entitlements in the sphere of health, education and welfare to ensure that the weakest members of society had the power to exercise their legal and political rights. In the third phase, sensitivity to difference has been broadened to take account of the extent to which public norms express little more than the values of the dominant cultural group and prevent the culturally marginal from feeling at home in their own society. These three stages have contributed to the triple transformation of political community.

The third stage creates interesting possibilities for extending the moral and political boundaries of the community because of the changes it makes to the social bond.[5] In this context, the social bond no longer rests on a totalising conception of community, or assumes a collective identity which all members are obliged to share. As Mouffe (1993) argues, the 'ethico-political bond' in this form of political community brings radical democrats together to promote certain 'common concerns' such as the eradication of the social barriers to fully-fledged membership.[6] What unites is the will to promote the freedom and equality of all, but what binds need not place the society at odds with the rest of humanity. Where the 'ethico-political bond' breaks with totalising conceptions of community, and 'where it is anchored in the universalistic rights of personhood' (Soysal, 1996, pp. 23–5), the prospects for widening the moral *and* political boundaries of the association so that citizens and aliens can participate in transnational rule are greatly enhanced (Linklater, 1990a, pp. 30–3 and 116–18). The developmental pressures which are present in societies which are committed to universalistic ethical codes are more likely to prevail as a result. New modes of transnational citizenship which bring insiders and outsiders together to promote their common concern with freedom and equality become possible.

The Problem of the Exclusionary Sovereign State

Citizenship has been central to the politics of inclusion and exclusion in modern states (Brubaker, 1992). Efforts to restrict citizenship have been a key weapon in the exercise of monopolising social privileges and opportunities, and struggles to extend citizenship rights have been crucial elements in the politics of challenging the uneven distribution of social entitlements. Systematically excluded groups have employed notions of second-class citizenship when contesting their allotted place within stratified social systems. Mobilised subaltern groups have challenged dominant elites to comply with the egalitarian principles which suffuse the dominant ideologies of modernity. Extensions of citizenship which followed prolonged intervals of social struggle to obtain full membership of the political community have helped create more inclusive societies.

Increased rivalry between more exclusionary sovereign states was one result of the development of more inclusive national communities in the early twentieth century, as Carr (1945) argued. The extension of citizenship rights sharpened the tension between obligations to the state and obligations to humanity within European international society. Carr believed that modern societies had accumulated sufficient moral capital to contemplate establishing wider political communities in which transnational governance would extend the achievements of national citizenship. In this form of international society, states would no longer purchase their individual autonomy by sacrificing or limiting the freedom of others or ground their collective identities in demeaning representations of other cultures. Exclusionary conceptions of national citizenship would be opened up to a wider ethical point of view.

It is clear that first impressions of national citizenship seem to rule out any significant movement beyond the nation-state. Citizenship remains one of the principal forms of closure in the modern world precisely because it confers exclusive rights on insiders. As refugees and aliens know only too well, the tightening of citizenship laws and immigration rules in affluent societies prevents 'the dilution of the benefits of industrialization' by excluding those who were born elsewhere (Murphy, 1988, p. 74). The modern unity of sovereignty, territoriality, citizenship and nationality has ensured that the basic moral tension between obligations to other citizens and obligations to the rest of humanity has persisted. But the debates surrounding the morality of war, global social justice and human rights nevertheless reveal that the ethical issue of whether obligations to co-nationals should have priority over obligations to outsiders is still deeply contested. Profound moral doubts about the rights and liberties which citizens can presume when dealing with outsiders are central to the nature of the modern social bond.

Many theories of the state and international relations argue that the state has to take account of duties beyond borders, though few go so far as to argue for transnational citizenship. Aristotle's analysis of the qualities of the citizen first raised the important moral question of whether arrangements between citizens could justify disregarding the interests of outsiders. In the sections of *The Politics* which explore the differences between the 'good man' and the 'good citizen', Aristotle stressed possible tensions between civic virtues and wider humanitarian considerations. The shame involved in treating outsiders 'in ways which [citizens] would refuse to acknowledge as just, or even expedient, among themselves' was an important theme in his thought. Good citizens had to ensure that what was 'lawful' in foreign policy outweighed calculations of sheer expediency (Aristotle, 1960, Book VII, ii, sections 12–14). A similar concern with balancing the rights of citizens and the rights of human beings has run through modern political theories of the state. The contention that the appropriate balance between civic and human morality is struck by the state's respect for the principles of international society has been a significant theme in the theory of international relations. There the matter might rest if states could be entrusted with ensuring that the interests of insiders and outsiders received appropriate moral consideration, but Rousseau's analysis of the tragic qualities of international relations stressed that this is a precarious moral equation (Hoffmann, 1965, ch. 3). Rousseau argued that the state's battle for survival and security was the cause of a deep division within the moral self in which the difficulty of being 'a good citizen of a nation and a good citizen of the world' at one and the same time was readily apparent. In Rousseau's judgement, this moral tension within the self could not be eradicated by creating new forms of political community which overcame the division between citizens and aliens. There was no obvious line of escape from the international state of nature. Kant, who was similarly troubled by the ease with which citizens could become 'the enemies of mankind', was the first leading modern political theorist to imagine new patterns of development in which world citizenship and the duty to extend hospitality to the whole of humankind would erode the ethical particularism of the sovereign state. For Kant, the obligation to evolve in this direction was grounded in the commitment to human autonomy which already underlies national conceptions of citizenship.

The belief that universal moral principles underpin citizenship was a central theme in the secularised natural law theories. Pufendorf and Vattel argued that citizenship of the state concretised and enforced the imperfect moral rights and duties which belonged to the whole of humanity in the original state of nature (Linklater, 1990a). Their supposition that national citizenship concretised universal human rights to freedom and equality was necessarily at odds with totalising projects which threaten to restrict membership of the moral community to insiders. Kant's miserable comforters recognised that sovereign states could not disown all obligations to outsiders without contradicting their essential nature, although they were anxious to defend the principle that states must have the right to determine their own international obligations. Constructed in this way, the modern idea of citizenship is laden with tensions and instabilities. On the one hand, citizenship embodies the right to freedom and equality which is the property of the whole of humanity; on the other hand, citizenship is invested in separate political communities which can happily purchase their own autonomy by limiting the freedom of others. Kant's response to this uneasy compromise argued that relations within and between states should similarly be governed by the rule of law. Answerability to the principle of publicity should apply equally in the two spheres of domestic and international politics. In this way national citizenship would cease being in opposition to the law of humanity.

Although Kant argued for a political condition in which moral agents would become co-legislators in a universal kingdom of ends, his defence of world citizenship called for a widening of humanity's moral horizons so that states would not secure their own autonomy by exporting harm to outsiders. Kant did not argue for the establishment of institutional arrangements which would permit citizens and aliens to come together as active participants in joint rule (Archibugi, 1995). His principal claim was that republican regimes were obliged because of the rise of economic and social interdependence to extend their commitment to constitutionalism by upholding the international rule of law. Modern conditions require more radical remedies. The very high levels of interdependence which exist between liberal democratic societies require close cooperation to create a transnational citizenry.

Three arguments have been made in support of this claim. First, citizens cannot rely on national democratic arrangements to give them much control over their individual and collective lives under conditions of complex interdependence.[7] The achievements of national citizenship are now threatened by the assumption that citizenship cannot exist apart from the sovereign nation-state. Second, the vast number of international organisations which have been designed to manage a more interdependent world face a democratic deficit because their decisions do not require popular consent. Third, democratic theory and practice has to break with the supposition that national populations have the sovereign right to withhold their consent from any developments within international organisations which clash with their conception of national interests. The sovereign state cannot claim to be the only relevant moral community as the level of transnational harm continues to rise with intensifications of interdependence (D. Held, 1995, p. 18). In these circumstances, like-minded states cannot assume that it is legitimate to perpetuate insular forms of life in which the differences between fellow-nationals and non-nationals are assumed to have deep moral significance. Attaching too much moral significance to the differences between citizens and aliens smacks of earlier practices of imputing more moral significance than is justified to the differences of class, gender, ethnicity or race. For these reasons, efforts to ensure that citizenship remains inextricably linked with sovereignty, territoriality and nationality lack normative justification. Increasing transnational harm confronts like-minded states with the obligation to promote the goals of greater freedom and autonomy by fostering the development of a transnational citizenry.

Progress in universalising rights of political participation on the grounds that the distinction between citizen and alien has lost its traditional moral relevance is important but insufficient without parallel advances in the culture of sensitivity to difference. Marshall's argument that full membership of the political community is impossible if citizens do not have sufficient economic and social power to be able to exercise their rights is equally relevant to national and international arrangements. It has special importance given the danger that the main agents and leading beneficiaries of globalisation will construct notions of world order and transnational citizenship which allow them to pursue their interests without much accountability to wider political constituencies (Falk, 1994). Progress in universalising legal, political and social rights, remote as it is, would be incomplete without important gains in sensitivity to cultural differences. The triple transformation of political communities is necessary to ensure a radical break with the totalising project. But in the context of globalisation, designing forms of citizenship which will promote a transnational, multicultural social democracy is essential to counterbalance the increased opportunities for elite dominance which accompany the decline of the modern territorial state.

Beyond the Westphalian State

To summarise the argument thus far, modern ideas about citizenship are contradictory and unstable on two planes. First, although the idea of citizenship has been used to deny insiders access to prized resources and meaningful opportunities, its radical potential has been turned against assorted systems of exclusion within nation-states. Calls for legal and political equality in the face of marked social distinctions, and efforts to achieve greater sensitivity to difference, have been important elements in the dialectics of national citizenship. Second, although citizenship confers rights on citizens which outsiders cannot claim, its radical potential can be turned against the very political framework within which citizens have defined their own rights and duties – the sovereign state which is one of the last bastions of exclusion to attract critical scrutiny (Murphy, 1988). The universalisation of citizenship rights is part of this radical potential, as is the movement towards greater respect for social and cultural differences. The ambiguities of citizenship have created the possibility of advances beyond the sovereign state to new forms of political association which release societal potentials for significant advances in universality and difference.

One response to the totalising project is to argue that while citizenship is one of the main achievements of modern states it has nevertheless been 'too puffed up and too compressed' (Wright, 1990): too puffed up, or universalistic, because the needs of those who do not exhibit the dominant cultural characteristics have frequently been disregarded; too compressed, or particularistic, because the interests of outsiders have typically been ignored. The upshot of this line of argument is that if citizenship is to be understood 'as a series of expanding circles which are pushed forward by the momentum of conflict and struggle' then the next stage of its expansion should be 'to go higher in our search for citizenship, but also lower and wider. Higher to the world, lower to the locality' (Wright, 1990). Few political theorists have attempted to develop this embryonic vision of an alternative to the sovereign nation-state (Turner, 1993b).

Two decades ago, Bull (1977, p. 267) observed that in the context of

Western Europe the time might indeed be ripe for enunciating new concepts of political organisation which would reveal how Wales, the United Kingdom and the European Community could each enjoy 'world political status' without laying claim to 'exclusive sovereignty'. The time was ripe, Bull surmised, for the enunciation of new political principles which would break with the tyranny of the concept of the sovereign state. While assuming that a return to a medievalist conception of international society was 'fanciful', he argued that it was realistic to envisage 'a modern and secular counterpart' which embodied one of its chief characteristics, namely, 'a system of overlapping authority and multiple loyalty'. For Bull, this potentially momentous shift in the organisation of European international society revolved around two main patterns of change. First, movement towards regional integration in Europe could reduce the sovereignty and autonomy of separate states without investing traditional state monopoly powers in new centralised, transnational institutions. Second, minority nations and separatist groups could aim to reduce the power of the nation-state without aiming for full sovereign status. What would eventuate as a result of this dual process of change was a system of multi-tiered political authority which corresponded with the multiple loyalties of European citizens. No authority would claim absolute sovereignty or 'superior jurisdiction', and none would seek to monopolise the political loyalties of groups or individuals. Should this ever occur, a 'genuine innovation' in the nature of European international society involving significant progress beyond the nation-state would have taken place (Bull, 1979, p. 114).

This process of moving higher to the world and lower to the locality would have major implications for sovereignty, state monopoly powers and national citizenship. Bull's comments on the possibility of a post-Westphalian European order clearly recognised the implications for sovereign statehood. Although there is rather less in his writings about the transcendence of monopoly powers and the reconstruction of citizenship, a great deal is implied. A new form of political community in which states shared their authority with regional or world authorities and with sub-state authorities would most clearly breach the state's traditional and exclusive right of representation in international organisations and its sole right to bind the whole community in international law. A 'Scottish authority in Edinburgh, a British authority in London, and a European authority in Brussels' could coexist as 'actors in world politics', each enjoying 'representation in world political organisations, together with rights and duties of various kinds in world law'. Clear implications for the traditional state monopoly power over matters of legal arbitration would follow. If none of the three levels of authority could claim the sovereign entitlement to deny the right of international representation to others, and if none could claim 'sovereignty or supremacy over the others', then rights of legal arbitration could be distributed across a number of different political authorities rather than concentrated in a single site of sovereign power. Bull's remarks on the nebulous quality of sovereignty in a foreseeable neo-medievalist Europe point towards this conclusion. Multi-layered structures of authority would not supersede the state entirely, but the state's role in world politics could be diminished to such an extent that there could be considerable doubt in theory and in practice as to whether sovereignty lay with the national governments or with the other levels of authority (Bull, 1977, p. 266). The modern counterpart to medieval international society could quickly provoke the question of whether the concept of sovereignty remained at all 'applicable'.[8]

The state's monopoly right to determine the order of priority of political allegiances – national before sub-state and transnational – would also be relinquished within a neo-medievalist international order. The mix of political authorities in Edinburgh, London and Brussels would not only surrender the sovereign rights already mentioned but suffer the loss of the right and capacity to regulate political allegiances. Under these conditions, 'a person living in Glasgow [would have] no exclusive or overriding loyalty to any of them.' Further, it might be argued, if the new political order granted recognition to cultures which had previously been denied significant representation, and if it allowed transnational solidarities equivalent voice, then the appropriateness of the state's monopoly power of taxation would immediately come under question. Similar doubts would inevitably be raised about its monopoly of control over the instruments of violence. It was precisely because the neo-medieval order would bring this last right into question that Bull was less than sanguine about alternatives to the sovereign state. Violence had been ubiquitous in the medieval world, and might become prevalent again in a 'neo-medieval order of overlapping sovereignties and jurisdictions' in which several potentially rival centres of power sought control of the instruments of force (Bull, 1979, p. 114).

Bull (1979) gave cautious support to the possibilities for a new kind of Western European international society but added that the regional integrationists and the sub-national disintegrationists had shown little interest in imagining alternatives to the sovereign state. At the time Bull was writing, this neglect was evident across the Political Sciences. Political theorists, who were with some exceptions firmly wedded to reflections upon the modern state, and students of International Relations who were concerned with analysing the relations between states, largely ignored questions about how alternative forms of political community and new principles of international relations might be conceptualised, or might evolve. The dearth of reflection on future possibilities is far less evident among regional integrationists and subnational disintegrationists in the current period than it was when Bull was writing in the 1970s. Compared with the dominant intellectual strands of that time, many recent approaches to the state and international relations are more curious about the nature of the social bond which unites the members of a society and shapes their conception of their rights and duties vis-à-vis the rest of the world. Images of Europe and the wider world which envisage the unravelling of sovereign states and the multiplication of human loyalties have gained support from several different strands of social and political theory in recent years.

A few illustrations will suffice. Foucault anticipated a world beyond state monopolies in which the recovery of local powers and identifications would occur alongside the development of an emergent international citizenry which 'promises to raise itself up against every abuse of power, no matter who the author or the victims' might be (Keenan, 1987, pp. 20–4). Several postmodernists have defended the diversification of local and transnational solidarities as a means of dislodging the stark contrasts between the domestic and the international, the inside and outside, which have been central to the way in which modern political community has been constructed and conceived (Walker, 1988, 1993). One of the principal aims of the postmodern turn in International Relations is to subvert the state's ability to use the dichotomy between domestic social harmony and international discord to construct and maintain totalising and exclusionary identities which obstruct movement higher to the world and lower to the locality. Reference has already been made to Derrida's vision of a European political framework which avoids the monopolisation of powers and the dispersal of loyalties to various centres of regressive particularism (see p. 74 above). Support for these themes is forthcoming from other branches of social and political theory such as Frankfurt School and neo-Marxist political theory. Bull's comments about a neo-medievalist European international society are echoed in the brief but more normatively focused remarks about future scenarios for Europe which appear in the writings of Habermas (1994) and Cox (1993, p. 263). Finally, the anarchist tradition has long argued for despatching state monopoly powers to local communities and transnational agencies in order to recover the potentials for universality and difference which were stifled by the rise of the modern territorial state (Weiss, 1975). These anarchistic sentiments resonate with recent critiques of the state's monopoly powers, exclusionary national identities and totalising political logics which invite further analysis of the nature of citizenship in a post-Westphalian society of states.

At this point it is worth recalling that Carr believed that the problem of modern politics was to restore the balance between national loyalties and internationalism which had collapsed with the spread of aggressive particularism. Movement beyond the classical sovereign nation-state was necessary to create a new balance between universality and difference. Similar conclusions are evident in more recent efforts to imagine political communities which are responsive to pressures for such a balance. Much recent social and political thought has argued that ethical universalism is incompatible with respect for human diversity, but the notion that state structures might be transformed in order to promote higher levels of universality *and* difference is an important trend within several different perspectives. Achieving the balance between universality and difference will certainly involve the state, but it requires states which shed many of their classical sovereign powers and nationalist presuppositions and proceed to engage sub-national, or sub-state, and transnational authorities in effective systems of joint rule.[9] The institutions of joint rule would not constitute a sovereign state since they would forgo conventional state monopolies and exclusionary claims on human loyalty and political identity. But they would inevitably impinge upon traditional state monopoly powers and encourage a proliferation of allegiances and identities which would inhibit the resumption of totalising projects. Questions regarding the distribution of membership, citizenship and global moral responsibilities would become matters of joint rule involving, at least in principle, each layer of a multi-tiered political authority; and each of these levels would be involved in creating the social and economic preconditions of the wider communities of discourse which unfold the progressive side of modernity.

These political structures would supersede traditional conceptions of sovereignty and state monopoly powers, and replace conventional notions of citizenship which assume that all, or most, citizens must share a common nationality and acknowledge the supreme authority of a single, sovereign power. Political transformation would involve the divorce of citizenship from the state, just as it was uncoupled earlier from the medieval town and the Renaissance city (Turner, 1993b, p. 15). Citizenship would have to be reworked in the light of multiple allegiances and authorities (Meehan, 1993, ch. 8). This project is immanent within the concept of citizenship itself, and one of the primary objectives of societies which are moved by its normative commitments should be to reconstruct citizenship with a view to expanding the boundaries of social interaction which are governed by dialogue and consent. In Hegel's thought, as noted earlier, the balancing of various affiliations is one of the more noble purposes of political activity and reflection. This observation is crucial to efforts to conceptualise the post-Westphalian state. One of the tasks of the post-Westphalian state is to harmonise the diversity of ethical spheres including sub-national or sub-state, national and wider regional and global affiliations, and to do so by creating forms of citizenship which pass beyond sovereignty to institutionalise advances in universality and diversity (Soysal, 1996, p. 19).

Citizenship in the Post-Westphalian State

Bull appeared to lament the fact that visions of a neo-medievalist order had failed to capture the imagination of the regional integrationists and the sub-national disintegrationists in the late 1970s. Various subsequent developments not only in theory but in practice have confirmed his observation that such visions are far from fanciful. The establishment of the Committee of the Regions in the Maastricht Treaty recognises the importance of sub-national or sub-state areas even though it stops short of securing their empowerment (McCarthy, forthcoming). Strong regional sentiments are evident amongst the German *Länder*, which were influential in the development of the Committee of the Regions, and in Italy, Belgium, France, Britain and Spain. The importance of national minority rights, a matter of increasing concern following the collapse of the Soviet sphere and the resurgence of ethnic particularism, is evident in the articles of the Council of Europe and the Organisation for Security and Cooperation in Europe. The European Charter of Regional or Minority Languages within the framework of the Council of Europe further reveals that issues concerning minority nations have impinged upon international law governing European international society to a greater extent than ever before. Opportunities for legal appeal beyond national courts as provided by the European Court of Human Rights are an important qualification of national sovereignty. Elements of transnational citizenship have been introduced in the European Union under the Maastricht Treaty in consequence of a democratic deficit which occurs because the harmonisation of national policies and the establishment of transnational legal agreements do not require the assent of national populations and legislatures. Erosions of sovereignty have yet to be accompanied by the radical alteration of traditional assumptions about citizenship. Even so, by virtue of their commitments to constitutional democracy, states are increasingly drawn into discussions about how the achievements of national citizenship can be retained and consolidated as the logics of globalisation and regionalisation transform modern political life. Recent institutional inventions are weak responses to these challenges, but they have introduced various alternative sites of political responsibility which different political actors will almost certainly seek to strengthen in their efforts to combat state monopoly powers and to withstand the effects of transnational business corporations and global market forces. The possibility of further breaches of state sovereignty to extend autonomy is immanent not only within state structures but in the welter of international conventions which affirm autonomy as a global normative ideal.

The Maastricht Treaty requires comment in this regard because it establishes the notion of the European citizen and in so doing creates ideological resources which can be mobilised in response to extensions of economic and political power. Limited though they are, these resources embody significant advances in reducing the moral significance of alien status. Article 8 of the Maastricht Treaty which holds that 'every person holding the nationality of a Member State shall be a citizen of the Union' affirms the following individual entitlements: the right of free movement within Europe, of residing in the territory of another member state, of petitioning the European Parliament or the European Union Ombudsman and of receiving assistance from the embassies of other member states when outside the Union. The Treaty sets out elementary political rights such as the right to vote and stand as a candidate in local elections in other countries and to vote or stand as a candidate for the European Parliament. Such developments extend previous measures which were designed to supplement national citizenship within the member states of the European Union. Those measures were largely concerned with installing elementary legal and social rights which would facilitate the free movement of people and goods between individual states. As Roche (1992, pp. 200–2) has argued, the development of the idea of European citizenship has therefore amended the sequence of legal, political and social rights which was at the centre of Marshall's analysis. Elementary legal and social rights were the first rights to be established within the European Union, with the promise that political rights would be added later.

What has been established within the European Union thus far is a thin conception of citizenship which brings an international civil society into existence rather than the thicker conception of citizenship which active membership of a political community is normally thought to imply. Democratising increasingly important regional institutions is necessary to secure meaningful transnational citizenship within Western Europe (Roche, 1992, p. 194). Adding extensive political rights to the legal and social entitlements which already exist is therefore a crucial task. The observation that national citizenship is all that exists in the context of greater interdependence 'which requires a new theory of internationalism and universalistic citizenship' captures the essential point, as does the related comment that the 'struggle for citizenship as a struggle for equality must begin again', given the emergence of 'a cosmopolis of communications and financial transactions' (see Turner, 1986, p. 140; Balibar, 1988, p. 723). If it is the case that citizenship has been too puffed up and too compressed, then efforts to universalise citizenship rights by bringing citizens and aliens together as co-legislators will have to be accompanied by efforts to ensure that transnational citizenship is sensitive to the meaning which most citizens attach to local identities and particular cultural differences (Turner, 1990, pp. 211–13). Attempts to thicken the conception of citizenship which currently exists within the European Union inevitably clash with the fusion of sovereignty, territoriality, nationality and citizenship which has been at the heart of modern political life for more than two centuries.

What is at issue is the conception of citizenship which emerged with the rise of sovereignty and territoriality and which is described in Bodin's writings. Bodin (1967, p. 21) argued that what 'makes a man a citizen [is] the mutual obligation between subject and sovereign' in which 'faith and obedience are exchanged for justice, counsel, assistance, encouragement and protection'. His writings stressed four main dimensions of the nexus between citizenship, territoriality and sovereignty which the age of nationalism would later reinforce: first, only one sovereign power can exercise legitimate rule within each territory; second, no person can be the subject of more than one sovereign; third, all citizens have the same legal status and stand in exactly the same relationship with the sovereign; and fourth, the ties which bind the citizen and sovereign totally exclude aliens.[10] These are the characteristics of the dominant conception of citizenship in the modern world which the post-Westphalian state rejects. Post-Westphalian structures which promote developmental pressures to recognise multiple authorities and loyalties must uncouple citizenship from sovereignty, shared nationality and territoriality. The practical task is to envisage forms of citizenship which are appropriate to the post-Westphalian condition of multiple political authorities and allegiances.

Some progress towards uncoupling citizenship from sovereignty is made by Article 8 of the Maastricht Treaty but European citizenship is a thin supplement to the rights which citizens already have within their respective nation-states. The higher normative goal is to ensure that the process of uncoupling citizenship from state sovereignty results in a thicker conception of citizenship in which societal potentials for increasing human autonomy prevail over competing logics of social control. These potentials cannot be realised as long as national identity is singled out and made central to political community. A revised version of Marshall's account of the dialectics of modern citizenship is necessary in this context. As noted earlier, Marshall set out the legal, political and social rights which citizens had to possess if they were to be at home in political communities in which state power and capitalist development were the principal threats to their autonomy. The current challenge is to set out the rights which are needed to ensure full membership of a post-Westphalian political community which takes up the quest for autonomy as globalisation and fragmentation erode the monopoly powers of the modern state.

Part of the challenge is to identify different arenas in which the extension of citizenship rights is possible. One approach to uncoupling citizenship from the sovereign state stresses four potential geographical sites on which citizenship can flourish: the locality or province, the state, the international region and the world as a whole (Heater, 1990, p. 319).[11] It is inconceivable that citizenship in each of these domains can be linked with sentiments which are similar to those associated with national identity; nor is it necessary to suppose, as Mouffe (1993) has indicated, that the ethico-political bond between the citizens of a locality or a nation-state must ultimately rest on the prior existence of a shared identity (see also Howe, 1995).[12] An interest in preventing environmental damage rather than the desire to preserve shared cultural attachments may be the factor which encourages individuals to transcend their various differences and organise as, say, a local community. National citizenship can be anchored in the commitment to abstract principles which question the grounds for social exclusion and invite the elimination of unjust forms of closure as much as in some sense of primordial attachments. More often than not, elements of common identity, shared interests and moral obligation combine to form the social bond between citizens at local and national levels. But large numbers of human beings have to find abstract principles and common interests as meaningful as cultural similarities before citizenship can be extended to members of a continental region. Inevitably, a sense of humanitarian obligation has to stand in for shared nationality or common interest in the case of world citizenship. Transnational citizenship cannot ignore human diversity, for the reasons given earlier.[13] It embodies the normative conviction that efforts to secure respect for cultural differences belong to the larger project of using the moral resources which have been accumulated in national struggles for citizenship for the purpose of extending the sphere of dialogic relations. The quest for new locations for citizenship exists because the sovereign state cannot, in Hegelian terms, reconcile the universal and the particular.

Identifying new locations for citizenship is one means of securing its development beyond the parochial world of the sovereign state (Turner, 1993b). Introducing international analogues of Marshall's triad of civil, political and social rights, and creating forms of transnational citizenship which are attuned to the demands for cultural rights, are additional ways of building on the achievements of national citizenship. Beginning with Marshall's famous triad, civil rights can be strengthened by granting individuals the right of legal appeal beyond national courts to international courts of law. Political rights can be deepened by ensuring that international organisations such as the European Union satisfy the normative requirement of democratic participation. Equivalent social rights are necessary to ensure that transnational civil and political rights are significant in the lives of individuals. To put this in Honneth's terms, transnational civil and political rights express the belief that certain differences between persons (in this case the differences between citizens and aliens) lack moral relevance; transnational social rights demonstrate sensitivity to the existence of striking differences of economic and political power.

All of these rights can contribute to the sense of fully-fledged membership of a post-Westphalian international society. But as with domestic society, so with post-Westphalian structures: the most successful experiments in effective political cooperation have to respect the diversity of human loyalties. (See Carr, pp. 161–3 above.) Sensitivity to difference within post-Westphalian arrangements therefore requires measures to reduce inequalities of economic power and forms of transnational citizenship which recognise the diversity of forms of life and culturally-specific needs. Respect for the special concerns of minority nations and indigenous peoples, recognition of the particular vulnerabilities of women and children, and regard for sexual difference are among the important means of ensuring that transnational citizenship does not simply deal with abstract individuals.[14] Intriguingly, to consider one of these domains further, many minority nations in contemporary Europe which wish to reclaim lost rights from sovereign states look to international institutions and law for endorsement of their claims (Howe, 1995, p. 37). Ensuring that the project of universalising civil, political and social rights takes particular account of the members of minority nations is one means of satisfying their aspirations (Garcia, 1993, pp. 27 and 126).

Several means of achieving this objective are available. Affirming the legal right to an education which respects differences of culture, religion and language, and permitting the right of appeal beyond the state where minorities suffer discrimination, are two ways in which post-Westphalian structures can accommodate the politics of recognition. As for political rights, the devolution of power to sub-national or sub-state authorities, their acquisition of the parallel right of representation in international organisations and the achievement of an independent status in international law are examples of inroads into state power which are essential if experiments in transnational democracy are to succeed (Wendt, 1994).[15] Involving citizens and aliens as co-legislators in a wider community of discourse is the promise of cosmopolitan democracy, but local rights of autonomy accompanied by the right of participation in international institutions are essential if the interests of vulnerable regions and cultures are not to be neglected by the strong. Transnational social rights are crucial innovations in this context, especially with the globalisation of capitalist relations of production and exchange. The dominant strata in the world economy may find notions of transnational citizenship congenial if they protect their legal and political rights without imposing burdensome duties to assist those who are powerless to withstand the impact of global market forces. Hegemonic groups gain most where international arrangements remain within the confines of a thin conception of citizenship. A thicker notion of citizenship involving economic and social support for the victims of uneven economic development and de-industrialisation is crucial if the achievements of national citizenship are to be carried forward into the international domain.

The need to go higher to the world and lower to the locality arises because national citizenship has long been 'too puffed up and too compressed'. Normative commitments to the civil, political, social and cultural rights of citizens require the widening and deepening of political community, especially when the members of like-minded societies are exposed to unprecedented levels of transnational harm. The possibility of higher forms of citizenship which embed these rights in the structure of European international society is already immanent within modern state structures and international law, as is the potential for lower forms of citizenship which increase the power of local communities and minority nations. Higher *and* lower forms of citizenship which realise societal potentials for involvement in wider communities of discourse are evident within the elementary steps which have been taken to represent ethnic minorities and regions in international institutions and international law. Europe remains the most encouraging site for the development of new forms of political community which take up the challenge of promoting human autonomy under conditions in which states have a reduced capacity to secure the rights of citizens. Post-Westphalian arrangements which break up the union of sovereignty, territoriality, citizenship and shared nationality can provide a more effective means of reconciling the claims of universality and difference. In the age of globalisation and fragmentation, a new stage in the development of citizenship rights is promised by efforts to strike the balance between concrete attachments to local or national communities and more abstract cosmopolitan affiliations (Reiner, 1995, p. 3). Progress in this direction requires new forms of political community which internationalise the struggle against unjust exclusion.

Cosmopolitan Citizenship

Europe gave birth to the modern state which was exported subsequently to the rest of the world. Whether the entire society of states has entered the post-Westphalian era is clearly a matter of dispute but within Western Europe, at any rate, some evidence of a transition from Westphalian to post-Westphalian principles of political organisation is already evident. A new polity of this kind would represent a momentous step forward for the peoples of Europe, and it is not inconceivable that it might come to be regarded as a historical watershed within the evolution of international society as a whole. Given the trend towards regionalism in many parts of the world, Europe may well become a model of post-Westphalian political organisation which is emulated by regions elsewhere (Roche, 1992, p. 194).[16] Be that as it may, large parts of Europe are distinguished from the rest of the world by having undergone the transition from a system of states in which rivalry and suspicion prevail to a more solidarist society of states and peoples which have become involved in an unusual experiment in transnational political cooperation. Devising forms of citizenship which will guide Europe towards a multicultural, transnational social democracy is one of the central challenges facing the contemporary political imagination. The related challenge is to link this experiment in close political cooperation in Europe with the larger project of increasing autonomy across the world. Derrida (1992) has argued for a Europe which is not closed in upon itself. Adding transnational citizenship to the national forms which already exist is an important reason for regional cooperation, but it is incomplete without larger efforts to promote the ideals of cosmopolitan citizenship.

As Falk (1994, p. 139) observes, the idea of global citizenship smacks of the sentimental and the absurd – especially, it might be added, when it is associated with the unfashionable belief that a single world-wide political authority should govern the whole human race. Recent exponents of global or cosmopolitan citizenship have less ambitious goals. They defend the normative project of uncoupling citizenship from the sovereign state so that a strong sense of moral obligation is felt to all members of the species.[17] Representing this position, Heater (1990, pp. 163–4) argues that citizenship should not simply refer to the rights and duties which bind the members of particular sovereign states: it should be used more broadly to describe the duties and loyalties which link individuals with an extraordinary range of associations which extend from the city to the whole of humanity. Heater (1990, pp. 163–4) uses the phrase 'world social citizenship' to stress the moral duties which the most affluent populations have to the poorest members of global society. In a similar vein, Shaw (1991, p. 187) argues that a new form of 'post-military citizenship' which replaces the classical civic duty to defend the state in war with obligations to protect the weak and duties to safeguard the natural environment is emerging in post-Cold War Europe.[18] Linking cosmopolitanism and citizenship has a dual purpose: it argues that states are not the only moral agents in international relations and it claims that individuals and non-state actors have important moral duties to the rest of humanity which their membership of sovereign communities has consistently overshadowed.

The emphasis of such appeals to cosmopolitan citizenship has invariably fallen on *duties* to non-nationals. Kant's support for a universal 'constitution formed by the laws of world citizenship', the *ius cosmopoliticum*, was an exercise in moral exhortation: it was an appeal to co-nationals to transcend the parochial world of the sovereign state by respecting the rights of all humanity (Kant, 1970b, p. 206). Kant argued that all human beings should be regarded as 'the citizens of a universal state of humanity'; extending hospitality to each other was their primary cosmopolitan duty. World citizenship invited fellow-nationals to extend feelings of compassion to outsiders. It involved few of the demands associated with conceptions of national citizenship which embrace the Aristotelian ideal of active participation in joint rule or modern notions of social and economic rights. For this reason, the advocates of cosmopolitan citizenship may seem vulnerable to the charge that compassion is not enough. As Ignatieff (1991, p. 34) maintains, citizenship is less about compassion than about 'ensuring for everyone the entitlements necessary for the exercise of their freedom'. Cosmopolitan citizenship suggests vague and ultimately unenforceable moral responsibilities to the rest of humanity, whereas national citizenship entails concrete rights which are guaranteed by the political community. By the terms of this argument, Kant is open to the criticism he made of Grotius, Pufendorf and Vattel of failing to convert imperfect moral duties into perfect political rights (see also Archibugi, 1995).

Most accounts of cosmopolitan citizenship do not defend perfect political rights, but the Kantian theme that individuals should act on principles which could emerge from a universal communication community provides the starting-point for more robust formulations of the concept. Kant's appeal to world citizenship can be enlarged to embrace two important injunctions. The obligation to create frameworks of action which will steadily bring a universal communication community into being is the first injunction (Apel, 1979, pp. 98–9); the second is the duty to create the social and economic conditions which will ensure that participation within appropriate communicative frameworks is meaningful for the largest possible number of the world's population.[19] Approached in this way, cosmopolitan citizenship is a 'promissory note' issued across time and space (Hoy and McCarthy, 1994, p. 75), one which is at least as demanding as national citizenship because it conveys the intention of securing the entitlements which are necessary for the exercise of freedom for all members of the human race.

The contrast between thin and thick conceptions of transnational citizenship is worth recalling at this point because a similar distinction holds for world citizenship. Thin conceptions of cosmopolitan citizenship revolve around compassion for the vulnerable but leave asymmetries of power and wealth intact; thick conceptions of cosmopolitan citizenship attempt to influence the structural conditions faced by vulnerable groups. Collective political action to dismantle unjust systems of exclusion and to create communicative frameworks which will ensure higher levels of autonomy for the disadvantaged is central to the thicker version of world citizenship. Each of these orientations contributes to the transformation of international society. As a petition for enlarging the boundaries of compassion, the thin version of cosmopolitan citizenship is an important intermediate step between the practice of confining the ethical constituency to co-nationals and the condition in which thicker versions of world citizenship achieve significant structural change. This condition may be said to exist when clearly defined civil, political, social and cultural rights are guaranteed by universal communities of discourse.

A combination of post-Westphalian states, as defined earlier, represents progress in institutionalising a thicker version of transnational citizenship because the members of different societies possess concrete rights and duties as citizens of a wider political community. The achievements of transnational citizenship are strictly regional or continental, and there is always a possibility that the new polity will become closed in on itself. The idea of cosmopolitan citizenship is crucial because it argues that member states and non-state actors within post-Westphalian structures have additional obligations to ensure just treatment for the rest of humanity. Concern for vulnerable groups which lack the economic and political power to resist any harm which the post-Westphalian association does to them is the most appropriate point of departure.[20] In this respect, cosmopolitan citizenship enlarges the social realm in which the achievements of national citizenship influence human conduct. The duties of national citizens require collective action to improve the life-chances of the unjustly excluded and to increase their level of autonomy within the nation-state. Cosmopolitan citizenship requires international joint action to ameliorate the condition of the most vulnerable groups in world society and to ensure that they can defend their legitimate interests by participating in effective universal communicative frameworks.

Pockets of solidarism, it was argued earlier, have developed within a pluralist international society, and still more intricate forms of close political cooperation have evolved within the solidarist zone of peace. A post-Westphalian configuration of states committed to the triple transformation of political community is the most involved system of joint rule which can be realised in the present era. To ensure that it does not close itself off unreasonably, a post-Westphalian order has to honour various obligations to other societies which do not share its principles of association. These societies may be adversaries within a pluralist society of states or associates within solidarist frameworks of communication. Compliance with the ideals of cosmopolitan citizenship requires efforts to accommodate the legitimate concerns of adversaries; it demands accountability to others within pluralist and solidarist arrangements and measures to promote any developmental pressures within these communicative frameworks which promise to free human beings from the burden of unjust constraints. Cosmopolitan citizenship acquires its most profound praxeological significance when it is regarded as a guide to the moral principles which should be observed in these circumstances.

Realists argue that adversaries can often best secure their basic objectives by accommodating one another's respective legitimate security interests: in so doing, the realists stress the virtue of prudence within the constraining environment of the system of states (Morgenthau, 1973; Kissinger, 1979). Rationalists have maintained that states are most likely to secure their primary goals if they preserve the basic principles and procedures of international society; in so doing, the rationalists emphasise the virtue of inter-state collaboration to reach agreement about the legal and moral foundations of international order.[21] Respect for sovereignty, observance of international law, recognition of the need for constraints on violence, cooperation to preserve the balance of power and the reliance on diplomacy to resolve international disputes are central themes in rationalist reflections upon state practice. Rationalists add that international order can survive in the absence of any consensus about principles of global justice, but its foundations will be stronger where a majority of states, including the great powers, agree not only on the preconditions of their orderly coexistence but on substantive questions of morality and justice (Bull, 1977, p. 95). Where states disagree fundamentally about ethical matters, rationalists argue, their efforts to promote competing views of international justice are likely to produce significant disorder.

For much of its history, European international society was pluralist rather than solidarist because its constitutive principles were designed to maintain order between independent political communities rather than to realise shared normative commitments such as greater justice (Bull, 1977, ch. 4). The interests of the great powers had priority over those of weaker powers; order triumphed over justice. Whether order inevitably prevails over justice is a central theme in rationalist thought (Bull, 1977, 1983a, 1983b; Vincent, 1990b; Wheeler and Dunne, 1996). Rationalists observe that the great powers invariably shape the diplomatic dialogue between states, but they also recognise that powerful developmental pressures in international society have made its communicative framework more responsive to considerations of justice. Support for the principle that affluent societies have moral obligations to assist the populations of the poorer states has increased in the latter part of the twentieth century. Recognition of the extent to which justice between peoples has become an important precondition of international order has occurred in the wake of the Third World revolt against Western dominance.

Bull and Watson (1984, pp. 220–4) identified five main dimensions of this revolt against the exclusionary nature of the Western-dominated international society: first, the legal revolt in which states such as China and Japan demanded the right to full membership of the society of states; second, the political revolt spearheaded by nationalist movements which contended that the colonies should have exactly the same rights as their imperial overlords; third, the racial revolt against notions of white supremacism; fourth, the economic revolt which was triggered by the realisation that the acquisition of national sovereignty had not resulted in greater economic and political independence; and, fifth, the cultural revolt against the dominance of Western ideas and practices which is an expression of the resurgence of the cultures which are indigenous to Asia, Africa and the Pacific, and testimony to their renewed confidence in the validity of local beliefs.

These five forms of revolt against international systems of unjust exclusion are not arbitrary and unrelated. They are the main elements of a broad pattern of global development in which the moral significance attached to the racial and cultural differences between Western and non-Western peoples has sharply declined. The grounds for denying non-Western societies the right of equal membership of the society of states have been eroded in the twentieth century, and the legal status which the West once monopolised has come to be shared with the former colonial territories. Awareness of the respects in which economic inequalities reduce the sovereign independence of many new states, and sensitivity to racial and cultural differences, have increased during the transition from a European to a universal international society, although that society still remains largely Western-dominated. Parallels with developments in

national citizenship are evident in the belief that fully-fledged membership of international society requires not only the achievement of
sovereign rights but continuing efforts to dismantle the forms of racial,
economic and cultural exclusion which emerged with Western imperialism. Echoes of the developmental pressures which have favoured the
triple transformation of domestic political communities are evident in
the claim that a radical redistribution of wealth and power in favour of
non-Western peoples, and the greater accommodation of non-Western
principles in international law, are necessary for the construction of a
just international order (Bull, 1977, pp. 316–17). One of the primary
functions of cosmopolitan citizenship is to urge the members of a post-
Westphalian society of states to create a wider communicative framework in which vulnerable societies can enjoy greater autonomy.
   The cultural revolt against the West may ensure that the wider
communicative framework remains pluralist rather than solidarist in
character. Be that as it may, efforts to secure democratic government,
respect for individual human rights and the protection of the rights of
national minorities demonstrate that a solidarist realm can exist alongside the pluralist and post-Westphalian international societies.[22] Modifying the principles of international society which have reserved full
membership for sovereign states is an important means of creating a
universal communicative framework which is responsive to diverse
societal preferences and interests. A post-Westphalian political order
which is not closed in on itself can widen the boundaries of dialogue by
recognising that a variety of non-state actors, including non-governmental associations, social movements and national minorities, can enjoy
membership of an international society which is not just a society of
states but a society of peoples and individuals. The promise of solidarism
is the partial dissolution of the international society of states within this
wider communicative domain.[23]
   Some remarks about important affinities between rationalism and
critical approaches to international relations conclude the discussion.
Rationalism is frequently associated with the conservative standpoint
which defends the sovereign states-system and legitimates the practice of
granting order priority over justice. It has been portrayed as a distinctively British variant on realism which denies the possibility of significant
international progress (but see Wheeler and Dunne, 1996, p. 4). This
interpretation is not unwarranted, as one strand of rationalism clearly
inclines towards the realist tradition, but it hardly does justice to its
competing intellectual tendencies which overlap with modes of universalistic thought that stress the virtues of dialogue and consent.[24] Rationalism is as sceptical as much recent social theory about the supposition
that immutable and universal moral truths reside in some transcendental

conception of the self or particular civilisation. It is emphatic that the pursuit of clashing conceptions of justice which no philosophical system has been able to reconcile can destroy the foundations of international order, but it is keen to stress that states have established basic universal principles of coexistence through diplomatic dialogue. Although rationalists often doubt that states can agree on universal principles of morality, they have suggested that some limited progress in this direction has occurred in the first global society of states.[25] Higher levels of moral agreement are not ruled out by rationalism, but the need for more radical forms of dialogue which are deeply sensitive to cultural differences is a pronounced theme within more recent formulations of the perspective (Vincent, 1986).

This commitment to dialogue is linked with the rationalist analysis of the transition in which non-Western societies were drawn into a society of states which originated in Europe and which is still largely governed by principles which enjoy most support in the West (Bull and Watson, 1984). Rationalists have been acutely aware that the society of states and various conceptions of the universal community of humankind have been as exclusionary as the forms of sovereign closure which they aspire to overcome, and they have been strong advocates of the view that the principles of international order will lack legitimacy unless they command the consent of the world's peoples as opposed to the majority of sovereign states. By advocating communities of discourse which are highly sensitive to cultural diversity, rationalists have explored important lines of inquiry which have been developed further by critical theories of international relations. A lack of enthusiasm for abstract philosophical inquiry has prevented a robust normative defence of a universal communication community in which equals participate in the knowledge that no argument is automatically privileged and no outcome predetermined, but rationalist thought is far from incompatible with this point of view (Linklater, 1996c, pp. 112–13). Critical theorists have analysed the prerequisites of the dialogic community in some detail, although rationalist thought contains important insights into how the ideal of a universal communication community might be promoted by developing the potentials which exist within different conceptions of the society of states. Rationalist and critical approaches therefore contribute to the realisation that cosmopolitan attachments to dialogue and consent are best nurtured and realised in these multiple communicative frameworks.

This interpretation of rationalism invites the conclusion that there are four communities of discourse which enable human beings, or their representatives, to engage in dialogue to determine the political conditions of their existence: the sovereign state, the pluralist international society, the solidarist society which is a society of states and peoples, and the post-Westphalian order which is host to bold experiments in creating a transnational citizenry. This interpretation also suggests that the participants in post-Westphalian arrangements can promote the ideals of cosmopolitan citizenship by ensuring that each communicative framework makes its appropriate contribution to the progressive transformation of international society. These multiple communities of discourse can ensure justice for states, minority nations and indigenous groups which may be primarily concerned with preserving cultural differences within a pluralist order; they can institutionalise the preferences of states which are agreed that respect for human rights and global social justice form the basis for more solidarist arrangements; and they can embody the preferences of states and other associations which are prepared to cede sovereignty, in whole or in part, to transnational democratic structures. Post-Westphalian structures have special obligations to establish and maintain these diverse communities of discourse and to assist any developmental tendencies which promise to eradicate unjust exclusion within them.

To ensure that each political community has access to the appropriate communicative framework is to increase the possibility that decisions about the nature and direction of international society enjoy the consent of all parties with important interests at stake. To reduce unjust exclusion within each framework is to increase the autonomy of all the parties involved. Cosmopolitan citizenship supports global arrangements in which human beings enlarge the spheres of social interaction which are governed by dialogue rather than force. It weds themes drawn from three perspectives: the Kantian ideal of equal membership of a universal kingdom of ends, the Marxian project of dismantling systems of exclusion which frustrate human autonomy, and the thesis which is derived from rationalism that multiple communities of discourse can promote new relations between universality and difference. The post-Westphalian era will begin when societies act as cosmopolitan citizens who aspire to make progress together towards the ethical ideal of a universal communication community. As part of that process, national and other particularistic ties would defer to efforts 'to secure the social bond of all with all precisely through equal consideration of the interests of each individual' (Habermas, 1987, p. 346).

Conclusions

Citizenship involves the enjoyment of civil, political, social and cultural rights, and corresponding duties to remove the barriers to equal membership of the political community. A society which is committed to realising the ideals of citizenship is obliged by this conviction to engage outsiders in open dialogue about the respects in which its actions may harm their interests. It has an obligation to transcend the dichotomy between citizens and aliens by establishing systems of joint rule. Post-Westphalian arrangements are the most elaborate experiments in close cooperation to achieve this goal which seem realisable in the present epoch; but they are necessarily confined to especially like-minded states, and the pluralist and solidarist versions of international society are also important means of endeavouring to make progress towards the ideal of a universal communication community. The moral capital which has been accumulated in the process of creating the rights and duties of national citizens provides the resources for reconfiguring international society in the light of this normative ideal.

Kant (Reiss, 1970, pp. 51–3) argued that establishing what each society had contributed to the cosmopolitan goal was a minor motive for writing a philosophy of history. The preceding discussion points to the conclusion that the societies which contribute most to world citizenship will aim to ensure that the universal communication frameworks in which they take part reflect the vision of the dialogic community. The task of cosmopolitan citizenship is to project the achievements of national citizenship out into the sphere of international relations. Its function is to promote the goal of the universal communication community by ensuring that pluralist, solidarist and post-Westphalian arrangements respect the principle of equal autonomy. The main point is to guarantee that the legitimacy of all practices, whether domestic or international, is decided in the same way, namely by engaging the systematically excluded in open dialogue and by cooperating to remove the constraints upon their effective participation. Promoting the Kantian vision of a universal kingdom of ends, and the parallel enterprise of realising the neo-Marxian ideal of overcoming asymmetries of power and wealth, form the essence of cosmopolitan citizenship.

Conclusion

The state-building process in the Westphalian era produced unusual territorial concentrations of power. Centralised political institutions established a complex ensemble of monopoly powers over clearly defined territorial frontiers and aimed, with varying levels of success, to create homogeneous national units. States asserted the sovereign right to decide all matters concerning the distribution of membership, the allocation of citizenship rights and the extent of their global obligations and responsibilities. They employed nationalist symbols to bring political and cultural boundaries into close alignment and to accentuate the differences between insiders and outsiders. A new stage in the development of the capacity to organise territorial populations and to control far-flung empires from a central administrative point opened with the rise of the modern state. Violent demonstrations of the differences between the modern state and all previous forms of social and political organisation were provided by the totalitarian states earlier this century. The high point of the totalising project was reached in Nazi Germany and Stalin's Russia, but these states failed to secure lasting close political cooperation. The collapse of communist monopoly power provides clear confirmation of Hegel's theme that the states which struck the appropriate balance between individual rights and loyalties to the community, between market social relations and support for the needy, and between national sovereignty and respect for the principles of international society grasped the secret of close cooperation.

Hegel's argument is a reminder that the rise of territorial concentrations of power has been checked by developments within two ethical domains. First, those who exercise state monopoly powers have not been entirely free from the moral constraints of international society, and they have not been at liberty to ignore all ethical appeals to the community of humankind. Second, the growth of state power has generated demands for citizenship rights which would shield populations from centralising and totalising tendencies. Although totalitarian states intensified developments which are evident in all states to some extent, they have proved to be the exception rather than the rule. Modern states have not been so different from their predecessors that they could eradicate all counter-weights to their monopoly powers. Forms of social learning which questioned the legitimacy of modern forms of power and exclusion have accompanied the development of the more sophisticated techniques of social and political control.

Logics which encourage the increase of state monopoly power and forces which resist the state's intrusion exist in all modern societies, but their relative significance has long been the subject of vigorous debate. Three phases in the history of this debate can be identified. First, in the eighteenth century, mercantilist thinkers argued that states were condemned to participate in a permanent struggle for power and wealth. The state-building project which aimed to secure national frontiers and to create highly protected and integrated national economies undermined earlier conceptions of Christian or European international society and precluded attempts to widen the moral and political boundaries of community. In the second phase, which began in the middle of the nineteenth century, the question of political community was reopened by the expansion of commercial relations and the introduction of industrial systems of production. Liberal and socialist writers pointed to powerful currents of social and economic change which would soon dissolve bounded national communities. Their abundant faith that globalisation would breed cosmopolitanism was destroyed by the First World War and the subsequent twenty years' crisis. In the third phase, realist perspectives argued that the inevitable competition and conflict between states prevented the emergence of alternative forms of political community. In the context of international anarchy, they argued, the normative appeal of international society and ethical universality would necessarily remain marginal and weak.

The tension between these competing intellectual tendencies or traditions has not been finally resolved; however, endemic struggle between the major powers secured the triumph of realist approaches to political community for most of the second half of the twentieth century. Realists argued that it was utopian to assume that commitments to the rights of citizens and to the moral equality of the human race foreshadowed more advanced forms of social and political organisation. However much national societies might have evolved domestically in the light of popular demands for citizenship, the conduct of their external relations revealed no clear pattern of advance (Wight, 1966). According to realism, geopolitical forces frustrated liberal and socialist predictions of world progress in the first part of the century, and they will continue to reveal the folly of all attempts to promote radical political change. For realists, the endemic struggle for security and survival means that the question of political community is effectively closed.

Neo-realism is the most robust contemporary formulation of this thesis. Its very existence is testimony to the success of the totalising project in creating the sharp divide between domestic and international politics and in encouraging the related understanding that the gulf between these two social worlds cannot be bridged. Neo-realism has assumed that the learning processes which led to the pacification and control of national territories, to the development of more sophisticated instruments of violence and to an appreciation of the stabilising role of the balance of power have triumphed over learning in the moral sphere. By denying the possibility of establishing new forms of life on the moral foundations which developed in the struggle against state monopoly power, neo-realism has legitimated conventional beliefs that the problem of community has been largely resolved.

Three criticisms of neo-realism deny this pessimistic conclusion. The first, which links Wight's analysis of international revolutions with more recent postmodern accounts of the incompleteness of states (Devetak, 1995b), emphasises the precarious nature of the modern form of political community. Current analyses of globalisation and fragmentation underline the central point that no form of political community is ever complete or immune from major disturbance and possible decay. A second criticism argues that neo-realism greatly underestimates the potential for the unit-driven transformation of international relations. A mild formulation of the point suggests that unit-level phenomena, such as constitutionalism, encouraged the development of an international society, as opposed to a system, of states. More radical in its implications is the contention that domestic liberal commitments to the politics of accommodation and consent have led to an inter-liberal zone of peace. A third criticism is that neo-realism is mistaken when it locates the ultimate source of competition and conflict in the anarchic nature of the international system. Conceptions of the inter-liberal peace reinforce the criticism that what was imputed to anarchy should have been attributed to its constituent parts. National actors can utilise their moral capital to join outsiders to extend the moral and political boundaries of community, and to pacify international society in the process. Neo-realism has denied that 'inside-out' approaches to international political change can succeed; competing liberal approaches offer a different conclusion with far-reaching implications, namely that the neo-realist enterprise of reducing the study of international relations to an analysis of the elements of recurrence and repetition is profoundly mistaken. The discipline has a deeper purpose which is normative and philosophical, and requires above all else the analysis of the potentials for the transformation of political community. As a branch of critical inquiry, the study of international relations has the primary task of considering the moral principles with which political communities are to be judged, of analysing the empirical forces which block or support the transition to more advanced forms of community, and of reflecting upon the practical opportunities for creating wider communities of discourse.

The logics of globalisation and fragmentation have drawn the eye back to the national boundary after several decades when it seemed that the problems which liberals and socialists had identified in their critique of sovereign statehood appeared to have been solved, and when the nation-state seemed to lack powerful rivals and to be immune from substantial change. Fragmentation has highlighted the disjunctions between the boundaries of cultural and political community in many parts of the world, while globalisation casts considerable doubt on the supposition that the nation-state is the only significant moral community. Growing doubts about the rationality of territorial concentrations of monopoly power indicate that the question of political community has been reopened at the end of the twentieth century.

Current reflections on the nature and purpose of political community suggest a return to the second of the three stages mentioned earlier. They lead back to the point before ethics, political theory and sociology became separate from the study of international relations, and before the analysis of how national societies interacted with one another, and how they were or could be organised internally, overshadowed the larger question of how bounded communities had been configured in the first place and might be reconstituted in future. Kant and Marx were the central figures in the second stage of the history of the debate about the rationality of bounded political communities because they raised key normative, sociological and praxeological questions about modern territorial concentrations of monopoly power. Their assumption that global commercial and industrial relations would lead to new forms of universal political cooperation defined the critical theory of political community between the late eighteenth and mid-nineteenth centuries. However, the claims of universality were privileged over the claims of difference in their writings, and the intensification of national sentiments and the extension of state power in the latter part of the nineteenth century revealed the limitations of their analyses.

Two responses occurred at this point. First, realist and neo-realist approaches drew the inference that the modern states-system would be reproduced indefinitely and that reformist projects would necessarily be confined to the inner world of the territorial state. Second, Marxist approaches to nationalism and imperialism responded to the forces which had contracted the boundaries of community – contrary to the earlier expectations of proletarian internationalism – by redefining the problem of community to take account of the logics of globalisation and fragmentation. The most sophisticated lines of argument which were developed by the Austro-Marxists envisaged new forms of political community in which the advancement of greater universality would be accompanied by greater respect for cultural differences. Realism and neo-realism prevailed over Marxism in this dispute about the fate of bounded political communities, but the combined influence of globalisation and fragmentation suggests that this victory has been temporary. Recent approaches to political community which envisage multiple authorities and loyalties resonate with the Austro-Marxists' theme that globalisation and fragmentation create the context in which new relations between universality and diversity can develop. A fourth stage in the debate about the nature of bounded communities is evident in the argument that totalising projects can, and should be, replaced by the collective enterprise of promoting the triple transformation of community.

Kant and Marx assumed that the moral capital which had developed in response to state monopoly powers made the reconstitution of political community possible. They recognised that modern conceptions of citizenship and universality checked the systems of unjust exclusion which were integral to bounded communities and their external relations. Kant believed that the paradox of violent conflict and growing international commerce forced societies to use their moral capital for the purpose of devising universal frameworks of cooperation; Marx assumed that the global spread of capitalism would pacify international relations and allow universal solidarity to triumph over the particularism of nation-states. Recent accounts suggest that globalisation has encouraged the pacification of relations between constitutionally secure industrial states; they also note how the obsolescence of force has removed one of the central pillars of bounded communities. Increased sensitivity to the moral problem of transnational harm and parallel sensibilities about the wrongs caused by assimilationist practices have combined to make novel forms of community and citizenship possible. Images of community which envisage the transfer of power and authority to new centres of decision-making inside and outside national boundaries promise to preserve the strengths and cancel the weakness of orthodox conceptions of citizenship. Sub-national and transnational forms of citizenship can extend the sphere of social interaction which is governed by dialogue and consent rather than by violence and power. Critical theories of community which pursue these themes retrieve the framework of analysis which Kant and Marx developed in their consideration of the possibilities for reconfiguring political community. But these critical approaches open up a fourth stage in the long debate about bounded communities by envisaging an end to the forms of cultural domination which have been woven into their domestic organisation and international relations.

The process which led to territorial concentrations of power in modern Europe (the simultaneous widening and contraction of human loyalties as emphasised in Wight's writings) is being reversed in many parts of the continent, and it has long been possible, but far from inevitable, that European international society would evolve in this direction. The ambiguities of the modern state contain different possibilities. Hegel observed that the modern state has had to balance competing ethical principles (individual liberty and the rights of the community, property rights and welfare provision, sovereignty and duties to other peoples). The majority of modern states have been Hegelian states which balanced these competing principles, albeit in different ways. Totalitarian states earlier in the century turned the national community into an ethical absolute, but the recognition of personal freedoms and the tolerance of the separate sphere of civil society have ensured that most national communities are exposed to radically different pressures. Totalising processes have confronted countervailing normative tendencies and a transnational civil society which has reduced state monopoly powers. Modern states have therefore contained the seeds of their own eventual destruction.

Alternative means of organising human beings which are already immanent within the modern states seem most likely to appear in Western Europe and in the neighbouring societies which are being drawn inside its orbit (Waller and Linklater, forthcoming). The idea of 'post-international politics' (Rosenau, 1990) and 'the post-Westphalian era' (Cox, 1992; Zacher, 1992) have special significance in that region where a lasting balance between the claims of the nation and the species may yet come to be struck – a balance which broke down in the first part of the century, as Carr pointed out in his critique of the modern state with its fusion of sovereignty, territoriality, citizenship and nationalism. Whether Europe will prove to be the first international region which is permanently transformed by peace rather than by war, whether it will be the setting for the triple transformation of political community and for a unique experiment in promoting multicultural, transnational social democracy, is unclear. What is clear is that it is improbable that such changes in the structure of European international society will be quickly emulated across the world as a whole. But although its practices might not be universalised, its principles would have relevance not only for the relations between the parts of Europe but for the relations between Europe and the rest of humanity. The principle that no one has the right to purchase autonomy by reducing the autonomy of others can be embedded in the project of creating a European security community which addresses the concerns of individuals and minorities and not merely the interests of nation-states. Societies which take this conviction seriously are bound to be troubled by the ways in which they export harms to outsiders or secure their own identity by demeaning or misrepresenting other cultures. Promoting the ideal of a universal communication community in which insiders and outsiders recognise one another as moral equals is essential where the nature of political community has become problematical in the lives of its own members.

Rousseau maintained that the problem of modern politics was how to create a society in which citizens could be as free as they had been in the original state of nature. The related problem was how to create a society in which the ties which bind citizens together would not make them enemies of the human race. Perhaps these are utopian aspirations; but whether or not that is the case, they capture the central problem of politics which is how to create communities which do not subject aliens and subaltern domestic groups to the tyranny of unjust exclusion. Rousseau believed that citizens could recover their original freedom in a dialogic community where the laws which obliged them were the laws which they made for themselves, but beyond the state stood the necessitous world of international relations. Rousseau's assumption that the state required a civil religion to bind citizens together neglected the possibility that the elements of social solidarity could be combined with wider dialogic commitments. Special ties and a particular harmony of dispositions need not preclude membership of a universal communication community; and the social bond need not be wholly reliant on the customs and traditions which distinguish a society from others. A commitment on the part of the members of a society to eradicate the unjust practices of exclusion which are imposed on aliens and subaltern groups can be a crucial element of social solidarity: *Moralität* can be fused with *Sittlichkeit* accordingly to constitute the social bond.

Political community is rounded out and closed off where social unity is derived from civil religion; it is necessarily incomplete and open to the concerns of outsiders where citizens are linked together in a post-national society. Kant believed that societies could widen the boundaries of discourse even while differences of language and religion prevented them from intermingling together. Their capacity to transcend local differences and to regard themselves as co-legislators in a universal kingdom of ends made the abolition of the necessitous state of international relations possible. For Kant, the transformation of international relations must begin with the reconstitution of political community. Peaceful change begins by problematising the basic systems of exclusion which arise in the relations between citizens and aliens, and by expanding the realm of dialogue and consent. Kant defended post-national societies which would avoid any actions which contradicted the normative ideal of a universal communication community or impeded its development. A revised formulation is that forms of political community which promote universal norms which recognise cultural claims and demands for the reduction of material inequalities have a unique role to play in bringing about the transformation of international relations. They alone have the capacity to develop a universal dialogic community in which the justice of all modes of exclusion is tested in open dialogue. It has been argued, paraphrasing Marx's observation that all history is the history of class struggle, that the whole of history has been a history of distorted communication (A. Wellmer, in J. M. Bernstein, 1995, p. 44). Maybe visions of a humanity united in domination-free communication will always be utopian. But by unfolding their distinctive moral potentials, modern societies may yet prove capable of creating dialogic arrangements which are unique in the history of world political organisation. Realising the promise of the post-Westphalian era is the essence of the unfinished project of modernity.

Notes

Chapter 1 Anarchy, Community and Critical International Theory

1 See Waltz (1959). For a careful scrutiny and critique of these assumptions, see Suganami (1996).
2 Waltz (1979) is the main exponent of this position although Mearsheimer (1990, 1994–5) is also important. Cox (1981) and Ashley (1982, 1984) are key papers in the critique of neo-realism and in the recovery of normative and critical orientations to the field. For an account of neo-realism in the aftermath of the Cold War era, see Linklater (1995a).
3 Bull (1977, p. 247) maintains that Kant failed to understand Hegel's point that 'it is the state *qua* state which is the source of tension and war, not the state *qua* this or that kind of state'.
4 Second-image analysis may seem to allow for this possibility. However, second-image explanation regards certain kinds of regime as the cause of international conflict – autocratic regimes for eighteenth- and nineteenth-century liberals and capitalist regimes for classical Marxists. The alternative image which is suggested here shifts the emphasis from the political predispositions of regimes to the particularism of bounded communities.
5 Neither problematises the nature of the political community which has generated the distinction between domestic and international politics and the stark contrast between the inside and outside that grants the contrast between reductionist and systemic theory its initial plausibility. See Walker (1993) for an account of these distinctions.
6 The term praxeology is derived from Raymond Aron's discussion of the antinomies of statecraft. See Aron (1966, pp. 577–9) where the tension between Machiavellian calculations of opportunity and the Kantian problem of justifying foreign policy acts and identifying the means to universal peace is defined as the central praxeological issue in international relations. The Kantian dimension of praxeology is the uppermost consideration in the present work.

7 For an account of the project of modernity in the context of international relations theory, see Devetak (1995a).

8 The central issues here were first set out in Horkheimer's essay *Traditional and Critical Theory*. See Horkheimer in Connerton (1978).

9 The practice of transferring the properties of human subjects to systems beyond their control is testimony to the existence of an alienated condition. For further discussion, see Linklater (1990a, ch. 8) and Rosenberg (1994, ch. 5).

10 It might be argued that anarchy does tend to generate self-interested political units, and that the security dilemma is the mechanism which triggers this reaction. The response to this observation is that under conditions of limited communication and low levels of trust, states are very likely to acquire the properties of egotistical subjects. Whether they are condemned to remain constituted in this way is the important question. Members of the English School argue that states have learned to cooperate to produce an anarchical society (Bull, 1977). Kant also argued that states have the capacity to abolish the international state of nature and to weave cosmopolitan principles into international society. That such forms of learning are possible is central to critical social theory and to other perspectives such as liberalism. T. H. Green's claim that states can learn to live peacefully even in the context of anarchy boldly formulates the crucial point (Linklater, 1990a, p. 229 n. 21).

11 Suganami (1989) describes these as world order proposals based on the domestic analogy and reveals that they are more subtle and sophisticated than is often realised.

12 For a statement of important affinities between critical social theory and genealogy in this regard, see Hoy and McCarthy (1994).

13 Attempts in the nineteenth century to explain the alleged inferiority of women or indigenous peoples by demonstrating their smaller cranial capacity illustrate the central point, as does the Nazi regime's obsession with the politics of eugenics in the twentieth century.

14 Wight and the English School more generally are not guilty of the ahistoricity which is so prevalent within neo-realism but Wight's awareness of the central historical ruptures and discontinuities was not combined with an analysis of the prospects for international political change. The notion that all earlier states-systems were finally destroyed by empires negated any interest in explaining how a progressivist interpretation of international politics might be possible. An unequalled grasp of the historical development of the European states-system was therefore combined with an emphasis on the recurrent and repetitious which later finds virtually identical expression in neo-realism.

15 The USSR is an intriguing exception whose completeness was widely taken for granted. For an example, see Waltz (1979, p. 95).

16 Incompleteness is the result of the failure of the totalising project, a consequence of the state's inability to hold universality in check and to keep difference at bay. The possibility of new forms of political community which are simultaneously more open to the claims of universality and difference has long been immanent within the dominant moral vocabulary of most modern states. Incompleteness, and the possibilities for new forms of life which that condition allows, give critical theory its purchase on international relations.

17 The distinction between immanent and transcendent ideologies is drawn from Mann (1986, pp. 22–4).

18 On the possibility of a new universality which escapes the particularistic agendas of the dominant powers, see Said (1993).

19 Complex issues are raised here. Chs 2 and 3 consider them in greater detail.

20 Rousseau in Forsyth et al. (1970, p. 132). For a more detailed discussion of this theme, see Hoffmann (1965).

21 This formulation is indebted to Wright's claim that modern forms of citizenship have simultaneously been 'too puffed up' and 'too compressed'. See Wright (1990) and also ch. 6 below.

22 On the importance of the first two monopoly powers, and on the significance of the modes of self-discipline, see Elias (1982, part 2).

23 The relationship between accumulations of power, the development of citizenship and the transformation of political community is considered in ch. 6.

24 'In India', Hegel (1952, para. 327, addition) argued, 'five hundred men conquered twenty thousand who were not cowards, but who only lacked [the] disposition to work in close cooperation with others.'

25 Globalisation refers to the forces which compress time and space (see D. Held and McGrew, 1995, p. 59). Marx's statement in the *Grundrisse* about the universalising logic of capitalism also captured the essential point: 'while capital must on one side strive to tear down every spatial barrier to intercourse, i.e. to exchange, and conquer the whole earth for its market, it strives on the other side to annihilate this space with time, i.e. to reduce to a minimum the time spent in motion from one place to another.' See Linklater (1990b, p. 39).

26 Tilly (1994) also emphasises the state's reduced ability to create national time.

27 Transnational harm refers to the harms which societies cause one another and to the harms to which all are exposed by global actors and processes.

28 Put the two together, as Gellner (1983) argued, and the result is a potent mixture.

29 See Crawford (1988) for a discussion of the changing place of national minorities and indigenous peoples in international law.

30 Whether the more powerful states in Asia will escape these tendencies is a question raised by Strange (1996, pp. 6–7), who concludes that many of the forces undercutting sovereign states in Europe are likely to shape Asia in the aftermath of the Cold War.

31 On some accounts, ethnic fragmentation seems most likely to prevail; others note the global trend towards democratisation and greater reliance on regional cooperation. For an overview, see Horsman and Marshall (1994).

32 As Carens (1995, p. 45) argues, moral and political community are not one and the same. Individuals can belong to moral communities which are 'wider or narrower than any political community to which [they] belong'.

33 The participants in this community would be the heads of government rather than individuals. See below, p. 174.

34 However ambiguous Marx's writings were on the subject of national and cultural differences under socialism, they clearly believed that individual differences would flourish in the future communist society.

35 On the democratic elements in Marx's thought, see D. Held (1996, ch. 4).
36 Kant (1970b, p. 216) believed that growing public outrage against violations of rights in other parts of the world was a major advance in the development of world citizenship. The function of praxeology was to elucidate the concrete maxims of foreign policy which would give force and direction to growing cosmopolitan sentiments.
37 This formulation borrows significantly from Mouffe (1993) and O'Neill (1989a, 1991). Mouffe relies on Oakeshottian themes to make the case for a political community in which the commitment to public principles replaces shared national identity as the essence of the social bond. For further comments, see pp. 188–9 below.
38 Although war continues to play that role insofar as the pacified realm resorts to force in its dealings with other states.

Chapter 2 Universality, Difference and the Emancipatory Project

1 'Liberating ourselves from the merely presumptive generality of selectively employed universalistic principles applied in a context-insensitive manner has always required . . . social movements and political struggles; we have to learn from the painful experiences and the irreparable suffering of those who have been humiliated, insulted, injured, and brutalised that nobody may be excluded in the name of moral universalism . . . Someone who in the name of universalism excludes another who has the right to *remain* [italics in orignal] alien or other betrays his own guiding idea. The universalism of equal respect for all and solidarity with everything that bears the mark of humanity is first put to the test by radical freedom in the choice of individual life histories and particular forms of life' (Habermas, 1993, p. 15).
2 Bull (1966a) distinguished between a pluralist and solidarist or Grotian conception of the society of states in this way. The 'central Grotian assumption is that of the solidarity, or potential solidarity, of the states comprising international society, with respect to the enforcement of the law'. The solidarity of international society has been manifested in the belief that there is a clear distinction between just and unjust wars and in the broader assumption 'from which [the] right of humanitarian intervention is derived: that individual human beings are subjects of international law and members of international society in their own right' (1966a, p. 64). The rival pluralist conception of international society argues that 'states do not exhibit solidarity of this kind, but are capable of agreeing only for certain minimum purposes which fall short of that of the enforcement of the law' (1966a, p. 52). According to the pluralist perspective, the members of that society are states rather than individuals (1966a, p. 68). We shall return to this distinction below, see pp. 59–61.
3 As Bader (1995) argues, Walzer's version of communitarianism is coupled with a defence of pluralist social democracy orientated towards universalistic concerns. For a defence of the right of free movement, see Carens (1987) and also Dummett's chapter in Goodin and Barry (1992).
4 One of Hegel's main arguments against Kant is that *Moralität* cannot cast

any light on the institutions which will enable individuals to lead free lives. Kantian reason acting alone cannot offer reasons for preferring one system of property relations over another. Hegel's contention is that private property and common ownership are equally compatible with the Kantian categorical imperative but that private property is a necessary condition of individuality (Hegel, 1952, para. 135).

5 Walzer (1994a, p. 29) draws out the significance of these claims for citizenship in an intriguing way. Walzer clearly rejects efforts to replace citizenship of the state with citizenship of some form of world political association: 'I am not a citizen of the world ... I am not even aware that there is a world such that one could be a citizen of it. No one has ever offered me citizenship, or described the naturalization process, or enlisted me in the world's institutional structures, or given me an account of its decision procedures ... or provided me with a list of the benefits and obligations of citizenship, or shown me the world's calendar and the common celebrations and commemorations of its citizens.' Walzer does not argue that communities can ignore moral duties to the rest of humanity. Indeed the question of how these might be balanced is an important part of his work (see below, pp. 79–81). But in his critique of the supposition that cosmopolitan morality requires the creation of a universal political association, Walzer asks whether it is not enough to be a 'cosmopolitan American'.

6 Very complex issues are involved in these debates. Gibney (1995) is an excellent guide to the main issues.

7 See Walzer (1995, pp. 52–61) on the 'tyranny' which results when those who have been allowed entry into a society are denied full citizenship rights.

8 The brief analysis of Hegel's view offered earlier also suggests as much. Large issues are involved here. For further discussion, see C. Brown (1992).

9 For a brief description of this position, and the rival standpoint, see MacIntyre (1984, p. 18).

10 See Connolly (1993, pp. 34–5) for a critique of the fixed moral order and Connolly (1994) for an approach to ethics which begins with the relationship between the constitution of moral subjectivity and the construction of otherness.

11 Emphasing the potentials for domination which are inherent in universalistic morality is a recurrent theme in much recent social theory. The response offered here is that ethical universalism asserts the rights of outsiders against communities which may profoundly affect their interests but which refuse them political representation and voice. By criticising the principle of state sovereignty, cosmopolitan thought challenges one of the most basic systems of exclusion in the modern world.

12 A third possibility – the post-Westphalian state – is considered in ch. 6.

13 The strongest affinity is with the pluralist conception of the society of states which argues that states, which are the exclusive subjects of international law, agree on the basic principles of coexistence but do not cooperate to realise shared moral ends. See n. 2, above.

14 We may regard this as marking the transition to a more solidarist conception of international society in which states cooperate to promote substantive moral ends such as the welfare of their inhabitants.

15 Close political cooperation to transnationalise the struggle against unjust

exclusion is one of the characteristics of the post-Westphalian state as it is understood in the present work. For further discussion, see ch. 6.

16 Postmodernism is critical, as a recent summary maintains, 'of universal claims, of totalizing theory, of impartial truth, of the Cartesian I' (D. Held, 1993, p. 12). Note that Habermas shares some of these suspicions, as his notion of an 'enlightened suspicion of enlightenment' reveals (see Roderick, 1986, p. 134). See also Giddens (1993, pp. 48–9) on the enigmatic qualities of modernity.

17 This was important in the critique of the position which Rawls took at least in *A Theory of Justice*. See Sandel (1984) for further details, and also Cochran (1996).

18 There are echoes here of Hegel's critique of Kantian *Moralität* and similar doubts about cosmopolitanism.

19 Anarchist versions of this theme are evident in the writings of Bakunin amongst others. See G. P. Maximoff, *The Political Philosophy of Bakunin* (New York: Free Press, 1953).

20 On the question of whether the ethic of care and responsibility is an essentially female ethic see Tronto (1993). To assume so is to risk condemning women indefinitely to the private sphere (Tronto, ibid.).

21 For a similar stress on the need to target state monopolies, see Derrida below, p. 74.

22 The point can be extended in relation to each of the five state monopolies discussed above on p. 28.

23 For further comments, see below, ch. 6.

24 For a different formulation which stems from post-structuralist theory, see Devetak (1995a, p. 44): 'The ethico-political moment in post-structuralism disavows the assertion or imposition of sovereign boundedness. Rather than correlate community with a clearly demarcated social space (territory) that asserts sovereignty, it prefers a position of openness: not just to keep open the boundaries of the community, but to keep open the question of community. The issue is not that of establishing a sovereign community, but of thinking what community without sovereignty might mean.' For support for a similar vision from a leading member of the English School, namely Hedley Bull, see below, pp. 193–5.

25 Interestingly Habermas (1994, pp. 103–4) expresses a preference for the language of understanding rather than the language of emancipation. Apel (1979, pp. 98–9) stresses emancipation as 'the progressive implementation of the standard of ideal communication and nonrepressive deliberation'. An emancipatory project with these intentions remains a valid ideal. See also below, p. 106.

Chapter 3 The Dialogic Ethic and the Transformation of Political Community

1 The term is derived from T. Nagel's book of the same title, Oxford, 1986.
2 See Wight (1977, p. 103) on Hellenic conceptions of Carthage, and H. Suganami, 'Japan's Entry into International Society', in Bull and Watson (1984).

3 On the relationship between ethnocentrism and transcultural validity claims, see R. Rorty and T. McCarthy, 'An Exchange on Truth, Freedom and Politics', *Critical Inquiry* (spring 1990). McCarthy argues that efforts to articulate transcultural validity claims are a means of transcending ethnocentrism while Rorty suggests that they are more likely to act as its conveyance. See also Rorty (1990, p. 198, and 1991, p. 213), where he remarks that 'the only common ground on which we can get together is that defined by the overlap between their communal beliefs and desires and our own.' Dialogue, it might be suggested, is a means of identifying the common ground and exploring the possibility of transcultural validity claims.

4 The emergence of these universalities of belief is a feature of the Axial Age civilisations (see Eisenstadt, 1986). Of course, different civilisations reached distinctive universalistic ethical positions by diverse routes, and what Butler (see p. 99 below) calls a complex labour of translation is still needed to produce a genuine universality. Yet these ethical convergences are deeply significant and reveal that different civilisations have made moral progress in similar ways.

5 The stress on slavery here does not underestimate the prevalence of bonded labour in many parts of the world including the Indian subcontinent.

6 One critique of Spanish conceptions of 'the newly-discovered Indians' stresses their enthusiasm for assuming that the other was already 'one of us', potentially if not actually Christian (Todorov, 1992). In the case of first contacts between civilisations, it might be argued, the central question is how to treat fellow human beings who are different from 'us'. Obligations to human beings *qua* human beings are all that exist in the absence of obligations based on pre-existing solidarities. See also Callinicos (1995, pp. 196–7) for a similar rejection of Rorty's statement that appeals to common humanity are weak and unconvincing. Rorty and Callinicos are agreed, however, that existing solidarities may be 'too narrow in an ethically relevant sense' to support duties to strangers. Both support a cosmopolitan ethic based on the 'recognition of the inadequacy of the narrower solidarities of nation or race or religion' (Callinicos, 1995, pp. 196–7).

7 The West might be said to have uncovered something of universal significance but to have expressed it in a culturally dominating way. Yet its own contradictions created the potential for working towards a universality which took account of the different starting-points of others. The formulation is indebted to Butler's argument that more advanced forms of universality require a complex labour of translation. See below, p. 99.

8 See Abu-Lughod (1963) on efforts to find Islamic counterparts to Western conceptions of deliberative politics in the nineteenth century. D. Rammage, *Democracy in Indonesia* (London, 1995) explores related themes in conjunction with notions of *musyawarah* (consultation) and *mufakat* (consensus).

9 It also requires the additional commitment that dialogue within wider communities of discourse should be guided simply by the force of the better argument. For further comments, see below, p. 92.

10 Owen (1995, pp. 160–4) uses Nietzschean resources to develop a similar approach to political community. George (1994, pp. 168–9) has argued for more careful analysis of the respects in which the Hegelian and Nietzschean perspectives criticise forms of social closure in Western theory and practice.

For a modernist approach to dialogue which also shares some of the features of Habermas's account, see Barry (1995, pp. 7–8, but also p. 196).

11 Coming to an agreement and reaching a consensus are not necessarily one and the same. See Benhabib (1993, p. 9). On the notion of a 'con-sensus' as a 'feeling or a sensing together', as in the enjoyment of contrapuntal music, see N. Love, 'What's Left of Marx', in White (1995, p. 62).

12 Rawls (1971) remains the most important statement of this crucial point.

13 These observations are taken further in connection with the nature of modern citizenship in ch. 6.

14 On the charge that transparency is a normative end of critical social theory and that the elimination of difference is the likely effect, see C. Brown (1994, p. 221). For Habermas's remarks on transparency and the elimination of difference, see p. 74 above. For a different reading of Habermas which draws on Benhabib's distinction between reaching an agreement and reaching an understanding, see Squires (1996, p. 631).

15 See also the earlier distinction between 'substitutionalist' and 'interactive universalism' in Benhabib and Cornell (1987, ch. 4).

16 Empathetic cooperation is a term introduced in Sylvester (1994, pp. 96–9).

17 As Dallmayr (Benhabib and Dallmayr, 1990, p. 8) points out, dialogue involves the hermeneutic commitment to understanding the viewpoint of all others.

18 In this context, it is worth noting Hutchings (1994, pp. 33–4) that the 'feminist ethic of care ... is neither confined by borders nor indifferent to them. Instead the feminist ethic of care opens up the possibility of mutual recognition across communities ... It is not therefore an ethics which implies an eventual, universal moral consensus but it does suggest the possibility of conversation, cooperation and also cross-border criticism in moral reasoning over questions of war and justice.'

19 Lyotard's statement that consensus is a horizon that is never reached resonates with Habermas's claim that human beings can only know that they are unfree and could never claim to have achieved absolute freedom. But there are important differences between their perspectives. Lyotard's observation that 'the poet is not concerned, after his statements are made, to enter into a dialogue with his readers in order to establish whether they understood him ...' suggests an unwillingness to attach too much importance to intelligibility between interlocutors. Discourse ethics is inevitably troubled by the notion of dialogue without dialectic. Some of these issues are discussed with considerable sophistication in Rosenau (1994). For comments on dialogue with, and without, dialectic, see Linklater (1994).

20 Hegel (1956, p. 144) made one telling point against the incommensurability thesis in his observations about the Indian caste-system in his lectures on the *Philosophy of History*. His argument was that nature rather than society was assumed to have created differences of caste. But human beings invested this power in nature and alienated their power to shape social structures to natural forces. To use Marx's terms, the caste-system was anchored in false consciousness. Such cross-cultural judgements may trouble some contemporary political critics. Yet it is an odd form of ethical nationalism which would immunise dominant cultures elsewhere from the kind of critique which has been used against powerful groups in the West. Without such cross-cultural

judgements, the legitimacy of those who wield notions of nature to impose power on others goes unchallenged and the ideal of the dialogic community is denied an important line of defence.

21 Rorty (1989, p. 68) argues for 'domination-free communication' and for a condition in which 'the idea of truth as correspondence to reality might gradually be replaced by the idea of truth as what comes to be believed in the course of free and open encounters'. But as Rorty (1990, p. 634) suggests, 'what [it] is really important to think about is what makes an encounter free from the influence of force.' See also Higgins (1996). On the need for a radical pluralism which develops the points made in this paragraph, see Connolly (1995).

22 The point here is not to rule out the theoretical possibility that the Archimedean standpoint might be retrieved at some distant point in the future. To rule out that possibility would be to endorse some notion of the end of history.

23 The 'we' in this formulation is the sum of all radical movements and perspectives which oppose unjust systems of exclusion across the world.

24 For a related formulation, see R. Bernstein (1986, p. 137).

25 This formulation is indebted to Keane's observation (1990, pp. 91–2) that postmodernism is not a radical break with modernisation but a dialectical intensification of its democratic impulses. See also Giddens's claim (1993, p. 5) that 'we have not moved beyond modernity but are living precisely through a phase of its radicalization.'

26 Investments in dialogue and consultation are not the preserve of Western societies. They are not uniquely exposed to the Socratic moment, and sensitivity to different phrasings which do not employ the vocabulary of the liberal-democratic West is of central importance. The nature of unconstrained dialogue must itself be decided through transcultural dialogue – otherwise there is a danger that one hegemonic account of discourse will prevail.

27 See, for example, the discussion of female genital mutilation in 'Symposium on Women and Human Rights', *Human Rights Quarterly*, 3 (1981).

28 The point here is that societies which are committed to the politics of dialogue must involve outsiders in appropriate communities of discourse if they are to demonstrate moral consistency. Whether such societies have the right to intervene in other societies remains a crucial question but it cannot be answered satisfactorily without ascertaining whether they have created systems of political cooperation which contribute to the goal of a universal communication community. Efforts to consider the ethics of intervention without considering these wider issues should be resisted. See pp. 204–12 for further remarks on the relationship between different forms of international society and the ideal of a universal communication community.

29 See D. C. Hendrickson, 'Political Realism and Migration in Law and Ethics' in Goodin and Barry (1992, p. 221).

30 On the subject of states as local agents, see Bull (1983a). For a different formulation, see Habermas (1994, p. 24) on 'multilaterally coordinated world domestic policy'.

31 The notion of the concentric-circle image of duty can be found in Shue (1988, pp. 692–3).

32 This is to take issue with Bauman (see above, p. 67) and to argue that morality can take the form of rules which disregard the differences between persons – although it is not exhausted by the quest for universalisable principles.

33 Brian Barry made a similar point in his analysis of Rawls's *A Theory of Justice*. See *The Liberal Theory of Justice* (Oxford: Clarendon Press, ch. 12). See also Rousseau's comment in *A Discourse on the Origins of Inequality*: 'Do you not know that numbers of your fellow-creatures are starving for want of what you have too much of? You ought to have had the express and universal consent of mankind, before appropriating more of the common subsistence than you needed for your own maintenance' (Rousseau, 1968, p. 204). See also the French revolutionary thinker Anacharsis Cloots, on the principle that 'sovereignty resides essentially in the entire human race' (Heater, 1996, p. 80).

34 To borrow Walzer's terminology, 'the thin morality is already very thick'. See Walzer (1994b, p. 12).

35 Bohler (1990, p. 133) formulates the central moral imperative in this way: 'Always engage in arguments that would also be capable of achieving consensus in an ideal community of argumentation and endeavour to bring about such circumstances as approximate more closely to the structures and conditions of an ideal community of argumentation.'

36 Alienation describes the condition in which the human race is at the mercy of the structures and forces which are its own creation. Exploitation refers to the condition in which particular groups directly control and profit from the labour-power of others. Estrangement describes the world of suspicion and hostility between separate national or cultural groups. For an analysis of the claim that the eradication of alienation, exploitation and estrangement from global society is the key political aspiration of the Marxist tradition, see Linklater (1996d).

37 These wider communities of discourse are the three conceptions of international society described earlier on pp. 74–5.

Chapter 4 The Modes of Exclusion and the Boundaries of Community

1 This formulation reworks the Marxian project of developing a sociology of the origins, reproduction and transformation of modes of production.

2 Hegel's views are set out in *The Philosophy of Right*, para. 324.

3 See Canny (1973) and Campbell (1990 and 1992).

4 The standard of civilisation distinguished the 'civilised' nations from 'barbaric' and 'savage' peoples.

5 For an astute analysis of forms of disciplinary power, see Ashley and Walker (1990) and the contributors to Rosenau (1994), especially the essays by Sylvester and Der Derian.

6 Habermas (1979) and Giddens (1985) are crucial works in this respect. Linklater (1990b) considers the significance of Marxism for critical international theory. Derrida (1994a) offers an appraisal of Marx's thought for the project of deconstruction.

7 For related observations about the ethical significance of the politics of resistance to unjust exclusion, see J. M. Bernstein (1995, pp. 193–4).

8 The question of how states learn the art of close cooperation has remained an influential theme in the literature on international organisations. See Haas (1990) and Modelski (1990).

9 This point resonates with the critique of neo-realism discussed above on pp. 18–19.

10 On the importance of Deutsch's themes, see Bull (1966b).

11 An interpretation of Marx criticised by Roderick (1986) amongst others.

12 Moral-practical learning is distinguished from technical-instrumental learning, which refers to advances in understanding how to master and exploit nature, and from strategic learning, which refers to advances in understanding how to administer, outmanoeuvre and control other human beings (see Habermas, 1979a).

13 Dahrendorf (1974) argues that citizenship is one of the key aspects of the positive side of modernity and one of the means by which it can realise its radical potential. This theme is developed below on pp. 168–75 and in ch. 6.

14 Strategic rationalisation refers to developments in understanding how to exercise control over others.

15 The transcendence of invidious dualisms often involved the denial of the other's right to a separate existence. See Todorov (1992).

16 On their significance for the development of capitalist modernity, see Nelson (1949) on 'universal otherhood'.

17 For accounts of these developments within the Islamic world, see G. E. Von Grundebaum, *Islam: Essays in the Nature and Growth of a Cultural Tradition* (New York, 1961), B. S. Turner, *Weber and Islam: A Critical Study* (London, 1974), M. Mahdi, *Ibn Khaldun's Philosophy of History: A Study in the Philosophic Foundation of the Science of Culture* (London, 1957), and E. Mortimer, *Faith and Power: The Politics of Islam* (London, 1980).

18 For a discussion of Islam, see Lewis (1982). The need to catch up with Western scientific and technological development was a major theme in the Middle East in the nineteenth century. For further details, see Abu-Lughod (1963).

19 On dialogue in international society, see Watson (1982). Bull and Watson (1984, p. 1) argued that a society of states was distinguished from a system of states by its emphasis on 'dialogue and consent' which facilitated the development of common rules, institutions and interests. The extent to which the society of states provides a dialogic framework for diverse states and cultures is a theme addressed by C. Brown (1988), Blaney and Inayatullah (1994) and Shapcott (1994). It provides one of the means by which fraternisation can find what Habermas (1984, p. 241) calls a 'foothold in institutions through which it [can] culturally reproduce itself in the long run'. The significance of the Grotian approach to international society for the normative ideals of the discourse theory of morality will be considered in ch. 6.

20 The important point here is that fraternisation does not necessarily take the

form of wider communities of discourse, although it may be a prior step in their formation.

21 Habermas (1979, pp. 37–8) maintained that Nelson assumed that the universalistic world-views of the European high Middle Ages were 'exclusively a Western phenomenon'. Habermas went on to deny that universalistic potentials 'were a peculiarity of occidental traditions' and referred, in this context, to Jasper's notion of the rise of a universal consciousness in many different civilisations during the Axial Age. For further analysis of the Axial Age and the development of cultural and religious collectivities which were distinct from ethnic and political ones, see Eisenstadt (1986, pp. 6 and 19).

22 Nelson (1973, pp. 101–2) believed that Marxism was the ideology which was most likely to offer resistance to the reassertion of particularism and privilege in the context of modernity.

23 This question is central to Bull and Watson (1984). See the introduction and conclusion.

24 This tripartite division is a refinement of the typology set out in Linklater (1990a, pp. 224–5). One response to Nelson's work argues that the 'sociology of civilisations' should pay serious attention to the 'sociology of empires' and, in so doing, to the 'comparative study of colonialism' (Tiryakian, 1974, p. 127). Tiryakian also emphasises the importance of 'intra-civilisational encounters'. Some systems of states such as the ancient Chinese, Graeco-Roman and modern European systems have some of the qualities of intra-civilisational encounters. The modern states-system which brings different civilisations within a universal society of states for the first time is not so easily categorised in this way. On this question, see Bull and Watson (1984).

25 Mann (1986, p. 28) eschews all claims about the primacy of any single factor throughout human history, and argues that different sources of power – the economic, ideological, political or military – have been the main tracklaying vehicles in different epochs. How they interact holds the key to extensions of power across space and to increasing concentrations of power.

26 Extensive power 'refers to the ability to organise large numbers of people over far-flung territories in order to engage in minimally stable cooperation'. Intensive power 'refers to the ability to organise tightly and command a high level of mobilisation or commitment from the participants, whether the area and numbers covered are great or small' (see Mann 1986, p. 5). Mann (1986, p. 8) also separates authoritative power from diffuse power. Authoritative power is 'willed by groups and institutions' and 'comprises definite commands and conscious obedience'; diffuse power, which is exemplified by the dissemination of ideology, 'spreads in a more spontaneous, unconscious, decentered way throughout a population'.

27 It should be stressed that these are not the terms in which Mann casts his analysis.

28 Put differently, the inquiry provides numerous insights into the relationship between the enlargement of political associations through extensive power, the emergence of greater concentrations of power within bounded communities through intensive and authoritative power, and the development of more inclusive solidarities and loyalties through the operation of diffuse power.

29 See W. H. McNeill, *A World History* (Oxford, 1979, ch. 3) on the rise of universal religions in this context. Interstitial power is a term used by Mann

(1986, pp. 363ff) to describe the rise of transcendent ideology in the form of monotheistic religion.

30 On the distinction between immanent and transcendent ideology, see Mann (1986, pp. 22–4). Transcendent ideology corresponds with the notion of Axial Age ideology. See Machinist, 'On Self-Consciousness in Mesopotamia' (Eisenstadt, 1986, p. 183) on the new ideologies which presented 'a comprehensive view of the world, not merely of any particular group, and argue[d] that the main task [was] to remake reality, corrupt and imperfect as it is, in accordance with the dictates of a higher moral order'.

31 On the limited efficacy of the universalisation of citizenship in the context of growing class inequalities, see Garnsey (1974).

32 Christians and Jews were similarly tolerated within the Islamic world though subjected to special taxes. Jews were invariably used as intermediaries – for example in commercial relations – to ensure that those of the Islamic faith were not corrupted by regular contact with the Christian world. For further discussion, see Lewis (1982).

33 Compromise with Rome occurred in the case of Christianity (Mann, 1986, pp. 326–31). Absorption within the state occurred in the case of Confucianism in Han China (1986, pp. 342–4).

34 It is important to note that a strong sense of answerability to others has not always been enshrined in the idea of the equality of states. See Wight (1977, chs 2–3) on the hegemonial character of Greece, and the shift towards the notion of the equality of city-states following the King's Peace in 387–386 BC with Persia.

35 Wight (1977, p. 33) makes little comment on the origins of universal moral perspectives but his observation that commerce is often the first main point of contact brings Mann and McNeill's point to mind that the expansion of the sphere of social and economic exchange has often been the context in which universalising moralities have developed.

36 For accounts of the tension between different conceptions of community in the Warring States Period in China, and especially the disputes between Legalist, Confucian and Mohist philosophies, see A. Waley, *Three Ways of Thought in Ancient China* (London, 1963), and R. L. Walker, *The Multi-State System of Ancient China* (New Haven, Connecticut, 1953).

37 Identification with Hellas appears to have developed gradually between the eighth and sixth centuries BC, and greatly increased as a result of the Persian Wars. See Hill (1989).

38 The rationalisation of the moral code is a term borrowed from L. T. Hobhouse, *Morals in Evolution* (New York, 1906), p. 34. Here it refers to the systematic scrutiny of the foundations of moral argument.

39 Eisenstadt (1986, pp. 35–7) refers to the 'tendency to universalise the political or cultural community' in ancient Greece but adds that its results were more evident in the symbolic than in the political sphere. Greeks were unable to transcend the legal and institutional framework of the local city-state which often drew upon Axial Age themes to couch its claims yet remained embedded in pre-Axial Age modes of consciousness.

40 A form of diplomatic dialogue existed in the society of states but this was rarely understood as involving equals. As Wight (1977, p. 65) argues, the dominant conception of international society in ancient Greece was hege-

monic. What is more, universalistic conceptions of ethics invariably appealed to notions of rationality which annihilated the difference of the other (Kristeva, 1991, p. 59). Visions of a universal communication community which brought the radically different together as equal participants in dialogue would have seemed absurd, given the widespread belief in the superiority of Hellenic culture.

41 The importance of the rationalisation of the symbolic sphere for the administration of polyethnic empires was noted earlier. Alexander's more cosmopolitan mode of governance following the conquest of Persia is a striking illustration of the creation of complex symbolic frameworks to legitimate imperial rule (Wallbank, 1981, ch. 2).

42 See Hill (1989) and also Walzer (1995, pp. 53–5) on the exclusion of the metic 'guest-workers' from full citizenship.

Chapter 5 State Power, Modernity and its Potentials

1 Held's observation about 'strategies of displacement' which 'disperse the worst effects of social and political problems onto vulnerable groups while appeasing those able to monopolise claims most effectively' is important in this context. See Held (1996, p. 252).

2 See Linklater (1990b). The importance of this dimension is stressed by Mann, however. For further details, see Mann (1986, p. 534) on 'normative regulation' in 'multi-power–actor civilisations'.

3 On the autonomy of the moral-cultural realm, see Bull and Watson (1984).

4 J. M. Bernstein (1995, p. 193) notes one dimension of the 'meaning of moral universalism' in the struggle against unjust exclusion. Resistance to entitlements which are denied on the basis of the characteristics of social class, ethnicity, gender or race is directed at 'scope restrictions that constitute the essence of domination and oppression'. The lifting of scope restrictions on the application of principles widens the circle of those who are recognised as free. These issues are taken further in the next chapter.

5 No single perspective embraces all of these dimensions although realism (which is principally concerned with strategic interaction), Marxism (which is largely preoccupied with systems of production and exchange), rationalism (which focuses on the nature of international order) and more recent critical-theoretical perspectives (which investigate modes of exclusion and potentials for dialogue) address particular aspects of the whole.

6 As Vincent (1990a, p. 243) argues, the 'idea, also reaching its apogee in the nineteenth century, that states were *exclusively* the subjects of international law, and individuals merely its objects, Grotius would have found a peculiar one' (italics in original).

7 'The European peoples form a family in accordance with the universal principle underlying their legal code, their customs and their civilisation. This principle has modified their international conduct accordingly in a state of affairs [i.e. war] otherwise dominated by the mutual infliction of evil' Hegel (1952, para. 339, addition).

8 The Marxist theory of imperialism addressed the point, as Lenin's discussion

of the labour aristocracy in *Imperialism: The Highest Stage of Capitalism* reveals.

9 'In no previous period of modern history have frontiers been so rigidly demarcated, or their character as barriers so ruthlessly enforced, as to-day; and in no period, as we have already seen, has it been so apparently impossible to organise and maintain any international form of power. Modern technique, military and economic, seems to have indissolubly welded together power and territory.' See Carr (1946, p. 228).

10 As previously noted, functionalism and neo-functionalism and especially the work of Karl Deutsch are important exceptions to this general neglect, and sociological writings from Weber to Mann have reached beyond the question of how bounded communities interact with one another to the issue of how boundaries are constituted in the first place. Doty (1996) approaches the latter issue by noting how the literature on nationalism has long been concerned with analysing the constitution of bounded communities.

11 On the notion of combinations of states as a level of analysis, see Linklater (1990b), especially chs 4, 6 and 7.

12 On welfare internationalism, see Suganami (1989, pp. 100ff).

13 'There is every reason to suppose that considerable numbers of Welshmen, Catalans and Uzbeks have quite satisfactorily solved the problem of regarding themselves as good Welshmen, Catalans and Uzbeks for some purposes and good British, Spanish and Soviet citizens for others . . . An extension of this system of divided but not incompatible loyalties is the only tolerable solution to the problem of self-determination; for it is the only one which will satisfy at one and the same time the needs of modern military and economic organisation and the urge of human beings to form groups based on common tradition, language and usage.' See Carr (1941, p. 50). Parallels with Bull's thought come to mind. See below, pp. 193–5.

14 The penultimate sentence of Carr (1946, p. 239) formulates the critical position in this way.

15 This may seem to suggest that immanent criticism is culture-bound and incapable of raising universalistic claims. The response is that modern conceptions of citizenship deny that differences of race, gender and ethnicity are legitimate grounds for treating persons differently and, in so doing, institutionalise universal principles. For further elaboration, see the earlier discussion on pp. 85–7.

16 On one level, as Carr (1945) argued, the development of citizenship rights in the first part of the century clashed with the internationalist project outlined here. But there is a deep connection between the two which Habermas (1996, p. 515) emphasises: 'Even if we still have a long way to go before fully achieving it, the cosmopolitan condition is no longer merely a mirage. State citizenship and world citizenship form a continuum whose contours, at least, are already becoming visible.' The relationship is discussed below in ch. 6.

17 See Suganami (1996) for an analysis of the theoretical issues raised in this paragraph.

18 As Ruggie argues, Waltz allows that the structure of international relations can only change in two ways: by the metamorphosis of the constitutive principles of world political organisation, as when anarchy is replaced by hierarchy, or by a change in the distribution of the military capabilities of

national units (Ruggie, 1983, pp. 266 and 271; Waltz, 1979, p. 93). Waltz fails to recognise that international political change can occur as a new configuration of state structures emerges. Ruggie illustrates the theme by arguing that the shift from medieval to modern international society occurred as political units replaced their image of themselves as the parts of a larger medieval unity with the notion that they were possessive individualists controlling 'mutually exclusive' jurisdictions (Ruggie, 1983, pp. 275 and 278). Carr's writings develop the point by observing that international political change would occur if nation-states no longer constituted themselves as territorially exclusive units. The approach strengthens Ruggie's observation that neo-realism is wrong to suppose that 'unit-level processes' are 'all product and are not at all productive' (Ruggie, 1983, p. 284). Wight's observation that domestic constitutionalism contributed to the development of a modern society of states strengthens the argument still further and reveals that the neo-realist distinction between systemic and reductionist theory is spurious. For further observations on this latter point, see Linklater (1990b). For further comments on constitutionalism, see below, pp. 169–71.

19 The notion of like-minded states is drawn from the like-minded group in international relations. For a discussion, see Dolman (1979).

20 'What we are required to surrender is not a mythical attribute called sovereignty, but the habit of framing our military and economic policy without regard for the needs and interests of other countries' (Carr, 1941, p. 61).

21 For an analysis of the different frameworks of action which are relevant to the foreign policy of liberal states, see Brewin (1988).

22 See above, p. 74. The trichotomy is derived from Linklater (1990a, ch. 10).

23 As noted earlier, groups such as the Amish and indigenous peoples which maintain some distance from the dominant society are often cited by way of illustration.

24 On the theoretical import of this claim, see ch. 5 n. 18 above.

25 Bull (Bull et al., 1990, pp. 73–4) also maintained that the development of constitutionalism prepared the way for an international society of states.

26 Bull (1983a, p. 6) provides the definitive summary: 'we have to remember that when these demands for justice were first put forward, the leaders of Third World peoples spoke as supplicants in a world in which the Western powers were still in a dominant position. The demands that were put forward had necessarily to be justified in terms of . . . conventions of which the Western powers were the principal authors; the moral appeal had to be cast in terms that would have most resonance in Western societies. But as . . . non-Western peoples have become stronger . . . and as the Westernised leaders of the early years of independence have been replaced in many countries by new leaders more representative of local or indigenous forces, Third World spokesmen have become freer to adopt a rhetoric that sets Western values aside, or . . . places different interpretations upon them. Today there is legitimate doubt as to how far the demands emanating from the Third World coalition are compatible with the moral ideas of the West'.

27 On functional similarity, see Waltz (1979, p. 97). See Deudney (1996) for

the argument that the Philadelphian system poses a similar challenge to neo-realist postulates.

Chapter 6 Community and Citizenship in the Post-Westphalian Era

1 For a parallel exercise which uses immanent critique in connection with democratic ideas, see D. Held (1995, ch. 8). Oakeshott's interpretation of Hegel's account of the ethical state outlines the method of immanent critique, and explains the approach which is adopted here. Hegel's rational state, according to Oakeshott, was 'intimated' – no more and no less – by the societies of his time. The ideal was clearly 'recognisable' in the pattern of their development yet radically 'incomplete'. For Hegel, the role of immanent critique under such conditions was to stress the achievements of the modern state and to highlight possibilities for further developments. Proceeding in this way, it was possible to imagine what Hoffmann (1960, p. 189) called 'relevant utopias', which take existing normative commitments to their logical conclusion. Returning to the present argument with these points in mind, some trends within existing states may provide evidence that higher possibilities are being realised, or might be realised in the near future. But in the end these are no more than illustrations of the paths which states should tread if they are to release the potential for continuing the struggle against unjustified exclusion which is already latent within established conceptions of national citizenship. Oakeshott's account of Hegel is set out in M. Oakeshott, *On Human Conduct* (Oxford, 1975), pp. 262–3.
2 For further details, see Garnsey (1974).
3 Others, such as Mouffe (1993, pp. 84–6), argue that the recognition of group-specific rights will simply entrench essentialist accounts of women, ethnic minorities and others in the public domain.
4 Migrants, national and other minorities and gypsies are three groups regularly cast down amongst the lumpen-citizenry in several European societies.
5 The cultural logic of questioning the moral significance of human differences also contributes to the end.
6 Mouffe (1993) argues that the 'ethico-political bond' is at odds with communitarian notions of a unifying common good and with the liberal belief that political community consists of elementary 'rules of civil intercourse' which leave individuals at liberty to promote their own interests. Similar themes are suggested by the idea of 'post-national civility' defended in Veit-Brause (1995, p. 72). See also Reiner (1995, p. 15) on 'civic nationalism' which avoids liberal-individualistic and national-collectivist conceptions of the social bond. These issues have particular reference in the European context, where the issue arises of how a European polity can be created in the absence of demos or nation. For a commentary on this latter theme which emphasises the importance of multiple loyalties (sub-state or sub-national, national and supranational), see Weiler (1996, p. 526).
7 As Habermas (1994, p. 165) notes, what 'was once meant by the idea of

popular sovereignty is doomed to decay into a mere chimera if it remains locked in the historical form of the self-asserting sovereign nation-state'.

8 Bull added that there might also be a short step from 'a situation of protracted uncertainty about the locus of sovereignty' to the condition where 'the concept of sovereignty is recognised to be irrelevant'. There is an interesting parallel with Carr's thinking about the concept of sovereignty. Carr (1946, p. 231) argued that the 'concept of sovereignty is more likely to become in the future even more blurred and indistinct than it is at present'. 'It is unlikely', he went on to write, 'that the future units of power will take much account of formal sovereignty. There is no reason why each unit should not consist of groups of several formally sovereign states so long as the effective (but not necessarily the nominal) authority is exercised from a single centre. The effective group unit of the future will in all probability not be the unit formally recognised as such by international law.'

9 Reflecting on this theme, MacCormack (1996, p. 566) argues that 'the members of a nation are as such in principle entitled to effective organs of political self-determination within the world order of sovereign or post-sovereign states; but these need not provide for self-government in the form of a sovereign state.' Parallel themes exist in the writings of Walzer, as noted above on pp. 59–60.

10 For a contemporary reformulation, see James (1986). The notion that insiders 'cannot seek legal redress because the door is closed against them' and the claim that 'outsiders have no right to complain about what goes on behind the door' (pp. 227–8) reaffirm the links between sovereignty and citizenship, as does the reference to the 'absence of any legal obligations to outsiders regarding one's internal conduct' (p. 226). See also the contention that the state is similar to a home which keeps its dirty washing to itself (p. 227) and the point that sovereignty entails 'functional exclusivity' so that the state 'does not let any of its functions fall into the direct grasp of externally based hands' (p. 227). A post-Westphalian state would not be wedded to any of these propositions.

11 Globalisation makes non-territorial conceptions of citizenship possible, for example by participation in transnational social movements. See Van Steenbergen (1994) for further discussion.

12 Owen (1995, p. 162) goes further by arguing that 'one can easily imagine a community in which formal respect for other persons (because they are willing to engage in argument and to exhibit the virtues appropriate to this engagement) is twinned with substantive disdain for them (because we hold that the ordered set of values they recommend is lacking by our lights).'

13 See the observations by Meinecke and Phillips cited on pp. 65 and 187 above.

14 See O'Neill's comments on the need for ethical reasoning to embrace abstract principles of justice and the sphere of particularity, as outlined on pp. 93–4.

15 The Austro-Marxists such as Bauer and Renner argued that minority nations could elect to be represented by their respective national associations rather than by the representatives of the areas in which they happened to reside (see Lowy, 1976, p. 92). On the merits of embedding this principle in the structure of European international relations, see Brewin (forthcoming).

16 It would be fanciful to press this point too far. Nonetheless, references to the

need to build political arrangements around 'the three-tiered edifice' of political loyalty in other continents do exist. See F. M. Deng et al. (eds) *Sovereignty as Responsibility: Conflict Management in Africa* (Washington, DC: Brookings Institute, 1996), p. 68 and the conclusion.

17 The world as well as the species because of obligations to the environment and to other species. See Falk (1994), and Van Steenbergen (1994) on global ecological citizenship.

18 Developments in the foreign policy world have also invoked some notion of world or international citizenship. The concept of the 'good international citizen' which asserted that states have duties to promote 'purposes beyond themselves' was an important theme in Australian foreign policy under the last Labour Government. Good international citizenship referred to the international role and obligations of the benevolent middle power. See Evans and Grant (1991). Linklater (1992b) related the concept to developments in the theory of international relations. For further comment, see Lawler (1992) and Hutchings (1996).

19 O'Neill (1991, pp. 301–2) maintains that the duty to avoid treating others in ways to which they could not consent requires more than a commitment to refrain from taking advantage of others' weaknesses: 'Just agents and agencies allow others, including those most vulnerable to them, the space to refuse and renegotiate offers.' Justice involves 'a commitment to transform the structure of institutions and the characters and powers of individual agents, i.e. the presuppositions of transactions, so as to reduce powerless and vulnerability'. Nancy Fraser distinguishes between accessibility to public spheres and the extent to which there is parity of participation within them. For further discussion, see Cochran (1996, pp. 295–300). The approach to communicative frameworks in this chapter echoes these sentiments. See also the comments by Bohler cited above in ch. 3 n. 35.

20 As noted earlier (p. 103) any temptation to begin the discussion of cosmopolitan citizenship by considering the rights and wrongs of humanitarian intervention is best resisted. In the first instance, cosmopolitan citizenship expresses the conviction that outsiders should not be at the mercy of the economic, political and military power which one's own society has at its disposal.

21 Bull (1977, pp. 9–10 and 13) distinguishes an international system from an international society in this way. A 'system of states (or international system) is formed when two or more states have sufficient contact between them, and have sufficient impact on one another's decisions to cause them to behave – at least in some measure – as parts of a whole.' A 'society of states . . . exists when a group of states, conscious of certain common interests and common values, form a society in the sense that they conceive themselves to be bound by a common set of rules in their relations with one another, and share in the working of common institutions.'

22 Ongoing controversies over human rights indicate that attempts to spread commitments to these values beyond Western liberal-democratic societies can provoke the robust defence of a pluralist conception of international society in which the principle of state sovereignty remains sacrosanct.

23 Willetts (1996) traces the entry of non-governmental organisations into the wider diplomatic dialogue promoted by the UN system.

24 Significantly, Bull and Watson (1984, p. 1) maintain that a society of states exists where states determine the principles of their coexistence by 'dialogue and consent'.
25 Bull (1982) argued that an agreement about the evils of apartheid was about as far as the universal moral consensus stretched in the late 1970s and early 1980s.

Select Bibliography

Abu-Lughod, I. 1963: *The Arab Discovery of Europe: A Study in Cultural Encounters*. Princeton: Princeton University Press.

Anderson, M., den Boer, M. and Miller, G. 1994: European Citizenship and Cooperation in Justice and Home Affairs. In A. Duff et al. (eds), *Maastricht and Beyond: Building the European Union*. London: Routledge.

Apel, K.-O. 1979: The Conflicts of our Time and the Problem of Political Ethics. In F. Dallmayr (ed.), *From Contract to Community*. New York: Marcel Dekker.

Apel, K.-O. 1980: *Towards a Transformation of Philosophy*. London: Routledge and Kegan Paul.

Archibugi, D. 1995: Immanuel Kant, Cosmopolitan Law and Peace. *European Journal of International Relations*, 1, 429–56.

Archibugi, Daniele and Held, D. (eds), 1995: *Cosmopolitan Democracy: An Agenda for a New World Order*. Cambridge: Polity Press.

Aristotle, 1960: *The Politics*, translated with notes by Ernest Barker. Oxford: Clarendon Press.

Armstrong, D. 1993: *Revolution and World Order: The Revolutionary State in International Society*. Oxford: Clarendon Press.

Aron, R. 1966: *Peace and War: A Theory of International Relations*. London: Weidenfeld and Nicolson.

Aron, R. 1968: *Progress and Disillusion: The Dialectic of Modern Society*. Harmondsworth: Penguin.

Ashley, R. K. 1982: Political Realism and Human Interests. *International Studies Quarterly*, 25, 204–46.

Ashley, R. K. 1984: The Poverty of Neo-Realism. *International Organisation*, 38, 225–86.

Ashley, R. K. 1988: Untying the Sovereign State: A Double Reading of the Anarchy Problematique. *Millennium*, 17, 227–62.

Ashley, R. K. and Walker, R. B. J. 1990: Reading Dissidence/Writing the Discipline: Crisis and the Question of Sovereignty in International Studies. *International Studies Quarterly*, 34, 367–416.

Bader, V. 1995: Citizenship and Exclusion: Radical Democracy, Community and Justice. Or, What is Wrong with Communitarianism. *Political Theory*, 23, 211–46.

Balibar, E. 1988: Propositions on Citizenship. *Ethics*, 98, 723–30.

Barry, B. 1995: *Justice as Impartiality*. Oxford: Clarendon Press.

Bartelson, J. 1995: *A Genealogy of Sovereignty*. Cambridge: Cambridge University Press.

Bauman, Z. 1993: *Postmodern Ethics*. Oxford: Basil Blackwell.

Bauman, Z. 1996: On Communitarianism and Human Freedom. Or, How to Square the Circle. *Theory, Culture and Society*, 13, 79–90.

Beck, U. 1992: *Risk Society: Towards a New Modernity*. London: Sage.

Beetham, D. 1984: The Future of the Nation-State. In G. McLennan, D. Held and S. Hall (eds), *The Idea of the Modern State*. Milton Keynes: Open University Press.

Beetham, D. forthcoming: Human Rights. In D. Held and D. Archibugi (eds), *Citizenship, Sovereignty and Cosmopolitanism: Studies in Cosmopolitan Democracy*. Cambridge: Polity Press.

Beiner, R. (ed.), 1995: *Theorizing Citizenship*. Albany: State University of New York Press.

Beitz, C. 1994: Cosmopolitan Liberalism and the States System. In C. Brown (ed.), *Political Restructuring in Europe: Ethical Perspectives*. London: Routledge.

Bendix, R. 1964: *Nation-Building and Citizenship: Our Changing Social Order*. New York: John Wiley and Sons.

Benhabib, S. 1993: *Situating the Self: Gender, Community and Postmodernism in Contemporary Ethics*. Cambridge: Polity Press.

Benhabib, S. and Cornell, D. (eds), 1987: *Feminism as Critique: Essays on the Politics of Gender in Late-Capitalist Societies*. Cambridge: Polity Press.

Benhabib, S. and Dallmayr, F. (eds), 1990: *The Communicative Ethic Controversy*. Cambridge, Massachusetts: MIT Press.

Berlin, I. 1976: *Vico and Herder: Two Studies in the History of Ideas*, London: Hogarth Press.

Bernstein, J. M. 1995: *Recovering Ethical Life: Jürgen Habermas and the Future of Critical Theory*. London: Routledge.

Bernstein, R. 1986: *Philosophical Profiles: Essays in a Pragmatic Mode*. Cambridge: Cambridge University Press.

Bernstein, R. 1988: Fred Dallmayr's Critique of Habermas. *Political Theory*, 16, 580–93.

Bernstein, R. 1991: *The New Constellation: The Ethical-Political Horizons of Modernity/Postmodernity*. Cambridge: Polity Press.

Biersteker, T. J. and Weber, C. (eds), 1996: *State Sovereignty as Social Construct*. Cambridge: Cambridge University Press.

Biro, G. 1994: Minority Rights in Eastern and Central Europe and the Role of International Institutions. In J. Laurenti (ed.), *Search for Moorings: East Central Europe in the International System*. New York: Sage.

Blaney D. and Inayatullah, N. 1994: Prelude to a Conversation of Cultures in International Society? Todorov and Nandy on the Possibility of Dialogue. *Alternatives*, 19, 23–51.

Bodin, J. 1967: *Six Books on the Commonwealth*. London: Blackwell.

Bohler, D. 1990: Transcendental Pragmatics and Critical Morality: On the Possibility and Moral Significance of a Self-Enlightenment of Reason. In S. Benhabib and F. Dallmayr (eds), *The Communicative Ethics Controversy.* Cambridge, Massachusetts: MIT Press.

Booth, K. 1991: Security in Anarchy: Utopian Realism in Theory and Practice. *International Affairs,* 67, 527–45.

Bottomore, T. B. and Goode, P. (eds), 1978: *Austro-Marxism.* Oxford: Oxford University Press.

Brewin, C. 1988: Liberal States and International Obligations. *Millennium,* 17, 321–38.

Brewin, C. forthcoming: Society as a Kind of Community: Problems in Creating a New Order of Citizen in Europe from Ataturk to the Treaty of Maastricht. In M. Waller and A. Linklater (eds), *Images of Europe: Community and Citizenship in the Remaking of Europe.*

Brown, C. 1988: The Modern Requirement? Reflections on Normative International Theory in a Post-Western World. *Millennium,* 17, 339–448.

Brown, C. 1992: *International Relations Theory: New Normative Approaches.* London: Harvester.

Brown, C. 1994: 'Turtles All the Way Down': Anti-Foundationalism, Critical Theory and International Relations. *Millennium,* 23, 213–36.

Brown, C. 1995: International Political Theory and the Idea of World Community. In K. Booth and S. Smith (eds), *International Relations Theory Today.* Cambridge: Polity Press.

Brown, R. 1995: Globalisation and the End of the National Project. In J. MacMillan and A. Linklater (eds), *Boundaries in Question: New Directions in International Relations.* London: Pinter.

Brubaker, R. 1992: *Citizenship and Nationhood in France and Germany.* Cambridge: Cambridge University Press.

Bull, H. 1966a: The Grotian Conception of International Society. In H. Butterfield and M. Wight (eds), *Diplomatic Investigations: Essays in the Theory of International Politics,* London: George Allen and Unwin.

Bull, H. 1966b: International Theory: The Case for a Classical Approach. *World Politics,* 18, 361–77.

Bull, H. 1977: *The Anarchical Society: A Study of Order in World Politics.* London: Macmillan.

Bull, H. 1979: The State's Positive Role in World Affairs. *Daedalus,* 108, 111–23.

Bull, H. 1982: The West and South Africa. *Daedalus,* 11, 255–70.

Bull, H. 1983a: *Justice and International Relations.* The Hagey Lectures, University of Waterloo, Canada.

Bull, H. 1983b: The International Anarchy in the 1980s. *Australian Outlook,* 37, 127–31.

Bull, H. and Watson, A. (eds), 1984: *The Expansion of International Society.* Oxford: Clarendon Press.

Bull, H. et al. (eds), 1990: *Hugo Grotius and International Relations.* Oxford: Clarendon Press.

Burchill, S. (ed.), 1996: *Theories of International Relations.* Basingstoke: Macmillan.

Butler, J. 1995: Contingent Foundations. In S. Benhabib, J. Butler, D. Cornell and N. Fraser, *Feminist Contentions*. London: Routledge.

Callinicos, A. 1995: *Theories and Narratives: Reflections on the Philosophy of History*. Cambridge: Polity Press.

Camilleri, J. and Falk, J. 1992: *The End of Sovereignty? The Politics of a Shrinking and Fragmenting World*. Aldershot: Edward Elgar.

Camilleri, J. A., Jarvis, A. P. and Paolini, A. J. (eds), 1995: *The State in Transition: Reimagining Political Space*. Boulder, Colorado: Lynne Rienner.

Campbell, D. 1990: Global Inscription: How Foreign Policy Constitutes the United States. *Alternatives*, 15, 263–86.

Campbell, D. 1992: *Writing Security: United States Foreign Policy and the Politics of Identity*. Manchester: Manchester University Press.

Campbell, D. 1994: The Deterritorialisation of Responsibility: Levinas, Derrida and Ethics after the End of Philosophy. *Alternatives*, 19, 455–84.

Canny, N. P. 1973: The Ideology of English Colonisation: From Ireland to America. *William and Mary Quarterly*, 30, 575–98.

Carens, J. 1987: Aliens & Citizens: The Case for Open Borders. *Review of Politics*, 49, 251–73.

Carens, J. 1995: Complex Justice, Cultural Difference and Political Community. In D. Miller and M. Walzer (eds), *Pluralism, Justice and Equality*. Oxford: Oxford University Press.

Carr, E. H. 1941: *The Future of Nations*. London: Macmillan.

Carr, E. H. 1945: *Nationalism and After*. London: Macmillan.

Carr, E. H. 1946: *The Twenty Years' Crisis: 1919–1939*. London: Macmillan.

Chase-Dunn, C. 1981: Interstate System and Capitalist World Economy: One Logic or Two? *International Studies Quarterly*, 25, 19–42.

Clark, I. 1989: *The Hierarchy of States: Reform and Resistance in the International Order*. Cambridge: Cambridge University Press.

Clarke, P. B. (ed.), 1994: *Citizenship*. London: Pluto Press.

Cochran, M. 1995: Cosmopolitanism and Communitarianism in a Post-Cold War World. In J. MacMillan and A. Linklater (eds), *Boundaries in Question: New Directions in International Relations*. London: Pinter.

Cochran, M. 1996: International Ethics as Pragmatic Critique: Confronting the Epistemological Impasse of the Cosmopolitan/Communitarian Debate. University of London Doctoral Thesis.

Cohen, J. 1990: Discourse Ethics and Civil Society. In D. Rasmussen (ed.), *Universalism vs. Communitarianism*. Cambridge, Massachusetts: MIT Press.

Connerton, P. (ed.), 1978: *Critical Sociology: Selected Readings*. Harmondsworth: Penguin.

Connolly, W. 1993: *The Augustinian Imperative: A Reflection on the Politics of Morality*. London: Sage.

Connolly, W. 1994: Cosmopolitanism and Difference. *Boston Review*, 19 (5), 25.

Connolly, W. 1995: *The Ethos of Pluralization*. Minneapolis: Minnesota University Press.

Corrigan, P. and Sayer, D. 1985: *The Great Arch: English State Formation as Cultural Revolution*. Oxford: Basil Blackwell.

Cox, R. W. 1981: Social Forces, States and World Orders: Beyond International Relations Theory. *Millennium*, 10, 126–55.

Cox, R. W. 1992: Multilateralism and World Order. *Review of International Studies*, 18, 161–80.

Cox, R. W. 1993: Structural Issues of Global Governance: Implications for Europe. In S. Gill (ed.), *Gramsci, Historical Materialism and International Relations*. Cambridge: Cambridge University Press.

Crawford, J. (ed.), 1988: *The Rights of Peoples*. Oxford: Oxford University Press.

Czempiel, E. O. 1974: The Citizen's Society: Lessons from Europe, *Social Research*, 41, 746–65.

Dahrendorf, R. 1974: Citizenship and Beyond: The Social Dynamics of an Idea. *Social Research*, 41, 673–701.

Debray, R. 1977: Marxism and the National Question. *New Left Review*, 105, 25–41.

D'Entreves, M. P. and Benhabib, S. (eds), 1996: *Habermas and the Unfinished Project of Modernity*. Cambridge: Polity Press.

Derrida, J. 1992: *The Other Heading: Reflections on Today's Europe*. Bloomington: Indiana University Press.

Derrida, J. 1994a: *Spectres of Marx: The State of the Debt, the Work of Mourning and the New International*. London: Routledge.

Derrida, J. 1994b: Spectres of Marx. *New Left Review*, 205 (May/June), 31–58.

Deudney, D. 1996: Binding Sovereigns: Authorities, Structures and Geopolitics in Philadelphian Systems. In T. J. Biersteker and C. Weber (eds), *State Sovereignty as Social Construct*. Cambridge: Cambridge University Press.

Deutsch, K. 1970: *Political Community at the International Level*. New York: Archon Books.

Devetak, R. 1995a: The Project of Modernity and International Relations Theory. *Millennium*, 24, 27–51.

Devetak, R. 1995b: Incomplete States. In J. MacMillan and A. Linklater (eds), *Boundaries in Question: New Directions in International Relations*. London: Pinter.

Devetak. R. 1996a: Critical Theory. In S. Burchill (ed.), *Theories of International Relations*. Basingstoke: Macmillan.

Devetak, R. 1996b: Postmodernism. In S. Burchill (ed.), *Theories of International Relations*. Basingstoke: Macmillan.

Dews, P. 1987: *Logics of Disintegration: Poststructuralist Thought and the Claims of Critical Theory*. London: Verso.

Dolman, A. 1979: The Like-Minded Countries and the New International Order: Past, Present and Future Prospects. *Cooperation and Conflict*, 14, 57–85.

Doty, R. L. 1996: Immigration and National Identity: Constituting the Nation. *Review of International Studies*, 22, 235–55.

Doyle, M. W. 1982: Kant, Liberal Legacies and Foreign Affairs. *Philosophy and Public Affairs*, 12, 205–35 and 323–53.

Doyle, M. 1986: Liberalism and World Politics, *American Political Science Review*, 80, 1151–69.

Dummett, A. 1992: The Transnational Migration of People Seen from a Natural Law Perspective. In R. Goodin and B. Barry (eds), *Free Movement: Ethical Issues in the Transnational Migration of People and Money*. Hemel Hempstead: Harvester.

Eisenstadt, S. (ed.), 1986: *The Origins and Diversity of the Axial Civilizations.* Albany: State University of New York Press.

Elias, N. 1982: *The Civilizing Process,* vol. 2: *State Formation and Civilization.* Oxford: Basil Blackwell.

Elshtain, J. B. 1994: Act V. In J. Rosenau (ed.), *Global Voices: Dialogues in International Relations.* Boulder, Colorado: Westview Press.

Evans, G. and Grant, B. 1991: *Australia's External Relations: The World of the 1990s.* Melbourne: Melbourne University Press.

Falk, R. 1990: Evasions of Sovereignty. In R. B. J. Walker and S. Mendlowitz (eds), *Contending Sovereignties: Redefining Political Community.* Boulder, Colorado: Lynne Rienner.

Falk, R. 1994: The Making of Global Citizenship. In Bart Van Steenbergen (ed.), *The Condition of Citizenship.* London: Sage.

Fidler, D. P. 1996: Desperately Changing the Grotian and Kantian Sheep: Rousseau's Attempted Escape from the State of War. In I. Clark and I. B. Neumann (eds), *Classical Theories of International Relations.* Basingstoke: Macmillan.

Filmer, Sir R. 1949: *Patriarcha and Other Political Works,* edited with an introduction by P. Laslett. Oxford: Oxford University Press.

Forsyth, M. et al. (eds), 1970: *Theories of International Relations.* London: Allen and Unwin.

Foucault, M. 1979: *Discipline and Punish: The Birth of the Prison.* Harmondsworth: Penguin.

Foucault, M. 1989: Rituals of Exclusion. In *Foucault Live: Interviews 1966–84.* New York: Semiotexte.

Fraser, N. 1989: *Unruly Practices: Power, Discourse and Gender in Contemporary Social Theory.* Cambridge: Polity Press.

Fraser, N. and Gordon, L. 1994: Civic Citizenship against Social Citizenship? In B. Van Steenbergen (ed.), *The Condition of Citizenship.* London: Sage.

Frazer, E. and Lacey, N. 1993: *The Politics of Community: A Feminist Critique of the Liberal-Communitarian Debate.* Hemel Hempstead: Harvester.

Fukuyama, F. 1992: *The End of History and the Last Man.* London: Hamish Hamilton.

Gallie, W. B. 1978: *Philosophers of Peace and War.* Cambridge: Cambridge University Press.

Garcia, S. (ed.), 1993: *European Identity and the Search for Legitimacy.* London: Pinter.

Garnsey P. 1974: Legal Privilege in the Roman Empire. In M. I. Finley (ed.), *Studies in Ancient History.* London: Routledge and Kegan Paul.

Gellner, E. 1983: *Nations and Nationalism.* Oxford: Basil Blackwell.

George, J. 1994: *Discourses of World Politics: A (Re)Introduction to International Relations.* Boulder, Colorado: Lynne Rienner.

Geras, N. 1995: *Solidarity in the Conversation of Humankind: The Ungroundable Liberalism of Richard Rorty.* London: Verso.

Gerth, H. H. and Mills, C. W. (eds), 1948: *From Max Weber: Essays in Sociology.* London: Routledge and Kegan Paul.

Gibney, M. 1995: Political Theory and the International Refugee Crisis. Cambridge University Doctoral Thesis.

Giddens, A. 1985: *The Nation-State and Violence.* Cambridge: Polity Press.

Giddens, A. 1993: *The Consequences of Modernity*. Cambridge: Polity Press.

Gilligan, C. 1993: *In a Different Voice*. Cambridge, Massachusetts: Harvard University Press.

Gong, G. W. 1984: *The Standard of 'Civilisation' in International Society*. Oxford: Clarendon Press.

Goodin, R. and Barry, B. (eds), 1992: *Free Movement: Ethical Issues in the Transnational Migration of People and Money*. Hemel Hempstead: Harvester.

Haas, E. B. 1990: Reason and Change in International Life: Justifying a Hypothesis. *Journal of International Affairs*, 44, 209–40.

Haber, H. F. 1994: *Beyond Postmodern Politics: Lyotard, Rorty, Foucault*. London: Routledge.

Habermas, J. 1972: *Knowledge and Human Interests*. London: Heinemann.

Habermas, J. 1979a: *Communication and the Evolution of Society*. London: Heinemann.

Habermas, J. 1979b: History and Evolution. *Telos*, 39, 5–44.

Habermas, J. 1980: Response to the Commentary of Bernstein and Dove. In D. P. Verene (ed.), *Hegel's Social and Political Thought: The Philosophy of Objective Spirit*. Atlantic Highlands, New Jersey: Humanities Press.

Habermas, J. 1984: *The Theory of Communicative Action*, vol. 1: *Reason and the Rationalization of Society*. Boston: Beacon Press.

Habermas, J. 1985: A Philosophical-Political Profile. *New Left Review*, 151, 75–105.

Habermas, J. 1987: *The Philosophical Discourse of Modernity: Twelve Lectures*. Cambridge: Polity Press.

Habermas, J. 1989: *The Theory of Communicative Action*, vol. 2: *The Critique of Functionalist Reason*. London: Heinemann.

Habermas, J. 1990a: *Moral Consciousness and Communicative Action*. Cambridge: Polity Press.

Habermas, J. 1990b: Ethics, Politics and History: An Interview with Jean-Marc Ferry. In D. Rasmussen (ed.), *Universalism vs. Communitarianism*. Cambridge, Massachusetts: MIT Press.

Habermas, J. 1992a: *Autonomy and Solidarity: Interviews with Jürgen Habermas*, edited by Peter Dews. London: Verso.

Habermas, J. 1992b: *The Structural Transformation of the Public Sphere: An Inquiry into a Category of Bourgeois Society*. Cambridge: Polity Press.

Habermas, J. 1993: *Justification and Application: Remarks on Discourse Ethics*. Cambridge: Polity Press.

Habermas, J. 1994: *The Past as Future*. Cambridge: Polity Press.

Habermas, J. 1996: *Between Facts and Norms: Contributions to a Discourse Theory of Law and Democracy*. Cambridge: Polity Press.

Halliday, F. 1994: *Rethinking International Relations*, London: Macmillan.

Hardimon, M. O. 1994: *Hegel's Social Philosophy: The Project of Reconciliation*. Cambridge: Cambridge University Press.

Heater, D. 1990: *Citizenship: The Civic Ideal in World History, Politics and Education*. London: Longman.

Heater, D. 1996: *World Citizenship and Government: Cosmopolitan Ideas in the History of Western Political Thought*. Basingstoke: Macmillan.

Hegel, G. W. F. 1952: *The Philosophy of Right*, translated by T. M. Knox. Oxford: Oxford University Press.

Hegel, G. W. F. 1956: *The Philosophy of History*. New York: Dover.
Held, D. 1995: *Democracy and the Global Order: From the Modern State to Cosmopolitan Governance*. Cambridge: Polity Press.
Held, D. and McGrew, A. 1995: Globalization and the Liberal Democratic State. In Y. Sakomoto (ed.), *Global Transformation: Challenges to the State System*. New York: United Nations University Press.
Held, D. 1996: *Models of Democracy*. Cambridge: Polity Press.
Held, V. 1993: *Feminist Morality: Transforming Culture, Society and Politics*. Chicago: University of Chicago Press.
Helman, G. B. and Ratner, S. R. 1992–3: Saving Failed States. *Foreign Policy*, 89, 3–20.
Higgins, N. 1996: A Question of Style: The Politics and Ethics of Cultural Conversation in Rorty and Connolly. *Global Society*, 10, 25–42.
Hill, E. 1989: *Inventing the Barbarian: Greek Self-Definition through Tragedy*. Oxford: Clarendon Press.
Hinsley, F. H. 1994: *Sovereignty*. Cambridge: Cambridge University Press.
Hintze, O. 1975: *The Historical Essays of Otto Hintze*, edited with an introduction by Felix Gilbert. New York: Oxford University Press.
Hoffmann, S. 1960: *Contemporary Theory in International Relations*. Englewood Cliffs, New Jersey: Prentice-Hall.
Hoffmann, S. 1965: *The State of War: Essays on the Theory and Practice of International Relations*. London: Pall Mall Press.
Hollis, M. and Smith, S. 1990: *Explaining and Understanding International Relations*. Oxford: Clarendon Press.
Honneth, A. 1995: *The Struggle for Recognition: The Moral Grammar of Social Conflicts*. Cambridge: Polity Press.
Horkheimer, M. 1972: *Critical Theory: Selected Essays*. New York: Free Press.
Horsman, M. and Marshall, A. 1994: *After the Nation-State: Citizens, Tribalism and the New World*. London: HarperCollins.
Howe, P. 1995: A Community of Europeans: The Requisite Underpinnings. *Journal of Common Market Studies*, 33, 27–46.
Hoy, D. C. (ed.), 1986: *Foucault: A Critical Reader*. Oxford: Basil Blackwell.
Hoy, D. C. and McCarthy, T. 1994: *Critical Theory*. Oxford: Blackwell Publishers.
Huff, T. E. (ed.), 1981: *On the Roads to Modernity: Conscience, Science and Civilization. Selected Writings by Benjamin Nelson*. Totowa, New Jersey: Rowman and Littlefield.
Huntington, S. 1993: The Clash of Civilisations. *Foreign Affairs*, 72, 22–49.
Hurrell, A. 1990: Kant and the Kantian Paradigm in International Relations. *Review of International Studies*, 16, 183–205.
Hurrell, A. 1994: A Crisis of Ecological Viability? Global Environmental Change and the Nation-State. *Political Studies*, 42, 146–65.
Hutchings, K. 1994: Feminist Morality and International Relations. *Paradigms*, 8, 23–35.
Hutchings, K. 1996: The Idea of International Citizenship. In B. Holden (ed.), *The Ethical Dimensions of Global Change*. Basingstoke: Macmillan.
Ignatieff, M. 1991: Citizenship and Moral Narcissism. In G. Andrews (ed.), *Citizenship*. London: Lawrence and Wishart.

Jabri, V. 1996: Textualising the Self: Moral Agency in Inter-Cultural Discourse. *Global Society*, 10, 57–68.

Jackson, R. 1990: *Quasi-States: Sovereignty, International Relations and the Third World.* Cambridge: Cambridge University Press.

James, A. 1986: *Sovereign Statehood: The Basis of International Society.* London: Allen and Unwin.

Kalberg, S. 1980: Max Weber's Types of Rationality: Cornerstones for the Analysis of Rationalization Processes in World History. *American Journal of Sociology*, 85, 1145–79.

Kalberg. S. 1994: *Max Weber's Comparative-Historical Sociology.* Cambridge: Polity Press.

Kant, I. 1970a: The Metaphysical Elements of Justice. In M. Forsyth, H. M. A. Keens-Soper and P. Savigear (eds), *The Theory of International Relations: Selected Texts from Gentili to Treitschke.* London: Allen and Unwin.

Kant, I. 1970b: Perpetual Peace, in M. Forsyth, H. M. A. Keens-Soper and P. Savigear (eds), *The Theory of International Relations: Selected Texts from Gentili to Treitschke,* London: Allen and Unwin.

Keane, J. 1990: The Modern Democratic Revolution: Reflections on Lyotard's *The PostModern Condition.* In A. Benjamin (ed.), *Judging Lyotard.* London: Routledge.

Keenan, T. 1987: The Paradox of Knowledge and Power: Reading Foucault on a Bias. *Political Theory*, 15, 5–30.

Kissinger, H. 1979: *White House Years.* London: Weidenfeld and Nicolson.

Kristeva, J. 1991: *Strangers to Ourselves.* Hemel Hempstead: Harvester Wheatsheaf.

Kumar, K. 1981: *Prophecy and Progress: The Sociology of Industrial and Post-Industrial Society.* Harmondsworth: Penguin.

Kymlicka, W. 1989: *Liberalism, Community and Culture.* Oxford: Oxford University Press.

Kymlicka, W. 1995: *Multicultural Citizenship: A Liberal Theory of Minority Rights.* Oxford: Clarendon Press.

Lawler, P. 1992: The Good Citizen Australia? *Asian Survey*, 16, 241–50.

Lawler, P. 1994: Constituting the Good State. In P. James (ed.), *Critical Politics.* Melbourne: Arena Publications.

Lawler, P. forthcoming: Scandinavian Exceptionalism. In M. Waller and A. Linklater (eds), *Images of Europe: Community and Citizenship in the Remaking of Europe.*

Lewis, B. 1982: *The Muslim Discovery of Europe.* London: Phoenix.

Linklater, A. 1990a: *Men and Citizens in the Theory of International Relations.* London: Macmillan.

Linklater, A. 1990b: *Beyond Realism and Marxism: Critical Theory and International Relations.* London: Macmillan.

Linklater, A. 1990c: The Problem of Community in International Relations. *Alternatives*, 15, 135–53.

Linklater, A. 1991: Marxism and International Relations: Antithesis, Reconciliation and Transcendence. In R. Higgott and J. L. Richardson (eds), *International Relations: Global and Australian Perspectives on an Evolving Discipline.* Canberra: Department of International Relations.

Linklater, A. 1992a: The Question of the Next Stage: A Critical-Theoretical Point of View. *Millennium,* 21, 77–98.

Linklater, A. 1992b: What is a Good International Citizen? In P. Keal (ed.), *Ethics and Foreign Policy.* Sydney: Allen and Unwin.

Linklater, A. 1993: Liberal Democracy, Constitutionalism and the New World Order. In J. L. Richardson and R. Leaver (eds), *The New World Order.* Boulder: Colorado: Westview Press.

Linklater, A. 1994: Dialogue, Dialectic and Emancipation in International Relations at the End of the Post-War Age. *Millennium,* 23, 119–31.

Linklater, A. 1995a: Neo-Realism in Theory and Practice. In S. Smith and K. Booth (eds), *International Political Theory Today.* Cambridge: Polity Press.

Linklater, A. 1995b: Community. In A. Danchev (ed.), *Fin de Siecle: The Meaning of the Twentieth Century.* London: Tauris Academic Studies.

Linklater, A. 1996a: The Achievements of Critical Theory. In S. Smith, K. Booth and M. Zalewski (eds), *International Theory: Positivism and Beyond.* Cambridge: Cambridge University Press.

Linklater, A. 1996b: Citizenship and Sovereignty in the Post-Westphalian State. *European Journal of International Relations,* 2, 77–103.

Linklater, A. 1996c: Rationalism. In S. Burchill (ed.), *Theories of International Relations.* London: Macmillan.

Linklater, A. 1996d: Marxism. In S. Burchill (ed.), *Theories of International Relations.* London: Macmillan.

Linklater, A. 1996e: Hegel, the State and International Relations. In I. Clark and I. B. Neumann (eds), *Classical Theories of International Relations.* Basingstoke: Macmillan.

Linklater, A. 1997: The Transformation of Political Community: E. H. Carr, Critical Theory and International Relations. *Review of International Studies.*

Long, D. and Wilson, P. (eds), 1995: *Thinkers of the Twenty Years' Crisis: Interwar Idealism Reassessed.* Oxford: Oxford University Press.

Lowy, M. 1976: Marxists and the National Question. *New Left Review,* 96, 81–100.

Lyotard, J.-F. 1984: *The Postmodern Condition: A Report on Knowledge.* Manchester: Manchester University Press.

Lyotard, J.-F. (with Thebaud, J.-F.) 1985: *Just Gaming.* Manchester: Manchester University Press.

Lyotard, J.-F. 1993: The Other's Rights. In S. Shute and S. Hurley (eds), *On Human Rights: The Oxford Amnesty Lectures.* New York: Basic Books.

McCarthy, R. forthcoming: The Committee of the Regions. In M. Waller and A. Linklater (eds), *Images of Europe: Community and Citizenship in the Remaking of Europe.*

McCarthy, T. 1981: *The Critical Theory of Jürgen Habermas.* London: MIT Press.

McCarthy, T. 1990: Private Irony and Public Decency: Richard Rorty's New Pragmatism. *Critical Inquiry,* 16, 355–70.

MacCormack, N. 1996: Liberalism, Nationalism and the Post-Sovereign State. *Political Studies,* 44, 553–67.

McIlwain, C. H. 1947: *Constitutionalism: Ancient and Modern.* Ithaca, New York: Cornell University Press.

MacIntyre, A. 1984: *Is Patriotism a Virtue?* Lawrence: University of Kansas.

Macmillan, J. and Linklater, A. (eds), 1995: *Boundaries in Question: New Directions in International Relations*. London: Pinter.

Mann, M. 1986: *The Sources of Social Power,* vol. 1: *A History of Power from the Beginning to AD 1760,* Cambridge: Cambridge University Press.

Mann, M. 1987: Ruling Class Strategies and Citizenship. *Sociology,* 21, 339–54.

Mann, M. 1994: *The Sources of Social Power,* vol. 2: *The Rise of Classes and Nation-States, 1760–1914*. Cambridge: Cambridge University Press.

Mann, M. 1996: Authoritarian and Liberal Militarism: A Contribution from Comparative and Historical Sociology. In S. Smith, K. Booth and M. Zalewski (eds), *International Theory: Positivism and Beyond*. Cambridge: Cambridge University Press.

Manville, P. B. 1990: *The Origins of Citizenship in Ancient Greece*. Princeton: Princeton University Press.

Marshall, T. H. 1973: *Class, Citizenship and Social Development*. Westport, Connecticut: Greenwood Press.

Mattingly, G. 1955: *Renaissance Diplomacy*. Harmondsworth: Penguin.

Mearsheimer, J. 1990: Back to the Future: Instability in Europe after the Cold War. *International Security,* 15, 5–56.

Mearsheimer, J. 1994–5: The False Promise of International Institutions. *International Security,* 19, 5–49.

Meehan, E. 1993: *Citizenship and the European Community*. London: Sage.

Meinecke, F. 1970: *Cosmopolitanism and the National State*. Princeton: Princeton University Press.

Miller, D. 1988: The Ethical Significance of Nationality. *Ethics*. 98, 647–62.

Miller, D. 1994: The Nation-State: A Modest Defence. In C. Brown (ed.), *Political Restructuring in Europe: Ethical Perspectives*. London: Routledge.

Miller, D. 1995: *On Nationality*. Oxford: Oxford University Press.

Miller, D. forthcoming: Bounded Citizenship. In K. Hutchings (ed.), *The Borders of Citizenship*. Basingstoke: Macmillan.

Modelski, G. 1978: The Long Cycle of Global Politics and the Nation-State. *Comparative Studies in Society and History,* 20, 214–35.

Modelski, G. 1990: Is World Political Evolutionary Learning Possible? *International Organisation,* 44 (1), 1–24.

Morgenthau, H. 1973: *Politics among Nations: The Struggle for Power and Peace*. New York: Alfred A. Knopf.

Mouffe, C. 1993: *The Return of the Political*. London: Verso.

Mueller, J. 1989: *Retreat from Doomsday: The Obsolescence of Major War*. New York: Basic Books.

Murphy, R. 1988: *Social Closure: The Theory of Monopolization and Closure*. Oxford: Oxford University Press.

Nardin, T. 1983: *Law, Morality and the Relations of States*. Princeton: Princeton University Press.

Nelson, B. 1949: *The Idea of Usury: From Tribal Brotherhood to Universal Otherhood*. Princeton: Princeton University Press.

Nelson, B. 1971: Note on the Notion of Civilisation by Emile Durkheim and Marcel Mauss. *Social Research,* 38, 808–13.

Nelson, B. 1973: Civilisational Complexes and Inter-Civilisational Relations. *Sociological Analysis,* 74, 79–105.

Nelson, B. 1976: On Occident and Orient in Max Weber. *Social Research*, 43, 114–29.

Neufeld, M. 1995: *The Restructuring of International Relations Theory*. Cambridge: Cambridge University Press.

Norman, R. 1995: *Ethics, Killing and War*. Cambridge: Cambridge University Press.

Nussbaum, M. et al. 1994: Patriotism or Cosmopolitanism? *Boston Review* (Oct./Nov.), 3–34.

O'Neill, O. 1988: Ethical Reasoning and Ideological Pluralism. *Ethics*, 98, 705–22.

O'Neill, O. 1989a: Justice, Gender and International Boundaries. *British Journal of Political Science*, 20, 439–59.

O'Neill, O. 1989b: *Constructions of Reason: Explorations of Kant's Political Philosophy*. Cambridge: Cambridge University Press.

O'Neill, O. 1991: Transnational Justice. In D. Held (ed.), *Political Theory Today*. Cambridge: Polity Press.

Owen, D. 1995: *Nietzsche, Politics and Modernity*. London: Sage.

Parekh, B. 1991: British Citizenship and Cultural Difference. In G. Andrews (ed.), *Citizenship*. London: Lawrence and Wishart.

Phillips, A. 1991: Citizenship and Feminist Theory. In G. Andrews (ed.), *Citizenship*. London: Lawrence and Wishart.

Phillips, A. 1993: *Democracy and Difference*. Cambridge: Polity Press.

Pogge, G. 1994: Cosmopolitanism and Sovereignty. In Chris Brown (ed.), *Political Restructuring in Europe: Ethical Perspectives*. London: Routledge.

Preuss, U. 1995: Citizenship and Identity: Aspects of a Political Theory of Citizenship. In R. Bellamy, V. Bafacchi and D. Castiglione (eds), *Democracy and Constitutional Culture in the Union of Europe*. London: Lothian Foundation Press.

Pufendorf, S. 1931: *Two Books of the Elements of Jurisprudence*. Classics of International Law. Oxford: Carnegie Foundation.

Rabinow, P. 1986: *The Foucault Reader*. Harmondsworth, Penguin.

Rawls, J. 1971: *A Theory of Justice*. Cambridge, Massachusetts: Harvard University Press.

Reiner, R. (ed.), 1995: *Theorizing Citizenship*. Albany: State University of New York Press.

Reiss, H. (ed.), 1970: *Kant's Political Writings*. Cambridge: Cambridge University Press.

Resnick, P. 1992: Isonomia, Isegoria and Isomoiria and Democracy at the International Level. *Praxis International*, 12, 35–49.

Richardson, J. 1993: The End of Geopolitics? In R. Leaver and J. Richardson (eds), *Charting the Post-Cold War*. Boulder, Colorado: Westview Press.

Roche, M. 1992: *Rethinking Citizenship: Welfare, Ideology and Change in Modern Society*. Cambridge: Polity Press.

Roderick, R. 1986: *Habermas and the Foundations of Critical Theory*. Basingstoke: Macmillan.

Rorty, R. 1989: *Contingency, Irony and Solidarity*. Cambridge: Cambridge University Press.

Rorty, R. 1990: Truth and Freedom: A Reply to Thomas McCarthy. *Critical Inquiry*, 16, 633–43.

Rorty, R. 1991: *Objectivity, Relativism and Truth: Philosophical Papers, Volume One.* Cambridge: Cambridge University Press.

Rosecrance, R. 1986: *The Rise of the Trading State: Commerce and Conquest in the Modern World.* New York: Basic Books.

Rosenau, J. 1990: *Turbulence and World Politics.* Princeton: Princeton University Press.

Rosenau, J. 1994: *Global Voices: Dialogues in International Relations.* Boulder, Colorado: Westview Press.

Rosenberg J. 1994: *The Empire of Civil Society: A Critique of the Realist Theory of International Relations.* London: Verso.

Rousseau, J. J. 1962: *The Political Writings,* edited by C. E. Vaughan. Oxford: Basil Blackwell.

Rousseau, J. J. 1968: *The Social Contract and Discourses.* London: Dent.

Ruggie, J. 1983: Continuity and Transformation in the World Polity: Towards a Neo-Realist Synthesis. *World Politics,* 35, 261–85.

Runyan, A. S. and Peterson, V. S. 1991: The Radical Future of Realism: Feminist Subversions of Realism. *Alternatives,* 16, 67–106.

Ryder, T. T. B. 1965: *Koine Eirene: General Peace and Local Independence in Ancient Greece.* Hull: University of Hull Publications.

Said. E. 1978: *Orientalism.* New York: Vintage Books.

Said, E. 1993: Nationalism, Human Rights and Interpretation. In B. Johnson (ed.), *Freedom and Interpretation: The Amnesty Lectures 1992.* New York: Basic Books.

Sandel, M. J. 1984: *Liberalism and its Critics.* Oxford: Basil Blackwell.

Shapcott, R. 1994: Conversation and Coexistence: Gadamer and the Interpretation of International Society. *Millennium,* 23, 57–83.

Shaw, M. 1991: *Post-Military Society: Militarism, Demilitarization and War at the End of the Twentieth Century.* Cambridge: Polity Press.

Shue, H. 1981: Exporting Hazards. In Peter G. Brown and Henry Shue (eds), *Boundaries: National Autonomy and its Limits.* Totowa, New Jersey: Rowman and Littlefield.

Shue, H. 1988: Mediating Duties. *Ethics,* 98, 687–704.

Skocpol. T. 1979: *States and Social Revolutions.* Cambridge: Cambridge University Press.

Smith, S. 1989: *Hegel's Critique of Liberalism: Rights in Context.* Chicago: Chicago University Press.

Soysal, Y. N. 1996: Changing Citizenship in Europe: Remarks on PostNational Membership and the National State. In D. Cesarani and M. Fulbrook (eds), *Citizenship, Nationality and Migration in Europe.* London: Routledge.

Squires, J. 1996: Liberal Constitutionalism, Identity and Difference. *Political Studies,* 44, 620–34.

Steans, J. forthcoming: *Gender, Feminism and International Relations.* Cambridge: Polity Press.

Sterling, R. W. 1958: *Ethics in a World of Power.* Princeton: Princeton University Press.

Strange, S. 1996: *The Retreat of the State: The Diffusion of Power in the World Economy.* Cambridge: Cambridge University Press.

Suganami, H. 1989: *Domestic Analogy and World Order.* Cambridge: Cambridge University Press.

Suganami, H. 1996: *On the Causes of War*. Oxford: Oxford University Press.

Sylvester, C. 1994: *Feminist Theory and International Relations in a Postmodern Era*. Cambridge: Cambridge University Press.

Tarn, W. W. 1930: *Hellenistic Civilisation*. London: Edward Arnold.

Taylor, C. 1985: Connolly, Foucault and Truth. *Political Theory*, 13, 377–85.

Taylor, C. 1994: *Multiculturalism and the Politics of Recognition*. Princeton: Princeton University Press.

Tickner, A. 1995: Inadequate Providers? A Gendered Analysis of States and Security. In J. A. Camilleri, A. P. Jarvis and A. J. Paolini (eds), *The State in Transition: Reimagining Political Space*. Boulder, Colorado: Lynne Rienner.

Tilly, C. (ed.), 1975: *The Formation of National States in Western Europe*. Princeton: Princeton University Press.

Tilly, C. 1992a: *Coercion, Capital and European States: AD 990–1992*. Oxford: Basil Blackwell.

Tilly, C. 1992b: The Futures of European States. *Social Research*, 59, 705–17.

Tilly, C. 1994: The Time of States. *Social Research*, 61, 269–95.

Tiryakian, E. 1974: Reflections on the Sociology of Civilisations. *Sociological Analysis*, 35, 122–8.

Todorov, T. 1992: *The Conquest of America*. New York: Harper.

Toennies, F. 1955: *Community and Association*. London: Routledge and Kegan Paul.

Toews, J. E. 1980: *Hegelianism: The Path towards Dialectical Humanism, 1805–1841*. Cambridge: Cambridge University Press.

Toynbee, A. 1978: *Mankind and Moral Earth*. London: Paladin.

Tronto, J. C. 1993: *Moral Boundaries: A Political Argument for an Ethic of Care*. London: Routledge.

True, J. 1996: Feminism. In S. Burchill (ed.), *Theories of International Relations*. London: Macmillan.

Turner, B. 1986: *Citizenship and Capitalism: The Debate over Reformism*. London: Allen and Unwin.

Turner, B. 1990: Outline of a Theory of Citizenship. *Sociology*, 24 (2), 189–217.

Turner, B. 1993a: Outline of a Theory of Human Rights. *Sociology*, 27 (3), 489–512.

Turner, B. 1993b: *Citizenship and Social Theory*. London: Sage.

Van Steenbergen, B. 1994: Towards a Global Ecological Citizenship. In B. Van Steenbergen (ed.), *The Condition of Citizenship*. London: Sage.

Vattel, E. de 1916: *The Law of Nations*, Washington, Classics of International Law: Carnegie Foundation.

Veit-Brause, I. 1995: Rethinking the State of the Nation. In J. A. Camilleri, A. P. Jarvis and A. J. Paolini (eds), *The State in Transition: Reimagining Political Space*. Boulder, Colorado: Lynne Rienner.

Vico, G. 1970: *The New Science*, translated by T. G. Bergin and M. H. Fisch. Ithaca, New York: Cornell University Press.

Vincent, R. J. 1986: *Human Rights and International Relations*. Cambridge: Cambridge University Press.

Vincent, R. J. 1990a: Grotius, Human Rights and Intervention. In H. Bull, B. Kingsbury and A. Roberts (eds), *Hugo Grotius and International Relations*. Oxford: Clarendon Press.

Vincent, R. J. 1990b: Order in International Politics. In J. D. B. Miller and R. J.

Vincent (eds), *Order and Violence: Hedley Bull and International Relations*. Oxford: Clarendon Press.

Vincent, R. J., and Wilson, P. 1993: Beyond Non-intervention. In I. Forbes and M. Hoffman (eds), *Political Theory, International Relations and the Ethics of Intervention*. Basingstoke: Macmillan.

Vogel, U. 1991: Is Citizenship Gender-Specific? In U. Vogel and M. Moran (eds), *The Frontiers of Citizenship*. Basingstoke: Macmillan.

Wagar, W. W. (ed.), 1971: *History and the Idea of Mankind*. Albuquerque: University of New Mexico Press.

Walby, S. 1994: Is Citizenship Gendered? *Sociology*, 28, 379–95.

Walker, R. B. J. 1988: *One World, Many Worlds: Struggles for a Just World Peace*. Boulder, Colorado: Lynne Rienner.

Walker, R. B. J. 1993: *Inside/Outside: International Relations as Political Theory*. Cambridge: Cambridge University Press.

Wallace, W. 1994: Rescue or Retreat? The Nation-State in Western Europe. *Political Studies*, 42, 52–76.

Wallbank, F. 1981: *The Hellenistic World*. Glasgow: Fontana.

Waller, M. 1993: *The End of the Communist Power Monopoly*. Manchester: Manchester University Press.

Waller, M. 1994: Voice, Choice and Loyalty: Democratisation in Eastern Europe. In G. Parry and M. Moran (eds), *Democracy and Democratisation*. London: Routledge.

Waller, M. and Linklater, A. (eds), forthcoming: *Images of Europe: Community and Citizenship in the Remaking of Europe*.

Waltz. K. N. 1959: *Man, the State and War: A Theoretical Analysis*. New York: Columbia University Press.

Waltz, K. N. 1979: *Theory of International Politics*. Reading, Massachusetts: Addison-Wesley.

Waltz, K. N. 1990: Realist Thought and NeoRealist Theory. *Journal of International Affairs*, 44, 21–37.

Walzer, M. 1979: *Just and Unjust Wars*. Harmondsworth: Penguin.

Walzer, M. 1994a: Spheres of Affection. *Boston Review*, 19 (5), 29.

Walzer, M. 1994b: *Thick and Thin: Moral Argument at Home and Abroad*. London: University of Notre Dame Press.

Walzer, M. 1995: *Spheres of Justice: A Defence of Pluralism and Equality*. Oxford: Blackwell Publishers.

Watson, A. 1982: *Diplomacy: The Dialogue between States*. London: Methuen.

Watson, A. 1987: Hedley Bull, States Systems and International Societies. *Review of International Studies*, 13, 147–53.

Weber, M. 1930: *The Protestant Ethic and the Spirit of Capitalism*. London: Unwin.

Weiler, J. H. H. 1996: European Neo-Constitutionalism: In Search of Foundations for the European Constitutional Order. *Political Studies*, 44, 517–33.

Weiss, T. G. 1975: The Tradition of Philosophical Anarchism and Future Directions in World Policy. *Journal of Peace Research*, 12, 1–17.

Wendt, A. 1987: The Agent-Structure Problem in International Relations Theory. *International Organisation*, 41, 335–70.

Wendt, A. 1992: Anarchy Is What States Make of It: The Social Construction of Power Politics. *International Organisation*, 46, 391–425.

Wendt, A. 1994: Collective Identity Formation and the International State. *American Political Science Review,* 88, 384–96.

Wheeler, N. 1996: Guardian Angel or Global Gangster? A Review of the Ethical Claims of International Society. *Political Studies,* 44, 123–35.

Wheeler, N. and Dunne, T. 1996: Hedley Bull's Pluralism of the Intellect and Solidarism of the Will. *International Affairs,* 72, 1–17.

White, S. K. 1988: *The Recent Work of Jürgen Habermas: Reason, Justice and Modernity.* Cambridge: Cambridge University Press.

White, S. K. 1991: *Political Theory and Post-Modernism.* Cambridge: Cambridge University Press.

White, S. K. (ed.), 1995: *The Cambridge Companion to Habermas.* Cambridge: Cambridge University Press.

Wight, M. 1966: Why Is There No International Theory? In H. Butterfield and M. Wight (eds), *Diplomatic Investigations.* London: George Allen and Unwin.

Wight, M. 1973: The Balance of Power and International Order. In A. James (ed.), *The Bases of International Order.* Oxford: Oxford University Press.

Wight, M. 1977: *System of States.* Leicester: Leicester University Press.

Wight, M. 1978: *Power Politics.* Leicester: Leicester University Press.

Wight, M. 1991: *International Theory: The Three Traditions.* Leicester: Leicester University Press.

Willetts. P. 1996: From Stockholm to Rio and Beyond: The Impact of the Environmental Movement on the United Nations Consultative Arrangements for NGOs. *Review of International Studies,* 22, 57–80.

Williams, H. and Booth, K. 1996: Kant: Theorist Beyond Limits. In I. Clark and I. B. Neumann (eds), *Classical Theories of International Relations.* Basingstoke: Macmillan.

Wise, M. and Gibb, R. 1993: *Single Market to Social Europe: The European Community in the 1990s.* London: Longman.

Wolin, S. 1960: *Politics and Vision: Continuity and Innovation in Western Political Thought.* Boston: Little Brown.

Wright, A. 1990: The Good Citizen. *New Statesman and Society,* 18 May, 31–2.

Young, I. M. 1987: Impartiality and the Civic Public: Some Implications of Feminist Critiques of Moral and Political Theory. In S. Benhabib and D. Cornell (eds), *Feminism as Critique: Essays on the Politics of Gender in Late-Capitalist Societies.* Cambridge: Polity Press.

Young, I. M. 1990: *Justice and the Politics of Difference.* Princeton: Princeton University Press.

Zacher, M. 1992: The Decaying Pillars of the Westphalian Temple. In J. Rosenau and E. O. Czempiel (eds), *Governance without Government: Order and Change in World Politics.* Cambridge: Cambridge University Press.

Zolberg, A. 1985: The Formation of New States as a Refugee Generating Process. In E. Ferris (ed.), *Refugees and World Politics.* New York: Praeger.

Index